True Crime

Assassination

TIME LIFE® By the Editors of
Time-Life Books

In a few days people will forget and there will be another president.

LEE HARVEY OSWALD

1

Enigma with a Gun

The wealthy Dallas neighborhood of Highland Park lay in darkness when the thin young man crept into position in the alley behind the sprawling house at 4011 Turtle Creek Boulevard. The intruder watched his quarry puttering in the rectangle of light that marked the dining room window, just 100 feet away. Hefting the 6.5-mm. Mannlicher-Carcano carbine to his shoulder, the former U.S. Marine trained the bolt-action rifle's four-power telescopic sight on his target, then perhaps relaxed for a moment to take a breath, steadying himself against a rising current of excitement. His life was about to change forever. Tonight, April 10, 1963, for the first time in his 23 years, Lee Harvey Oswald was about to become *somebody*.

A sudden murmur of voices marked the completion of Holy Week service for the Mormon church at the end of the alley. Oswald had chosen this exact moment to strike, the instant before the secluded suburb emptied of its last crowd—before a man seen on the streets at 9 p.m. would be a lonely curiosity, easily recalled. He turned his attention back to the man at the illuminated table: Retired Army major-general Edwin A. Walker—a species of fascist, an enemy of revolution, a right-wing superpatriot, a man who drew mobs into the street to oppose civil rights, a leader of the ultraconservative John Birch Society, an implacable foe of Fidel Castro's Cuba. Walker had just come back from leading a cross-country evangelizing crusade against communism under the inflammatory name of Operation Midnight Ride—a clear reference, for anyone in the South, to the racist terror of the Ku Klux Klan. To the gunman, Walker must have personified all that was wrong in the world.

Killing such a man, Oswald believed, would be a blow against fascism and U.S. imperialism—a heroic act. He badly wanted to be remembered for something, to have left some kind of mark upon the world; perhaps he hoped that it would be a distinctively ideological one. In any case, everyone would know what he did tonight.

At home he'd left a carefully collected and organized dossier that explained how he had planned this necessary murder, how he'd photographed the house and reconnoitered his avenues of escape, how he'd come to the decision to shoot Walker.

The moment had come. Cradling the rifle in a makeshift sling he'd fashioned from a leather strap, Oswald pulled the butt firmly against his right shoulder; he took a shallow breath and held it as his finger squeezed the trigger. The rifle bucked; its sharp sound echoed in the alley. Without stopping to verify that he'd hit his target, the slight, grim-faced assassin quickly fled, stopping only to bury the rifle in the woods near Walker's house.

Police would be looking for any suspicious man in a car—everybody in America had a car, except Oswald, who could not even drive one. In Dallas, where life was lived on four wheels, he used the buses. On this April night, he would escape by walking until he got to a bus stop and then vanish into the city's public transportation system. The police would never catch him. He'd thought of everything.

About two and a half hours later, Oswald, white-faced, panting, and glistening with sweat, walked into the cramped apartment at 214 West Neely Street that he shared with his Soviet wife, Marina, and one-year-old daughter, June. Marina stared at him with a combination of confusion and terror. She'd discovered a note that laid out a bewildering and ominous list of chores for her to perform—as if he were never coming home. "If I am alive and taken prisoner," the list ended, "the city jail is at the end of the bridge we always used to cross when we went to town." Like all communication between them, it was in Russian; Marina spoke little English and Oswald would not permit her to learn, supposedly to maintain his own fluency in Russian.

Now, according to her recollection of that night, she faced her husband in a panic. "What's happened?"

"I shot Walker."

Oswald evidently stalked retired major general Edwin Walker *(left)* for weeks and photographed his Dallas house *(right)*. The unexplained excision of the parked car's license plate occurred while the photo was in police hands.

"Did you kill him?"

"I don't know."

"My God. The police will be here any minute. What did you do with the rifle?"

"Buried it. Don't ask any questions. And for God's sake don't bother me."

Oswald turned on the radio to listen for news of his exploit. There wasn't any. Pulling off his clothes, he fell on the bed and was immediately asleep, leaving Marina Oswald to ponder once again the frightening, secretive, dogmatic little man she had married two years earlier in the Soviet Union.

In fact, Oswald's murderous odyssey had failed. While the assassin stalked him, the superpatriot general was completing an all-American ritual: He was doing his income tax return. Suddenly the window on his right shattered, sowing him with shards of glass. He heard a riffle of wind past his head, the crack of a rifle shot, then the impact of a high-velocity bullet plowing through a nearby wall. At first he thought it was kids with firecrackers. Then the grizzled combat veteran realized that he'd come within an inch or so of losing his life. He later told a reporter that the shot had been flawless and would have killed him had the bullet not been slightly deflected by the window sash. But a near miss was still a miss. Lee Harvey Oswald would remain a nobody, a dangerously frustrated cipher of a man, for another seven and a half months. Then he would step into history.

Yet Oswald would have despised the kind of fame he finally achieved. His defining act, it is generally believed, was the assassination of the 35th president of the United States, John F. Kennedy, in Dallas, on November 22, 1963. Almost immediately after the fatal shooting of Kennedy from ambush, Oswald's involvement became clouded with ambiguity; two days later it became nearly opaque when another antisocial nonentity, nightclub operator Jack Ruby, stepped past a cordon of police and shot the man accused of killing JFK.

Lee Harvey Oswald could not have committed the crime at all, said some. Others maintained that he could not have succeeded alone. Indeed, despite the dossier Oswald apparently compiled before the attempt on Edwin Walker and despite the testimony of his wife, there is even some question that he fired the errant shot in April. The entrance of Jack Ruby, many believe, is proof of wide conspiracy in the Kennedy assassination and, perhaps, of the involvement of the Mob. The tragic act in Dallas buzzes with inconsistency and coincidence, and a community of assassination historians has sprung up to spend entire careers studying it, hunting for a version of that terrible November day that accommodates their host of competing theories.

These hypotheses are like tributaries, however, to the single stream that is the story of Lee Harvey Oswald, reeling through a pinched, mean-spirited, disappointing life, trying to call attention to himself first as a dropout, then as a defector, a revolutionary, a man who was not afraid to kill. For many, this account is far too simple. It fails to probe all the tributaries, which remain irresistible. No matter that they lead off into an abyss of speculation, tangles of skewed fact, suspicions of every possible kind of plot—their very existence compels the explorers of assassination to follow them.

For Oswald, it would be a final, crushing irony, to have killed a man considered great by many, to have flooded the world with grief, and to have brought it off alone—and then to discover that many still doubted his ability to do it. The immortality he achieved, therefore, is the itchy kind usually reserved for wandering spirits; Lee Harvey Oswald inhabits history's stage as the forever-dubious assassin, whose thwarted ghost will never be allowed its final rest.

The central mystery of those events is the web of deception and contradiction spun by Oswald himself. A thin-lipped, humorless, prematurely balding, perennially angry 10th-grade dropout, he habitually tried to square the difference between fantasy and reality by telling lies, taking aliases, pledging allegiance in every direction. The ex-Marine tried to reject his U.S.

citizenship in defecting to the Soviet Union, then returned to America a couple of years later with a Russian wife and baby girl only to begin plotting a new defection to Cuba. At a time when most Americans invested communism with almost supernatural powers of conspiracy, Oswald trekked across the least stable political fault lines of the Cold War—a trait that immediately imparted a sinister international dimension to his involvement in the Kennedy assassination.

In fact, that aura of ideological intrigue was at stark odds with the hard actuality of his life, for Lee Harvey Oswald was a failure at virtually everything he tried. His short, unhappy adult existence was spent searching for mean jobs to sustain him and his family in poverty while he clung desperately to the idea that he was somehow different, and important. Dogmatically Marxist in his public views, pathologically secretive in private, paranoid and compulsively deceptive by nature, he lived a complicated and self-destructive life of rage, rejection, betrayal, and heroic fantasy that toyed with the most dangerous conflicts of the Cold War era—but always, until the very end, on the margins of politics and reality.

Emotionally, Oswald was hollowed out from within: a cold, manipulative, self-absorbed young man whose feelings of rage and hate were focused almost entirely through an ideological lens. "In a few days people will forget and there will be another President," he declared after his arrest for John Kennedy's murder in 1963—a startling example of his strange insensitivity to the world outside himself. Yet at the same time Oswald lived a florid and overheated inner life, in which his secret comings and goings were somehow part of a grand tapestry of power—if only others would recognize it.

The external world had been a void for Lee Harvey Oswald from the beginning. When he was born on October 18, 1939, in the Old French Hospital in New Orleans, his father, Robert E. Lee Oswald, an insurance premium collector, had been dead for two months. The boy's lonely life revolved around his strong-willed mother, Marguerite Claverie Oswald. The fifth of six children in a streetcar conductor's family, Marguerite had lost her own mother when she was four. She left school in the ninth grade and at 22 married Edward John Pic Jr., a shipping clerk. The couple separated when Marguerite was three months pregnant. She gave birth to a boy,

John Edward Pic in January 1932; 18 months later, in July 1933, she married Robert Oswald. Their first son, Robert Jr., was born in 1934. When Marguerite became pregnant four years later, the Oswalds hoped for a baby girl. But it was Lee Harvey.

Marguerite Oswald possessed many of the traits later attributed to her younger son. In the view of educational psychologists who examined Lee in his early teens and interviewed Marguerite, she was "very self-possessed and alert," easygoing and sociable on the surface, but beneath that thin veneer lay "a defensive, rigid, self-involved person who had real difficulty in accepting and relating to people." She had quicksilver loyalties, a talent for repeated failure, and a reflex toward free and inventive lying. Marguerite buffered her discontent with excuses—she and her boys were somehow special and deserved better, although her conviction seems to have carried little warmth. Her children were habitually scanted on food and clothing, and she repeatedly told her older boys what a burden they'd become.

Her children would later recall that Marguerite Oswald tried to control their lives to the last detail, but her spates of dominating interest alternated with calculated spells of abandonment. After her husband's death in 1939, Marguerite tried to survive by opening a notions shop in their New Orleans home. It soon failed, and she sold the house, placed her two elder sons in an orphanage, and sought work as a telephone operator. She kept Lee at her side, mainly because the orphanage refused to accept a charge so young whose mother was still alive. The struggling pair depended heavily on the charitable instincts of her sister Lillian and brother-in-law Charles "Dutz" Murrett, a prizefight promoter and, it later transpired, a well-known New Orleans bookie.

Young Lee was often in the care of babysitters, who would hit him for his misbehavior. At three years and two months he too was placed in the Evangelical Lutheran Bethlehem Orphan Asylum with his brothers. Like a library book, he would be checked out by his mother for two or three weeks at a time, then returned.

When Lee was four, Marguerite and he moved to Dallas, Texas, with her new boyfriend, electrical engineer Edwin Ekdahl. A few months later the older boys joined their mother and brother, and within a year

Marguerite and Edwin married. At first, the marriage looked like the break she and her sons needed. Ekdahl was a willing stepfather who put the family up in a roomy stone house in Benbrook, a suburb of Dallas's twin city, Fort Worth. The older boys were sent to private military school, and Lee started first grade at the Benbrook Common School. It was not long, however, before the marriage dissolved into bickering, and eventually Marguerite caught her husband with a mistress. In 1948 they were divorced.

The comfortable middle-class world that the Oswald boys had only begun to enjoy suddenly evaporated. Marguerite moved to a small, shabby house near the Fort Worth railway tracks and scraped by on a variety of ill-paying jobs. Although she began to push the older boys out of the nest, they resisted until they had finished high school, then escaped into the military; John chose the Coast Guard and Robert the Marines.

Lee, still just a boy—and his mother's favorite—stayed home, but hardly in one place. By the age of 10, in the fifth grade, he had attended six different schools. He was also showing signs of violent abnormality. At age eight, he'd pulled a knife on one of his brothers and chased him around the house. "They have these little scuffles all the time," Marguerite explained. His usual weapons, however, were withdrawal, rudeness, and sullen silence—the tactics of a youngster filled with rage but unable or afraid to vent it.

In August 1952 Marguerite suddenly moved again—to New York City and in with her son John, his wife, and infant child. Young Lee was enrolled in the Trinity Evangelical Lutheran School. Friction increased as the older son discovered that his mother was less than eager to find a job or an apartment of her own. Finally, she and Lee were more or less pushed out—into the Bronx. Lee, nearing 14, found himself the butt of schoolyard taunts from tough kids who jeered at his southern accent, his bumpkin clothes, and his passivity. He began to skip school more often than he attended. Sometimes he would spend the day riding nonstop on the New York subway system. Other days he would sit at home watching television. One of his favorite shows was *I Led Three Lives*, the adventures of an FBI agent who posed as a Communist spy. In spring of 1953 he was nabbed as a truant while wandering around the Bronx Zoo and sentenced to six weeks' detention for official observation.

The educational experts, psychologists, and social workers who examined Lee painted a bleak picture of the relatively bright, emotionally starved child who'd come under their scrutiny. Lee's IQ measured 118, well above average, but he was described as "seriously withdrawn, detached and very hard to reach." A social worker reported that Lee felt his mother "never gave a damn for him. He always felt like a burden she had to tolerate." Another social worker on the case evidently agreed, noting that Marguerite did not see Lee as an independent person but as "an extension of herself."

Lee compensated by fantasizing about being omnipotent and killing people. Social worker Evelyn Strickman concluded that he had suffered "serious personality damage," noting poignantly that there was "a rather pleasant, appealing quality about this emotionally starved, affectionless youngster." The psychologist more or less concurred with Strickman's downbeat but sympathetic assessment and declared Lee was not psychotic.

The analysts recommended that Lee be placed on academic probation and also that Marguerite Oswald be enrolled in therapy. She tartly refused. New York authorities, she asserted, knew nothing about Texas children, who often remained away from school for months. When classes resumed in the autumn of 1953, Lee once more became a disruptive presence, and his mother helped him miss his probation appointments. Authorities recommended that he be removed from parental control and placed in a children's home. A week after that ruling came down, Marguerite Oswald and her son abruptly departed for New Orleans, where they took up residence above a pool hall in the old French Quarter.

But the New York interlude had left a fresh, indelible mark on Lee Oswald's personality. It was in New York, he later claimed, that he discovered Marxism, the system of thought that advocates socialism and a classless society. His interest was first aroused, he said, when he was handed a pamphlet protesting the impending execution of Julius and Ethel Rosenberg, brought to trial in 1951 for passing atomic secrets to the Soviet Union. The Rosenberg trial was a celebrated cause among leftists of the '50s; they accused the conservative establishment of railroading the couple to the electric chair in 1953 for

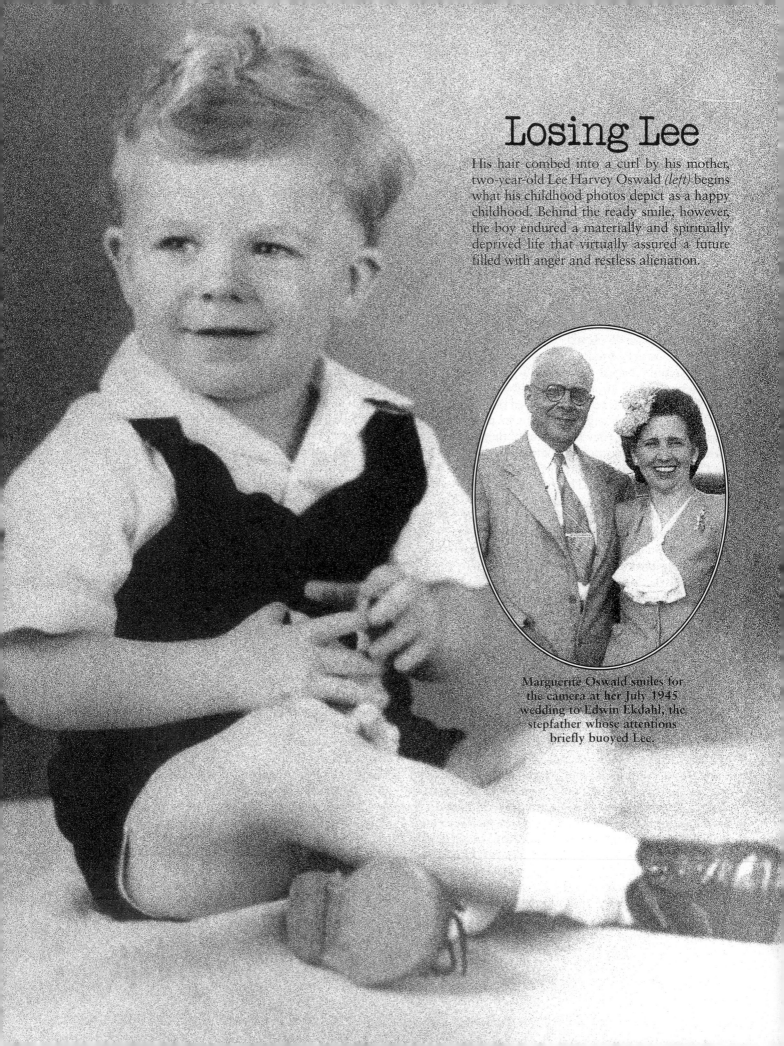

Losing Lee

His hair combed into a curl by his mother, two-year-old Lee Harvey Oswald *(left)* begins what his childhood photos depict as a happy childhood. Behind the ready smile, however, the boy endured a materially and spiritually deprived life that virtually assured a future filled with anger and restless alienation.

Marguerite Oswald smiles for the camera at her July 1945 wedding to Edwin Ekdahl, the stepfather whose attentions briefly buoyed Lee.

Sharing a happy moment, five-year-old **Lee** *(center)* laughs with brother Robert *(left)* and half-brother John Pic.

Not yet 10, Lee wears an expression that seems to foreshadow the angry young man he will become.

Streetwise and truant at 13, Lee leans against a fence at New York's Bronx Zoo.

Always hungry for attention, Lee *(left foreground)* clowns for the camera during a ninth grade New Orleans English class, which he squeaked through.

their socialist beliefs. Subsequent investigations have confirmed that the pair were Soviet spies.

The notion of a beleaguered couple battered by a hostile state could hardly fail to strike a chord in the teenager whose mother had repeatedly railed against the injustice of a society that kept her poor and her talented young son unrecognized. "My mother had been a worker all her life," he said years later in Moscow. "All her life she had to produce profits for capitalists."

But that sense of injustice was always coupled with a burning sense of selfishness. Marguerite believed in her right to any advantage, earned or not, that would correct the balance of her unfair lot in life—a rationalization for ingratitude that her son shared. As one acquaintance put it in later years, Lee "appreciated absolutely nothing you did for him. He never thanked you for anything. He seemed to expect it of you."

High-school sophomore Oswald wears the military-style uniform of his New Orleans Civil Air Patrol squadron, which he joined even as Marxism began to attract him.

As he neared 15 in New Orleans, Lee Oswald was variously described by those who knew him as spoiled, arrogant, and aggressively rude, especially toward his mother. But his interval in psychological observation and his political conversion seem to have placed his bad behavior in check. His school attendance improved. He became quiet and aloof, spending his time in the library reading the socialist doctrines of Karl Marx and his collaborator Friedrich Engels. The only outbreak of the old unruliness occurred when he was thrown off the Beauregard Junior High School football team: He alleged the coach's regulations violated his constitutional rights.

Oswald also joined the Civil Air Patrol, where his squadron leader was Captain David W. Ferrie, an airline pilot who would later develop Mafia and anti-Castro Cuban connections. The appearance of this shadowy figure in Oswald's youth is portentous to conspiracists, who suggest that Ferrie encouraged young Lee to feign a Marxist tilt as a cover for a career as an American spy.

But if Oswald was better behaved on the surface, he did not abandon his talent for falsehood. In the 10th grade he dropped out of school after forging a note from his mother announcing that the family was moving to San Diego. He persuaded Marguerite to write a letter saying he was 17 and took it to the U.S. Marine recruiting station, where he tried to enlist. The recruiters knew a 16-year-old when they saw one, however, and they turned him down.

In a curious ideological counterpoint, Oswald began to wear his pro-Communist sympathies provocatively on his sleeve. In a nation that had just finished fighting Communist forces in Korea and where a witch-hunting anti-Communist spirit still flourished at home, the expression of pro-Soviet sympathies was instantly infuriating. Oswald worked as a messenger at a dental laboratory, where he earned a reputation as a vocal supporter of Soviet premier Nikita Khrushchev.

In July 1956 the Oswalds moved back to Texas, where Lee entered the 10th grade at Arlington Heights High

School in Fort Worth. He quit within weeks—it would be his last formal schooling—and shortly thereafter he sent a coupon to the Socialist Party of America, asking for more information on their youth league. "I am a Marxist," he wrote, "and have been studying socialist principles for well over 15 months." But such contacts seem to have been mere dabbling, for he was soon on his way to greater, and more conventional, things. In October, 17 years old at last, Oswald signed up for a three-year hitch in the Marine Corps.

Lee Oswald was not exactly a model member of one of America's most fearsome warrior subcultures. At five feet eight inches and 135 pounds, he was physically unprepossessing and mildly unhealthy: He was afflicted with ear, nose, and throat problems. Nonetheless, he survived 10 weeks of boot camp at the San Diego Marine Recruit Depot. There he took rifle training, learning to fire at targets at ranges of up to 500 yards. In December 1956, as part of his "graduation," he scored 212 points with an M-1 rifle on the firing range, two points above the minimum for the designation sharpshooter, the middle grade of attainment, between marksman and expert.

Then it was on to Camp Pendleton for advanced combat training. In March Oswald was sent to the Naval Air Technical Training Center in Jacksonville, Florida, where he learned to be a radar surveillance specialist. He moved up in grade from recruit to private first class and, like most of his colleagues, received a low-grade confidential security clearance. He completed his specialist training at Keesler Air Force Base, Mississippi, where he learned to be a military air-traffic controller. In August 1957 he was shipped off to Atsugi, Japan.

For some, Oswald's posting to Atsugi rings with latent conspiracy. Located about 35 miles southwest of Tokyo, the field was a key overseas nerve center of the Cold War. Originally a Japanese facility, the sprawling base had become the most important U.S. aerial defense center in the northern Pacific, a vital command post in the event of war with the Soviet Union. It was also a hub of U.S. aerial espionage. Hidden from prying eyes in a huge hangar at Atsugi were the most advanced spy planes of the day: the high-flying aircraft known as U-2s. The camera-laden U-2s could fly above 70,000 feet, beyond the reach of Soviet antiaircraft rockets, and gave the Pentagon a bird's-eye peek at the most secret Soviet weapons complexes.

The ungainly craft could be watched as they took off and returned to Atsugi, and their high-altitude paths westward from Japan would have been visible on Oswald's radar. Why, ask conspiracists, would a professed Marxist be sent to such a well of secrecy? Indeed, why would a country that declared the Communist Party subversive accept a professed Marxist into the Marines? Perhaps, note some observers, Oswald's outspoken politics, like Oswald himself, weren't taken very seriously.

In any event Oswald behaved more like a Marine than a Marxist at Atsugi. He worked four-hour stints in the overheated, overcrowded radar bubble, tracking a variety of aircraft, plotting their courses, and identifying them as friend or foe. His superiors were impressed. Oswald "minds his business," one officer reported, "and does his job well."

Socially, Oswald had a harder time of it. He wasn't the outgoing, hyperconfident, guts-and-glory type that Marine ideology extolled. His roommate, Corporal Thomas Bagshaw, later remembered him as "very thin, almost frail, shy and quiet." He was the introverted little guy found in every military barracks and a natural butt for the jokes of his pushier companions. Oswald took it all in silence. He refused to talk about himself and rebuffed wisecracks with an inoffensive half-smile. Sometimes he would deflect tensions by doing a strange facial imitation of Bugs Bunny: wiggling his ears and extending his teeth over his lower lip. This earned him the not-very-warlike nickname of Bugs. Ozzie was one of the kinder things he was called; he was also known as Mrs. Oswald because he refused to join his mates on their beer-drinking, skirt-chasing leaves in Tokyo, admitting that, at 17, he was still a virgin.

Instead, Oswald spent his first liberties in the base TV room, watching American Bandstand and recorded replays of NFL football games. He also liked to sit around for hours watching other Marines gamble, though he would never take part. His annoyed mates responded to his aloof attitude by occasionally throwing him in the shower fully clothed. Said one Marine who knew him at Atsugi: "Ozzie reacted to most of the crap by looking at you with that half-grin on his face."

Not all of Oswald's comrades in arms found him so remote. One barracks-mate taught him how to use a 35-mm. camera; another recalled that Oswald "used to do me favors, like lending me money until payday." Gradually, the silent loner learned how to relax a little in the company of his fellow Marines. After a time he began to disappear into Tokyo on liberties without ever saying where he'd gone—later he would say that he'd become involved with a cell of Japanese communists; it could have been true. He told one barracks-mate that he'd begun seeing a Japanese hostess at the Queen Bee nightclub in Tokyo, one of the most high-priced hangouts catering to the U.S. military trade. Conspiracists raise their skeptical eyebrows at this: Oswald earned less than $85 per month, and dates with such ladies were expensive. Perhaps, they have suggested, his Marine pay was being supplemented by his wages as an American spy. It is equally possible, however, that Oswald may have been exercising the strict frugality that later let him survive on very little.

Barely two months after Oswald arrived at Atsugi, his unit began making preparations to ship out to the Philippines and the South China Sea, in part to monitor an ongoing political crisis in Indonesia. Perhaps coincidentally, on October 27, Oswald stained his Marine Corps career. While sitting in his barracks that morning, he was wounded in one elbow when he dropped a .22-caliber derringer pocket pistol he'd secretly obtained by mail order. "I believe I shot myself," he declared solemnly to his agitated comrades. He'd done more than that: Suspicion that the wound was self-inflicted and possession of a private firearm meant he would have to face a court-martial.

The wound got Oswald three weeks in the hospital, but he was still able to sail with his outfit. For the next four months, his Marine group shifted from island to island for exercises or practiced shipboard readiness. Part of that time was spent at the huge U.S. Navy installation at Subic Bay in the Philippines, where Oswald later claimed that he'd learned to hate American "militarist imperialism" and its exploitation of Filipino workers. He sympathized, he said later, with local communists. Part of his disaffection may have come from being moved out of the radar dome and given mess-hall duty.

When Oswald returned to Japan, a court-martial ruled that his wound had been accidental but found him guilty of possessing an illegal weapon. He was given a 20-day jail sentence, a $50 fine, and a reduction in rank to buck private. Although the confinement was suspended for six months on promise of good behavior, the young Marine did not go quite free: Instead of being restored to radar duty, Oswald was sent back to work in the mess hall.

The indignities of kitchen police duty summoned up the bedrock bitterness in Oswald's personality that his go-along manner had formerly concealed. He'd been singled out unfairly for the onerous assignment, he was convinced, and he focused on Technical Sergeant Miguel Rodriguez, the noncom who'd sent him back to the mess hall. Once more his innate self-destructiveness took over. He picked a fight with Rodriguez in a bar and spilled a drink on him. The sergeant signed a complaint and once again Oswald faced a military court. Oswald acted as his own defense attorney but failed to move the judges. He was sentenced to 28 days in the brig, plus his original time—48 days in all—and fined $55. In the event, he served only 17 days.

Still, in the late 1950s a Navy brig experience was far worse than mere detention. Inmates were subjected to heavy, humiliating doses of discipline interspersed with menial work details performed under the watchful eye of an armed guard. The strain was unrelenting and intense and forever changed the young man who'd gone into the brig as Ozzie.

To some conspiracists, the transformation of Lee Harvey Oswald has suggested the emergence of a harder, more capable operative—Oswald the spy. But in fact, this "new" Oswald remained very much in character, a cold, withdrawn, and frustrated young man. Only the former easygoing manner was gone—evidently, the socially uncomfortable Oswald no longer needed such a shield. The disciplinary sequence of events had toughened him but also left him thoroughly embittered. "I've seen enough of a democratic society here," he sarcastically remarked to another young radar operator. "When I get out I'm going to try something else." He began traveling to Tokyo whenever he could, but he tended to associate with a Japanese crowd unlike the party girls favored by his mates.

Still apparently enjoying his three-year hitch in the Marines, Oswald playfully flexes his muscles *(left)* in Atsugi, Japan; relaxes for a moment *(below left, circled)* with fellow Marines while training in the Philippines in 1958; and, stateside again, grins beneath a camouflaged combat helmet.

These pages from Oswald's so-called Historic Diary detail his suicide attempt in Moscow but also reveal great difficulty with spelling and grammar caused by acute dyslexia, a disorder that inverts written information.

Oswald's 15-month stint in Japan ended in November 1958, and he returned to California for the rest of his hitch. He also embarked on some carefully calculated self-improvement. Within three months of his return, he took the Marines' proficiency examination for Russian. He did not do well compared with peers who'd received formal instruction, but it was clear that he had somehow acquired a rudimentary command of the language. He also passed his high-school equivalency examinations.

In his barracks Oswald took a new tack: He became a vocal and public supporter of the Soviet Union, albeit a good-humored one. He began subscribing to a Russian-language Soviet newspaper and, when his superiors questioned him, said he was only following instructions to immerse himself in the enemy's culture. When playing chess, he would always choose red over black, saying in a thick mock accent, "the Red Army is always victorious." His barracks-mates nicknamed him Oswaldskovich; he called them Comrade and ostentatiously answered their questions with *Nyet* and *Da*.

Oswald also began to praise Fidel Castro, the charismatic guerrilla leader who had marched to power against the Cuban dictatorship of Fulgencio Batista on January 1, 1959, and whose ambiguous leftist pronouncements were causing concern in Washington, D.C. Oswald was especially drawn by the story of one William Morgan, a former United States Army sergeant who, after defecting to join Castro's forces, had quickly risen to the rank of major in that army. Oswald was already thinking of something similar for himself.

His time in the brig had moved his discharge date from October to early December 1959, an intolerable extension for a young man who itched to be free of the Corps. Like many short-timers, Oswald began waiting to get out and did little more. His work habits fell apart; he was taken off radar duty and put on janitorial jobs. Finally, in August, he sought a hardship discharge, citing a need to support his mother. Working through the Red Cross and armed with the cooperative Marguerite Oswald's corroborating letters, he received his discharge three weeks later.

On September 11, 1959, just 43 days shy of completing his original three-year enlistment—and one week after applying for a passport—Lee Harvey Oswald was released from active duty with an honorable discharge and

Historic Diary

"FROM Oct. 16 1959 ARRIVAL —"

Oct. 16. ARRIVE FROM HELSINKI BY TRAIN; AM MET BY INTOURIST REPRE. AND IN CAR TO HOTEL "BERLIN". REGES AS "STUDET" 5 DA. LUX. TOURIST. TICKET.) MEET MY INTOURIST GUIDE RIMMA SHO... I EXPLAIN TO HER I WISH TO APPL. FOR RUS. CITIZENSHIP. SHE IS FLABBERGASSED, BUT AGGREES TO HELP. SHE CHECKS WITH HER BOSS, MAIN OFFICE INTOUR; MAN HELPS ME ADD. A LETTER TO SUP. SOVIT. FOR CITIZENSHIP MEAN WHILE BOSS TELEPHONS PASSPORT & VISA OFFICE AND NOTIFIES THEM ABOUT ME.

Oct. 17 - RIMMA MEETS ME FOR INTOURIST SIGHTSEEING SAYS WE MUST CONTIN. WITH THIS ALTHOUGH I AM TOO NEVOUS SHE IS "SURE" ILL HAVE AN ANSEWER SOON. ASKS ME ABOUT MYSELF AND MY REASONS FOR DOING THIS I EXPLAIN ? + AM A COMMUNIST. ect. SHE IS POLITIY SYM. BUT UNEASY NOW. SHE TRIES TO BE A FRIEND TO ME. SHE FEELS SORRY FOR ME I AM SOMETH. NEW.

Oct. 18. MY 20th BIRTHDAY, WE VIST EXHIB. IN MORNING and IN THE AFTER NOON The LEAIN - STALIN TOMB. SHE GIDES ME A PRESENT BOOK "IDEOT" BY DESTOEVSKI.

Oct. 19. TOURISM. AM ANXIOUS SINCE MY VISA IS GOOD FOR FIVE DAYS ONLY AND STILL NO WORD FROM KRUM AUTH. ABOUT MY REGEST.

Oct. 20 RIMMA IN THE AFTER NOON SAYS INTOURIST WAS NOTIFIED BY THE PASS. & VISA DEPT. THAT THEY WANT TO SEE ME I AM EXCITED GREATLY BY THIS NEWS.

Oct. 21. (MOR)MEETING WITH SIGLE OFFICAL. BALDING STOUT, BLACK SUIT FAIRLY. GOOD ENGLISH) ASKES WHAT DO I WANT?, I SAY SOVITE CITIZENSHIP HE ASK WHY I GIVE VAUGE ANSEWER ABOUT "GREAT SOVIET UNION" HE TELLS ME "USSR ONLY GREAT IN LITERATURE WANTS ME TO BE BACK HOME" I AM STUNDED I REITERATE HE SAYS HE SHALL CHECK AND LET ME KNOW WEATHER MY VISA WILL BE (EXTENDED IT EXINERS TODAY) EVE. 6.00 RECIVE WORD FROM POLICE OFFICAL. I MUST LEAVE COUNTRY TONIGHT AT 8.00 PM AS VISA EXPIRS. I AM SHOCKED!! MY DREAMS! I RETIRE TO MY ROOM. I HAVE PLAND TO BE ACCEPTED BECM... LEFT. I HAVE WAITED FOR 2 YEAR TO BE ACCEPTED. BECM OF BAD PLANNING I PLANNING I FIANNED SO MUCH. I DECIDE TO END IT. SOAK RIST IN COLD WATER TO NUMB THE PAIN. THAN S... MY FONDLY DREAMS ARE SHATTERED BECAUSE OF A PETTY OFFINL. 7.00 PM. MY LEFT WRIST. I ... WATER.. INTO BATHTUM OF HOT WAT... I THINK "WHEN RIMMA COMES ... TO FIND ME DEAD IT ... BE A GREAT SHOCK.

transferred to the rolls of the inactive U.S. Marine Reserve. He signed a secrecy oath, promising to protect any military information he'd gained during his stint. Then he went back to Fort Worth briefly to visit his mother and to deliver the news that he had no intention of staying. He was going to New Orleans, he said, to work for an export firm.

But in New Orleans, Oswald booked passage on a freighter to France. On October 8, 1959, he landed in Le Havre, and took the boat train to Britain, then caught a flight to Finland, where he stayed for the better part of a week—and obtained a tourist visa for the Soviet Union. On October 15, three days before his 20th birthday, he left Helsinki by train and crossed the border, headed for Moscow. In a world still sharply divided by the Cold War, he had gone over to the enemy.

Oswald's motives for defecting and the details of his stay in the Soviet Union are difficult to verify—ominously so, say conspiracists. To some observers, the only way to explain his actions is to render him an American spy. To others, the only credible interpretation is that Oswald was not an American spy going in, but was a KGB spy coming out. It may very well be, however, that Oswald's own, more ordinary account was largely true in its depiction of a young man propelled mainly by his longing to be someone, and somewhere, else.

That account was contained in a diary—in his grandiose way, Oswald called it his Historic Diary—that he kept while in the USSR. According to this document, Oswald arrived in Moscow as a tourist, traveling on a visa valid for only six days. As with all Western visitors in those days, he was assigned to a guide-minder-interpreter from the Soviet Intourist agency, a woman named Rimma Shirokova. Two days after his arrival in Moscow—and a day shy of his 20th birthday—Oswald told her he wanted to defect. She was surprised and offered little encouragement. He insisted.

The following day Oswald was interviewed by someone who claimed to be a Radio Moscow correspondent but in all likelihood was taking Oswald's measure for the KGB; the interview never aired. On October 21, 1959—the day his tourist visa was to elapse—Oswald had an interview with officials of the MVD, the Soviet internal security ministry. According to his journal, he was told that his petition to obtain Soviet citizenship, which he'd drafted with the help of his Intourist guide, was likely to be rejected.

Oswald quickly raised the ante. Back at his hotel, he wrote later, he held his left wrist under cold water to numb it, then slashed a blood vessel with a razor blade and plunged his arm into a hot bath. He did so fully aware that Rimma Shirokova was returning to the hotel within the hour to help with his departure. When she found him, he was rushed to the hospital and given five stitches and a blood transfusion. He spent the next week under medical and psychiatric observation. At the end of that stint he was moved to a new hotel. His suicide attempt seems to have rattled the Soviet bureaucracy, which found itself suddenly with a dangerously unstable American defector on its hands. Officials from the Soviet visa office interviewed Oswald and asked if he still wanted citizenship. When Oswald said he did, they told him that the matter was under consideration and would be for quite a while. He would have to wait, but he could wait in the Soviet Union.

That story has ever since been suspect to conspiracists and considered improbable by some in American counterintelligence circles. The enormity of Oswald's defection in that era of intense Cold War rivalry is difficult to overstate—such defections were tantamount to treason. Oswald had worked with classified American radar equipment and procedures and had been stationed at fields from which U-2s were launched to spy on the Soviet Union. Depending upon the depth of his knowledge, he might have been considered a valuable catch. At the same time, Oswald almost certainly knew less about the U-2 than the Soviets, who'd been chasing the spy planes with jet fighters and antiaircraft missiles for years. The Korean War-vintage radars he'd used in the Marines were nothing new to the Soviets. Thus his defection had little technical value to the Soviet Union. He had nothing to offer besides a demonstrated, unstable impulsiveness. Said one Soviet defector later, "The KGB didn't want Oswald from day one."

Near the end of October, three days after his new hosts had given him that provisional welcome, Oswald performed another rash, puzzling act: He marched into the U.S. embassy and announced that he wanted to "dissolve his citizenship." He spoke to U.S. consular official Richard Snyder—a CIA intelligence agent operating under diplomatic cover—and handed the man a letter stating his wishes. He told Snyder he'd been a Marine Corps radar technician and would make that knowledge available to the Soviet Union. Why did he want to give up his citizenship? "I am a Marxist." Playing for time, and possibly touched by Oswald's immaturity, Snyder suggested he wait until he had been granted Soviet citizenship before taking such a rash step, and in any case to return in two days. Oswald stalked out, leaving his passport and letter. Snyder duly sent cables to the U.S. Department of State, which fanned word of Oswald's intentions out to the CIA, FBI, and Office of Naval Intelligence.

If Oswald's version of the defection is taken at face value, the recantation of his U.S. citizenship at the embassy may have been his way of burning his bridges back to America, effectively trapping himself in the Soviet Union. It may also have been a way of proving his seriousness—typically a problem with the very immature. Certainly it fed the loner's ego, as squadrons of U.S. reporters sought interviews when they heard that a young American ex-Marine wanted to defect. He refused to be interviewed, but their attention, Oswald wrote in his diary, made him feel "exhilarated, and not so lonely."

On November 3 Oswald wrote another letter to the U.S. ambassador in Moscow, protesting Snyder's refusal to accept his surrender of citizenship. Snyder replied by mail, inviting him to show up in person at the embassy to renounce his allegiance. Oswald stayed in his hotel. Then, 10 days later, he began to give interviews to the U.S. press about his conversion to Marxism—reading Marx, he told one reporter, was like "a very religious man opening the Bible for the first time." He also wrote to his brother Robert, declaring "I will never return to the United States, which is a country I hate."

Oswald spent the next two months in a Moscow hotel room studying Russian, with the help of Intourist guides. On January 4, 1960, the Soviet authorities announced that he had been granted residence papers and would be sent to the Byelorussian capital of Minsk,

about 420 miles from Moscow. He would not receive Soviet citizenship but would live in Minsk as a stateless person. He would be given a metal-working job in a Soviet radio and television factory and paid the equivalent of $70 to $90 a month, bolstered by a $70 monthly stipend ostensibly from the Soviet Red Cross. For relocation, he received the equivalent of about $500. Oswald, according to notes he made at the time, recognized that the extra cash really came from the Soviet interior ministry. It was "payment for my denunciation of the U.S. in Moscow," he wrote, "and a clear promise that as long as I lived in the USSR, life would be very good." It was more money than he had ever earned. Oswald had finally attained the land of his dreams.

When the young defector arrived in Minsk, he was greeted by the mayor and billeted rent-free in a furnished one-bedroom apartment that was large by Soviet standards and would normally have housed an entire family. For a man who had never owned his own home or even had his own bedroom for very long, this was star treatment. His work at the factory was boring but undemanding, and he seems to have been popular with his colleagues, who called their shy foreign comrade Alik, which sounded less Asian than Lee to a Russian ear. He lived in the heart of the bustling little city, close to the Foreign Language Institute, where he could find people, especially women, as eager to practice their English as he was to practice his Russian. The bashful American eventually had affairs with five of them. Oswald told his diary that he went to the "theater, movies, or opera almost every day. I'm living big and am very satisfied."

A little more than a year after his hero's welcome in Minsk, Oswald didn't seem to think he was living quite so big after all. When, in January 1961, Soviet authorities asked him if he still wanted Soviet citizenship, he said no. Having abandoned that option, in February Oswald wrote the U.S. embassy in Moscow, asking if he could have his passport back and return to the United States—"if we could come to some agreement concerning the dropping of any legal proceedings against me." As he had earlier, consular officer Richard Snyder suggested that the wavering defector come to Moscow to make his request in person.

Oswald's concern about legal proceedings stemmed from his threat to share his knowledge of military radars with the Soviets—it violated his secrecy oath; for all he knew, it constituted treason. In fact, although the ex-Marine would not learn of it for more than a year, his ill-considered threat had already branded him. In September 1960, after the embassy's notification of his attempted expatriation, the Marine Corps had stricken Oswald from the reserve rolls and downgraded his discharge from honorable to undesirable, a stigma that would dog Oswald's later efforts to find work in the United States. He also fretted about the legality of the stipend he'd been receiving indirectly from the MVD and about his having applied for Soviet citizenship. America might not want him back.

The motive for Oswald's growing disaffection with the land of his dreams has never been established. One factor may have been his rebuff by a woman with whom he'd fallen heavily in love: Ella Germann, a foreign-language student. But one woman's rejection hardly seemed justification for the sudden turnaround in Oswald's attitude toward the Soviet Union—especially since he would soon marry another Russian woman.

In the Historic Diary Oswald attributed his change of heart to the counsel he was beginning to receive from friends like the manager of his factory, Alexander Ziger, who advised him to go home. "He says many things and relates many things I do not know about the USSR," wrote Oswald. "I feel inside, it's true!!" He began to make querulous comments about the regimentation of Soviet life, the omnipresence of the Communist Party bureaucracy, and the quality of the life he had so recently praised. "The work is drab," he wrote. "The money I get has nowhere to be spent. No nightclubs or bowling alleys. No places of recreation except the trade union dances. I have had enough." His natural ingratitude settled on his Soviet hosts.

Although the restless American privately denigrated the dances held at the local Palace of Culture, where leisure activities were planned for Minsk residents, he didn't give them up. It was at a medical student's ball there, in fact, that he first met 19-year-old Marina Nikolayevna Prusakova, on March 17, 1961. He spent the evening in the swarm of young men who followed in the wake of this pretty, delicately made young woman. A week later they met again. Marina has said she was intrigued by the thin, dark-eyed American defector, who quietly defended his native country when it came under attack from his Soviet acquaintances. They met at another dance a week later and made a date. But in a few days Oswald called from the hospital, where he was undergoing an adenoids operation. Would Marina come to see him there? She agreed.

For more than two weeks they met in the hospital. When he was discharged on April 11, he met her family. On April 18—only a month after their first encounter—Oswald proposed and she accepted. On April 30 they were married before a civil registrar—and Marina Oswald discovered that her new husband had lied to her: He was 21, not 24, as he'd told her. She would learn that lying was one of the few things Oswald did well.

Although Marina could not have known it, she'd begun a life of almost total dependency on a man who would remain opaque to her, as he would later to students of the Kennedy assassination. And the close family bonds she had apparently missed as a child were not to be found with him. Born illegitimate on July 17, 1941, in Molotovsk, on the White Sea, Marina never knew her father, or even his name. When her mother married an electrical engineer named Alexander Ivanovich Medvedev, the new family moved to a more comfortable life among his relations in Leningrad, now St. Petersburg.

Marina's pharmacist training at a Leningrad technical college was interrupted when her mother died, leaving the girl alone among the Medvedevs, with whom she felt uncomfortably out of place. In June 1959 she completed her training and, unable to stay with her step-relations, moved to Minsk to live in the household of her maternal uncle, Ilya Vasilyevich Prusakov—an engineer who worked for the MVD. His rank and his ministry made him a highly influential member of the Communist community—and would later provide fodder for conspiracists searching for a Soviet link to the Kennedy killing, although no verifiable connection has ever been found.

When Oswald asked for her hand in marriage, Marina later admitted, she didn't love him. "I married him because I liked him," she said. As it happened, Oswald was not in love with her either. He was still moping over his rejection by Ella Germann and had fastened on Marina on the rebound. Nonetheless, when her uncle reluctantly gave his consent—it would not help his career to have a niece married to an American—the unlikely arrangement was as good as done.

That the pair came together speaks volumes about how little they expected from this most intimate of life's relationships. Over the next couple of years, their marriage would increasingly be held together with perverse ties of anger and abuse—physical on his part, verbal on hers—alternating with genuine, often deep, affection. But even as they first set up housekeeping together, Marina noticed her husband had various tics and obsessions, which offered a glimpse into his upbringing and evoked his travails with his mother.

Marina found that he was consumed with cleanliness and was forever washing dishes and mopping the floor. He went so far in his fetish as to refuse to kiss women on the mouth if they were wearing lipstick. Oswald was ashamed of his manual labor and would never let Marina launder his soiled work clothes—like anything else that caused him pain or embarrassment, he preferred to take care of it himself in isolation. He was excessively jealous of any time that Marina spent away from him; even if she was a few minutes late in returning home, he demanded an explanation. When she attended Communist Youth League meetings, he accused her of seeing old boyfriends. Like his mother, he was inordinately stingy in doling out money for clothing and food. And, as his mother had kept him dependent, he further clipped Marina's wings by forbidding her to learn English—even as it became clear that he planned a return to the homeland he despised.

Lee Harvey Oswald had one other noteworthy obsession: a love of guns. He'd bought a shotgun almost as soon as he had arrived in Minsk and had joined a hunting club. From the first days of their marriage, Marina recalled, he kept the weapon mounted on a wall of their apartment and often cleaned and polished it. But she could recall his taking it on a shooting expedition into the countryside just once. The rest of the time it rested on its supports, a silent harbinger of other guns to come.

During the month before his marriage, Oswald had once again rudely demanded that the U.S. embassy return his passport and had said he could not leave Minsk to pick it up in Moscow without offending Sovi-

Lee Harvey Oswald and his Russian bride, Marina Nikolayevna Prusakova, pose for a photo on their wedding day in April 1961.

At the Minsk train station, Soviet friends Maria, Alexander, and Eleanor Ziger (holding Oswald baby) bid Lee and Marina (*far right*) goodbye as they begin their long journey back to America in May 1962.

et authorities. After receiving guidance from Washington, the embassy had replied that his passport could only be returned to him in person. Moreover, before he could have his passport back, Oswald would be made to swear under oath regarding "the circumstances of his presence in the Soviet Union and his possible commitment of an act or acts of expatriation." The U.S. government took seriously the possibility that he had, in fact, repudiated his citizenship.

Oswald tried again. On May 16, 1961, he wrote that he was "asking not only for the right to return to the United States, but also for full guarantees that I shall not, under any circumstances, be persecuted for any act pertaining to this case." Then he threw the embassy a curve ball: "Since my last letter I have gotten married." Mentioning that his spouse was Russian, he said, "Arrangements would have to be made for her to leave at the same time I do."

As he had for years with Marguerite, Oswald took a bullying, ungracious tone to get what he wanted. The embassy continued to hold out for a personal interview. At home, these tensions took the form of marital strife and sexual trouble. Marina countered with unexpected good news: She was pregnant.

In July Oswald flew to Moscow to win back his passport. In a face-to-face interview with Richard Snyder, and under oath, he told some of the most serious lies of his life. He had never applied for Soviet citizenship, he said, nor belonged to a trade union at his factory—that would have made him a member of a Communist organization. Then he claimed that Soviet officials had never questioned him about his life in the United States. While admitting to a Radio Moscow interview, Snyder reported, Oswald testified that he had "made no statements at any time of an exploitable nature concerning his original decision to reside in the Soviet Union." In other words, he said he hadn't betrayed his native country either in word or in deed.

Perhaps more important than what Oswald said was how he said it. The old arrogance and bravado were gone, Snyder noted approvingly. In their place were some unabashed attempts to gain sympathy. Oswald contended that Marina was being harassed at work for choosing to leave the country with him, and he falsely claimed she had been hospitalized for nervous exhaus-

tion as a result. He said he was penniless and in need of financial aid to get home. By now, his passport had expired; he needed a new one.

Oswald seemed to have made his case well enough in Moscow. Marina joined him there for her own interview, and also squeezed through the ordeal by denying her membership in Komsomol, the Communist Youth League. Gradually, the Oswalds passed through the bureaucratic straits of immigration, supplying whatever new information the embassy in Moscow needed to satisfy the reservations of such agencies as the U.S. Immigration and Naturalization Service, then leery of Soviet women marrying Americans just to gain entry to the United States.

Leaving the Soviet Union appears to have been easier for the Oswalds than for most. Although they had not yet been cleared for entry by the United States, by Christmas Day 1961 they had received exit visas from the Soviet authorities. For some, this facile release from a police state later raised suspicions of KGB involvement—the deployment of two spies back to the United States, perhaps. More likely, the Soviet Union was anxious to return its vacillating, nervous defector and didn't mind his Russian wife going with him. As a young pharmacist, she took no secrets with her.

The delays were all on the U.S. side, as the embassy demanded more information about Marina and proof that Oswald would provide her support. In fact, a behind-the-scenes struggle was going on. The Immigration and Naturalization Service outright opposed Oswald's return, arguing that his loyalty was in question. The State Department argued, however, that it was better to have volatile malcontents like Oswald at home than abroad. He was, in their view, an "unstable character, whose actions are entirely unpredictable." Besides, on the Cold War tally sheet, it was always positive to have a defector come home.

Meanwhile Oswald staged another of his bullying campaigns, this time aimed at the U.S. Marine Corps. In the course of his efforts to return to the United States, he'd learned that the Corps had changed his honorable discharge to an undesirable discharge and dropped him from the inactive reserves. Now he launched a blustering correspondence to get that stigmatizing decision reversed. In a long petition, he argued that he was not a

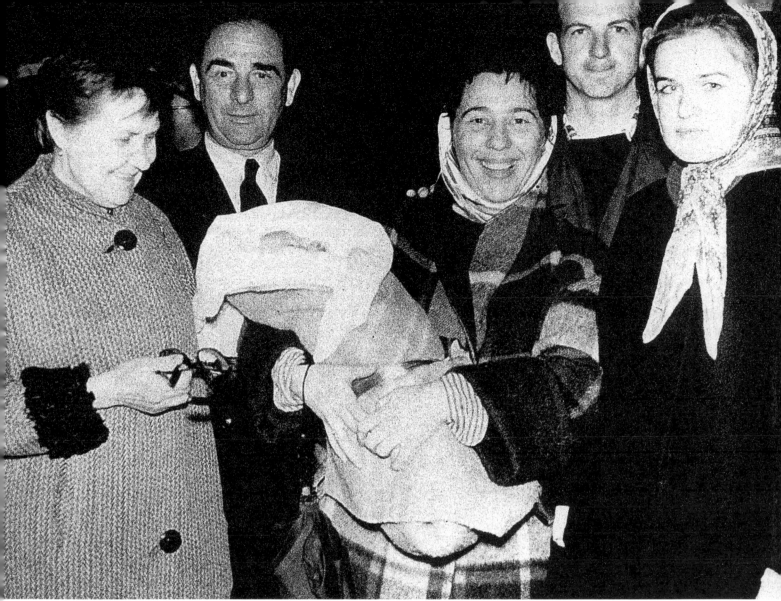

defector at all but had been forcibly detained by the Soviets—and even offered to hand over any useful information on the Soviets he had gleaned during his stay. One of those he wrote was soon-to-be governor of Texas John Connally, apparently under the mistaken impression that he had been Secretary of the Navy when Oswald's discharge status was changed.

While the couple waited, their daughter was born on February 14, 1962. Oswald had hoped for a boy and wanted his son born on American soil—American children born abroad, he explained to Marina, could never be president. They named the girl June Lee, since Soviet tradition dictated that there must be some reference to the father for her middle name. Oswald became a devoted parent, in his fashion.

Finally, on May 10, Marina received her U.S. visa; two weeks later, Oswald received his renewed passport—good only for travel to the United States. The State Department loaned him $435.71 to make the trip home.

The little family departed by train from Moscow on June 1 and traveled to Rotterdam, where they boarded a ship for New York.

On the voyage across the Atlantic, according to Marina, Oswald grew increasingly nervous. He anticipated a press mob at dockside, questioning him about his defection and his return. He closeted himself in the ship's library to compose a disingenuous double set of replies about the questionable aspects of his defection. In one set of answers, he admitted to everything that he had just denied under oath: seeking Soviet citizenship, accepting payment for broadcasts against the United States, offering to reveal military secrets. In the second set, he denied everything. As always, his persona flickered between extremes—would he be the unrepentant defector or the returning prodigal son?

In further anticipation that the world would be waiting on the Hoboken quay to hear his political views, Os-

Oswald's trans-Atlantic political musings, jotted down on
Holland-America ship's sta-
tionery, reflect the anxiety he
felt as he returned to the
United States.

wald also composed a rambling, disjointed dissertation. There he attacked not only capitalist but communist, fascist, anarchic, and religious beliefs, declaring them all destructive of the United States. What was required, he said, was to take the "ideological best" from both the left and right, "and yet be utterly opposed to both." In his own case, that meant a bitter attack on the existence of the state. In the end he foresaw a vaguely apocalyptic confrontation between socialism and capitalism and suggested that he would emerge in the vanguard of a peace movement that would break with both camps. The point he most aimed to impress upon his imagined audience was that he'd returned from the Soviet Union declaring a pox on both houses. "I have lived under both systems," he grandly declared. "I have sought the answers and, although it would be very easy to dupe myself into believing one system is better than the other, I know they are not."

As it turned out, he had no need for his manifesto. The only person awaiting them at dockside on June 13, 1962, when the ship landed at Hoboken, was a Traveler's Aid Society representative, present to escort them across the harbor to Manhattan. Oswald was tense. "Thank God there are no reporters," he told his wife. But he could not have been too pleased, after his perilous Cold War adventures, to be the same unknown little man he'd been two years before. To the Traveler's Aid person, he explained why he had been in Moscow: He'd been a Marine stationed at the U.S. embassy. In New York he learned that the New York City Department of Welfare had scraped up $200 for the family's

airfare to Fort Worth by calling his brother Robert. Oswald was livid and tried to refuse the money. The welfare organization stood firm.

The family flew to Fort Worth, where Robert met them. "What? No photographers or anything?" Lee asked his older brother. Robert explained that the *Fort Worth Star-Telegram* had already run a front-page story about the defector, under the headline: "Ex-Marine from Ft. Worth Ends Stay in Soviet Union"—he may not have mentioned that the story ran a mere 15 lines.

Inevitably, Marguerite swept upon the scene and, true to form, tried to bring the focus of the occasion around to herself with the announcement that she planned to write her autobiography, inspired by her son's defection. Lee bridled at the notion—he had intended to do something similar. Within days of touching down in Fort Worth, he was on the hunt for a typist-stenographer to turn his scribbled, disorganized Historic Diary into a manuscript. Typically, he melodramatized the nature of the document, telling the steno that he had smuggled it out of Russia under his clothes. Over three days, they managed to turn out about 10 single-spaced pages, about a third of the manuscript. Then Oswald announced that he had run out of money. When the typist offered to do the rest of the work without pay, he refused, saying, "I don't work that way." The diary project petered out.

On the home front, it didn't take long for the euphoria of Oswald's family reunion to wear off. Within days, he and Marina had an argument at their brother's dinner table. When she refused to break off the squabble in public, Lee followed her into the bedroom and hit her across the face with his open hand. Whatever secret angers and uncertainties he bottled up inside would increasingly come to the surface in the form of a slap or punch for his wife.

Some of Oswald's jitters undoubtedly involved the authorities. Despite the lack of a reception when he returned to the United States, he surely knew that he would be under some form of official surveillance, at least for a while. Within two weeks of his arrival in Fort Worth he was invited by the local FBI office to come for an interview. He was questioned intensely about his motives for going to the Soviet Union. What the FBI really wanted to know, however, was whether they had a returning Soviet spy on their hands—he might have traded his services as a mole for his family's exit visas. Oswald repeatedly denied any such involvement and finally informed the interviewing agents sharply that he did not "care to relive the past." He refused a polygraph test. The G-men found him impatient, arrogant, and evasive, and they recommended that he be questioned again. Back at his brother's house, Oswald explained the brush with the law in typical fashion: The FBI, he said, had wanted to know whether he had ever worked as a U.S. government agent.

The FBI was not the only threatening presence moving in on Oswald. Marguerite announced that she'd quit her job in a neighboring town in order to be close to her dear young son and his family. She'd rented a two-room apartment in Fort Worth and wanted them to move in with her. Marina was delighted at the news, her husband much less so. But he was broke and unemployed, and they acceded. Within a short time, however, he found a job as a sheet-metal worker at the Leslie Welding Company—he lied about his experience to get the work. As always, he was a hard but taciturn worker. And, as always, he aimed to live rent-free with his mother while he dutifully paid off the money he owed to Robert and the State Department.

Marguerite, meanwhile, brought Marina more closely into the Oswald family circle by accusing her, as she had her other sons' wives, of alienating Lee's filial affections. Oswald soon found the situation intolerable, and less than a month after moving in, he, Marina, and June moved out, in a scene worthy of a Tennessee Williams play. When brother Robert pulled up to the apartment to help with the move, he found his mother screaming and crying at the unexpected turn of events. When they drove off, Marguerite ran a few steps after the accelerating car. "She'll be all right," Lee coldly advised. "It's not the first time."

Oswald's flight was a short one. He'd rented a shabby duplex at 2703 Mercedes Street, a poorly furnished but clean apartment about half a mile from Marguerite Oswald's place. Six days after their move two FBI agents knocked at the door. They wanted to talk to him again about any "deal" he might have struck before leaving Russia. Again, Oswald flatly denied the idea. The FBI did not push too hard; later it recommended that the case on Oswald be closed. "He had gotten a job, and he wasn't as tense," one of the agents reported. But Oswald did remark that "he might have to return to the Soviet Union in about five years to take his wife back home to see her relatives." And a day or two later, Oswald wrote to the Soviet embassy in Washington, asking them to send periodicals that might be of interest to Soviet citizens living "for a time" in the United States.

The rootless family needed to connect to this new— and, for Marina, bewildering—Texas homeland. Unable to speak English and housebound in their meager apartment, she lived in almost Arctic isolation. Then, searching for someone to certify him as a Russian translator, Oswald happened upon Fort Worth's community of Russian émigrés. That small group of expatriates, always eager for new membership, soon drew the Oswalds in. Marina, naturally enough, was the focus of most of the attention: She was frailly attractive, impoverished, and stranded in a mother tongue that few people spoke in America.

Paul Gregory, the son of an expatriate Russian consulting engineer, became a frequent visitor at the Oswald home, hoping to improve his Russian with Marina. Inevitably, he found himself embroiled in political conversations with her husband, who still saw in Communism the wave of a better future. He fervidly praised Nikita Khrushchev and Cuba's Fidel Castro, and even had favorable words to say about John F. Kennedy, whom he described as a "good leader." Gregory found Oswald "hot tempered, not very smart and slightly mixed up." He was struck by Lee's increasingly brutal tone toward

Marina, the way he starved her of money, and the extent to which he seemed intent on maintaining her isolation. When Gregory suggested that Marina get English lessons, her husband strenuously objected—if they began speaking English at home, he said, he would lose his fluency in Russian.

The Oswalds were soon known among the émigrés as a charity case, but when food and clothing were offered, Oswald rudely turned most of the supplies away and accepted the rest without thanks. In the same fashion, he allowed the émigrés to fix Marina's badly decayed teeth, yet he blamed Marina both for the charitable attention and for the friendships she struck up among the expatriates, at one point calling them a "betrayal." The number of beatings increased; Marina began appearing in public with black eyes. Gradually, opinion hardened against Oswald, especially when his political fulminations revealed that he did not share the hardened anticommunism that was universal among Russians in exile. "I am scared of this man," said George Bouhe, an elderly expatriate who had taken an avuncular fancy to Marina. "He is a lunatic."

Oswald's willingness to exploit the émigrés even while insulting them politically reached a peak in early October 1962, when he announced that he had been fired from his sheet-metal job—it was another calculated Oswald lie. An unofficial rescue committee was formed; Marina and little June were packed off to the home of a couple in the expatriate circle. With his family safely in the care of others, Oswald then quit his sheet-metal job—he'd earned enough to pay off his debt to his brother. The ploy had been a cold-blooded move to get his family off his hands while he changed jobs and cities. He set out for Dallas, 30 miles east, to look for work. Not once did he offer to pay for his family's expenses while he was away, nor did he tell anyone where he'd gone. Within a few days, he signed on as a trainee cameraman at Jaggars-Chiles-Stovall, a graphic arts firm, using his references from the Russian community. The episode clearly confirmed the assessment of one émigré that Oswald would "trample over you in hobnail boots in order to get what he wanted."

The Oswalds remained apart for a month, with the destitute Marina and June moving from one home to another. No one knows where Oswald lived during his first week in Dallas or during a second period from October 21 to November 2. He claimed to be staying at the YMCA, then in the Carlton Boarding House in Dallas's Oak Cliff section. His stay at the Y, however, only lasted one workweek, and he never registered at the boardinghouse. Conspiracists have viewed these blanks with alarm, suggesting that, since Oswald's lodgings could not be verified, he must have been up to some secret business somewhere else. In fact, his days, at least, are accounted for: He was learning the photography trade at Jaggars-Chiles-Stovall and made periodic visits to his wife and child in Fort Worth.

During the second, two-week-long period for which Oswald's living place is unknown, the world's attention riveted on events farther south, in the Caribbean, where, for four days, nuclear war between the United States and Soviet Union seemed imminent. A standoff had developed over the issue of Soviet intermediate-range missiles that Nikita Khrushchev and Fidel Castro were secretly emplacing in Cuba. On October 22 President Kennedy had declared a naval blockade, raising the possibility that American warships would be forced to fire on Soviet freighters steaming toward the island. Tensions between the superpowers had never been higher. The crisis lasted until October 28, when the Soviet leader ordered his freighters to come home in exchange for certain U.S. concessions. The peaceful ending was no surprise to Oswald. On one of his periodic trips to Fort Worth, he discounted the threat of conflict. He'd been to the Soviet Union, he said, and he was sure the Soviet government would never start a nuclear war.

As tensions eased between the superpowers, however, hostilities in the Oswald family reached new heights. Lee Oswald's manner toward his wife was becoming overtly brutal. The couple quarreled incessantly; he ordered her around and belittled her in front of friends. The émigré community was given a dramatic firsthand view on November 3, the day after Oswald had finally announced that he was taking his family to a new home in Dallas. After he arrived to pick them up, he noted that the zipper on Marina's skirt was not fully closed. He ordered her to approach him, and when she did, he slapped her across the face while she held their baby in her arms.

The Oswalds' new home was at 604 Elsbeth Street, in

the Oak Cliff district. It was a dirty, unkempt apartment in a garbage-infested neighborhood—a "pigsty," Marina remembered calling it, as she balked at moving in. Eventually she relented, but the battle continued to rage over the next few days. Oswald accused her of "whoring" after the émigré community that had spoiled her. "If you like them so much, go live with them," he ordered. Somehow Marina found the courage to comply. She bolted from the house with June and returned to the home of one of her expatriate protectors. The community gathered and told her she was right to leave. Yet within two weeks, after repeated entreaties by Oswald, the two were back together again. The disappointed Fort Worth Russians washed their hands of a situation that offered so little hope of improvement.

The one émigré who did not seem to sour on Lee Oswald was himself a mystery man—and a man who, for conspiracists, added mystery to Oswald as well. George de Mohrenschildt was tall and handsome, with a Russian aristocratic background, an exotic fashion-designer wife named Jeanne, a Polish and Belgian education, a background in petroleum engineering, and a disdain for middle-class convention. It was de Mohrenschildt's daughter and son-in-law who first put up Marina and June while Oswald went off to Dallas.

De Mohrenschildt's past political loyalties were as murky, in their way, as Oswald's. During World War II he'd worked with the Free French in New York and had made trips across the United States to recruit intelligence agents with petroleum expertise. But he was also associated with Baron Konstantin Von Maydell, a Nazi agent arrested in the United States in 1942 as a "dangerous alien" and interned in North Dakota. De Mohrenschildt had made an abortive attempt to join the Office of Strategic Services, precursor of the CIA, but was turned down on security grounds. A CIA background check in 1957 called him a "dubious character."

For all his differences with the scruffy, dogmatic Oswald, however, de Mohrenschildt conceived a sympathy for the man he considered a "semi-educated hillbilly." It may have been his well-known passion for underdogs; De Mohrenschildt's wife Jeanne referred to the one-time defector as "a puppy dog everybody kicked." It may have been something of a father-son relationship: De Mohrenschildt's only son had died.

Oswald in turn was fascinated by the dashing, unconventional blue blood, going so far as to show him an essay he'd written called "The Collective," which described life and work in regimented Communist society. He even agreed with some of de Mohrenschildt's opinions. Privately, the aristocrat sneered. Oswald, he said, was a man of "exceedingly poor background who read rather advanced books and did not understand even the words in them." Oswald, he observed, got no fun out of life; he mused that even Oswald's defection to the Soviet Union had been accomplished without "the enjoyment of adventure."

It was de Mohrenschildt, however, who first tried to help the Oswalds toward reconciliation, lecturing Lee on his wife beating and trying to extract a promise that he would stop. When the couple reconciled, the de Mohrenschildt's did not join the rest of the émigrés in ostracizing them. Unlike the other expatriates, de Mohrenschildt frankly enjoyed talking politics with Oswald—perhaps because his own opinions were too unconventional for that community. The pair agreed on Fidel Castro—another underdog—on civil rights issues, and above all on the loathsomeness of white racist opposition to the desegregation battle, then in full swing.

Just before the Cuban crisis erupted, U.S. attention had been fixed on the University of Mississippi, where retired major general Edwin Walker was leading white mobs against federal agents trying to enroll the school's first African American student, James Meredith. De Mohrenschildt and Oswald talked long and often about Walker, a man who had, paradoxically enough, led a battalion of U.S. troops into Little Rock, Arkansas, to integrate Central High School at the behest of President Dwight Eisenhower only five years before. After his retirement to Dallas, Walker had become one of America's leading exponents of militant action against communists, civil rights activists, and liberals of every stripe. Although de Mohrenschildt's disdain for Walker was deep, it was abstract; Oswald's animosity would prove to have a sharper edge.

Oswald and his family were reunited, but it was clear that the cankers in his soul were more inflamed than ever. As usual, Marina and her child bore the brunt of it. It was only weeks after her return that Marina phoned an acquaintance in panic: Ten-month-old June had a

The coupon Oswald used to order a revolver bears the signatures of A. J. Hidell and D. F. Drittal—two favorite aliases.

bothering about who was working there. He also started reading *Krokodil*, a Soviet humor magazine, with ostentatious pleasure.

Oswald had been so grimly intent on paying off his debts that he'd forsaken almost every other amusement. But finally that burden lifted in early 1963, and on January 27 he celebrated his new solvency by ordering a gun. Oswald sent off a form to the Seaport Traders Inc. in Los Angeles, with a $10 deposit, and ordered a Smith & Wesson .38-caliber revolver, a model with a five-inch barrel that had been shortened to two and one-fourth inches. The balance, $19.95, plus postage and handling, was due on delivery. He filled out the mail-order form in the name of A. J. Hidell and then forged the name of a witness to his testimony that he had never been convicted of a felony. The 23-year-old Oswald also lied about his age, declaring that "Hidell" was 28. The revolver was to be sent to Post Office Box 2915, Dallas. He had apparently rented the box during his October job-finding stint in the city, as soon as he had secured a promise of employment.

The next day Oswald enrolled in a typing course at a nearby high school. The course meant he would be away from home three evenings a week until it ended at 7:15, but Marina later testified that he was never home before 7:00 p.m. on any night. For at least a portion of that time, he was learning photo-typesetting techniques after regular working hours and offered to do work for two New York-based leftist newspapers: the *Militant,* an organ of the Trotskyist Socialist Worker's Party, and the *Worker,* house organ of the Communist Party in the United States.

When he did show up at home, Oswald spent hours alone in the kitchen, poring over what he said was a typing test. In fact, it appears that he was studying bus schedules and maps of Dallas to determine his way in to a target and his way out—the apprentice assassin had not learned to drive. Judging from the evidence of advance planning later found in the family's dwelling, Oswald had spent weeks ruminating over the killing of General Walker.

Clearly, some kind of violence had begun to take root in his mind. His beatings of Marina grew worse, and his frictions at work became more intense, nearly coming to blows on several occasions. During this period Oswald

103-degree fever and Lee wasn't home; she needed a ride to the Parkland Memorial Hospital's emergency room. At the hospital Marina was told to come back when a pediatrician would be on duty. But only after another explosive argument did Oswald, who by then had returned home, agree to let the child see a doctor—he feared he couldn't pay. Once at the hospital, he gave a false address and said that he was unemployed to avoid paying more than a token amount.

Oswald's chronic edginess was on the rise. Marina noticed that he avoided their neighbors and invariably used the back door of the apartment building to enter. At work he'd been promoted from trainee to a regular employee, but that modicum of success seemed to affect him adversely. He began making mistakes that his bosses noticed. His relationships with his fellow employees began to deteriorate. Among other things, he developed a habit of walking into the company darkroom without may have rifled the files at Jaggars-Chiles-Stovall, since he was later to attach copies of the company's tax returns to his résumé in order to establish his photo-reproduction—and spying—skills. He may also have forged a Selective Service notice of classification and Marine Corps certificate of service in the name of Alek James Hidell; both would be found among his effects. And, ominously, he notified Marina that he might soon be sending her and the baby back to the Soviet Union. It was too hard to support a family in the United States, he said. They would be better off there. As if to reinforce the point, his open-handed slaps more frequently became punches with a closed fist. In early February, fearing his wrath, Marina broke the news to Oswald that she was pregnant; to her surprise, he expressed delight but then seemed to forget about it as he returned to the deadly matter at hand.

On February 14—baby June's first birthday—the *Dallas Morning News* announced that General Edwin Walker's anticommunist, anti-Castro crusade, Operation Midnight Ride, would begin on February 27 in Miami, and the paper followed that up within days with a feature story on the upcoming event. On February 17, according to Marina, Oswald forced her to write to the Soviet embassy in Washington, expressing her desire to return home and, in typical Oswald fashion, asking the Soviets to pay her way. He seemed to be arranging a life for her and June without him.

No one knows whether Oswald's restless planning was intended to spare his family or whether it was meant merely to detach them from his life. Browsing among his grand fantasies, he may have seen his death in the attempt on Walker or envisaged going off alone to fight in Cuba, like the mythic Major William Morgan he so admired—in either case, Marina and June would be better off among her relatives in Minsk. He may also have wanted to pave the way for his own return to the Soviet Union.

On February 23, Walker's last Saturday in Dallas before hitting the crusading trail, Oswald didn't report for work. His whereabouts are unknown; he may have been studying the lay of the land around his future prey. Marina recalled that the following week was the most violent of their marriage; it was so bad that their landlord was forced to intervene. Neighbors had been complaining, he warned; the battling had to stop. Oswald's reaction was to move out. On March 2 he moved the family into a new apartment a block away at 214 West Neely Street. The new place was cleaner and cheaper, and it had a balcony. It also had a closet-sized study, with a separate entrance from the outside stairs. With the inside door to the study shut, Oswald could come and go freely, unobserved.

Just over a week later, according to the detailed record Oswald left behind, he began stalking Walker in earnest, taking pictures of the general's house and compiling a scheme that he meticulously recorded in his diary. On March 12, using a coupon clipped from the *American Rifleman* magazine, he sent away to Klein's Sporting Goods Company in Chicago for their advertised 6.5-mm. Mannlicher-Carcano carbine, a World War II-vintage Italian military rifle; the weapon cost $21.45, telescopic sight included. Oswald ordered the gun in the name of A. Hidell, and he requested that it be sent to his post-office box.

Locked away in his tiny alcove, Oswald added further to his vague political philosophy for the enlightenment of future readers. In a wandering manifesto he once again predicted that a "total crisis" would destroy the U.S. government, leaving the pieces to be picked up by a small elite party that would establish a "separate, democratic, pure communist society." He added a second document that laid out elements of his personal creed for the organization: It included free speech, racial and religious tolerance, abolition of all organized armies—and gun control.

One thing was missing from this increasingly comprehensive record: an image of the freedom fighter himself. On March 31 Oswald asked Marina to take a picture of him with their Imperial Reflex camera. He appeared in the backyard of their apartment building dressed all in black, carrying his rifle in one hand, his revolver at his hip. In his other hand he held copies of the *Worker* and a March 11 edition of the *Militant,* in which he apparently had published a letter under the initials LH. The next day he developed the photos and inscribed one "For Junie from Papa." He said it was "to remember Papa by sometimes."

That same April Fool's Day, Oswald was informed by his boss at Jaggars-Chiles-Stovall that he'd been fired for

In early 1963 Oswald ordered a Mannlicher-Carcano carbine from Klein's Sporting Goods and faked a Marine Corps certificate of service, again using the Alek James Hidell alias.

substandard work, effective April 6. His only response was a quiet "Well, thank you." He didn't tell Marina the bad news. During his last week at work he began serious target practice, even telling his wife, who had discovered the gun in his study. Only on April 10 did Oswald confess that he'd lost his job. He blamed it on the FBI, who, he said, had visited his shop. "When will they leave me alone?" he asked rhetorically. He could not resist a lie, even when he seemed to believe the end was near. The tone of his notebook entries and manifestoes was that of a man

CERTIFICATE OF SERVICE
ARMED FORCES OF THE UNITED STATES

THIS IS TO CERTIFY THAT

ALEK JAMES HIDELL

HONORABLY SERVED ON ACTIVE DUTY IN THE

United States Marine Corps

DD FORM 217 MC   1 JAN 51

who doesn't believe he will see the dawn. That night, Oswald began his journey toward Walker, glory—and, he evidently fantasized, his death.

The next morning, the story of the attempted assassination was in all the newspapers. By then Oswald had recovered enough aplomb to be amused. The police erroneously announced that the badly damaged bullet buried in Walker's wall was 30.06 caliber, not the 6.5 mm. of his Carcano rifle. Reports also announced that a 14-year-old witness had spotted two men escaping in separate cars. Oswald snorted, even as he lashed himself verbally for missing the shot—"A perfect shot if only he hadn't moved." Despite the failure, however, Oswald had silenced his demons by firing at Walker. Calm now, he revealed his meticulous notebook plan to Marina, who later said that she had urged him immediately to destroy it. He burned the plan and flushed the cinders down the toilet. But he saved the photographs and the philosophical musings. He wasn't finished with such important, soul-healing work.

On the following Saturday George and Jeanne de Mohrenschildt stopped by the Oswald home for a visit. With characteristic heavy-handed humor, de Mohrenschildt asked, "Hey Lee, how come you missed?" The Oswalds were horrified by his prescience. In fact, as de Mohrenschildt later explained, his remark was a fairly obvious joke, given Oswald's expressed hatred for Walker. It was the last time the couples saw each other; the de Mohrenschildts were leaving town, not to return until 1966. Waiting for them would be a package containing some records Lee had borrowed and a photograph of Oswald with his guns, inscribed: "Fighter Against Fascism, Ha-ha-ha."

The day after the de Mohrenschildt visit Oswald retrieved his rifle from its hiding place near Walker's home; some think he risked capture hoping to have his brave deed revealed to the world. A few days later he did the next best thing to proclaiming himself the mysterious assassin—he stood on a Dallas street corner with a sign around his neck that warned Hands Off Cuba! Viva Fidel! and passed out pro-Castro political leaflets. He may not have slain the dragon, as intended, but he could still flaunt his radical allegiances. He later wrote to the Fair Play for Cuba Committee in New York to report

that he'd handed out 15 leaflets in the space of 40 minutes, and he asked for more. They were mailed to him on April 19.

Two weeks after shooting at Walker, Lee Harvey Oswald, unemployed since early April, left for New Orleans. He took with him his personal belongings—including his rifle—but not his family. They went to live with Ruth Paine, a quiet housewife who'd met Marina a few weeks earlier. Paine welcomed the abandoned wife and child to her comfortable home in the Dallas suburb of Irving. Recently separated from her husband, Michael, a physicist at the nearby Bell Helicopter plant, and living alone with her two children, she was glad for the company and for the opportunity to practice her beginning Russian.

On April 25 Oswald turned up at the New Orleans home of his Uncle Charles Murret and Aunt Lillian. In his customarily methodical way, he set about looking for work. That posed a problem: His only references were bad ones, and even his military service had been tainted by an undesirable discharge. Undaunted, he simply lied about his background and after two weeks landed a $1.50-an-hour job as a maintenance man at a coffee distribution company, where he oiled and cleaned the large grinders. He immediately sent for Marina and June. The obliging Ruth Paine drove the family to New Orleans, where Lee had found a ground floor apartment at 4907 Magazine Street, a seedy neighborhood between Canal Street and the Mississippi River. They resumed the life of poverty that, to his miserable, pregnant wife, must have looked by now like the human condition.

Oswald started work on May 10 and soon joined the public library; the first book he took out was a biography of Mao Zedong. Within days after that, he was once again burnishing his credentials as a militant supporter of Cuba, writing to the Fair Play for Cuba Committee for information about how to start a local chapter.

Even here, appearances apparently mattered more to Oswald than realities. Rather than wait for a go-ahead from the Fair Play headquarters, he had his own Hands Off! leaflets printed up, under the name Lee Osborne, along with 500 chapter membership applications and 300 membership cards. He had Marina forge the name of A. J. Hidell as chapter president. Even as he was doing so, he received a warm but skeptical letter from the real president of the Fair Play committee, Vincent Lee, saying that he did not think Oswald would be able to recruit many members in the South and warning him to operate out of his home and to use a post-office box as a mailing address; an office might attract the feds. In the second week of June, Oswald mailed off a letter to the *Worker,* announcing his formation of the New Orleans chapter, and sent honorary membership cards to U.S. Communist Party leaders Gus Hall and Benjamin Davis.

What Oswald was really doing, he told his wife, was planning trips to Cuba—illegal for U.S. citizens—and China. His Fair Play ruse was evidently intended to establish his revolutionary credentials for the Cubans, who could hardly be expected to welcome every ex-Marine who turned up at their door asking to join the struggle. Oswald told Marina coldly, "I love to travel and with you I can't" and informed her that he still intended to send her and June back to Russia, where they could wait for him. As always, his egocentric revolutionary fantasy dominated his interior stage, which had little room for his family. As part of his preparation for a tropical trip he obtained an international vaccination certificate in his own name and forged the signature of a doctor—once again, A. J. Hidell. A few days later, in a strange taunting of his former branch of the armed forces, Lee Oswald took his Fair Play for Cuba leaflets down to the New Orleans waterfront and began handing them out at the dock where an American aircraft carrier was berthed. He was soon told to leave.

On June 24 Oswald applied for a new U.S. passport. He said that he planned to travel to England, France, Germany, Holland, the Soviet Union, Finland, Italy, and Poland; he'd be leaving, he said, on the Lykes Steamship line—the same line he'd taken to Europe in 1959—sometime between October and December 1963. Oswald also changed his tactics with Marina, saying he would accompany her to the Soviet Union. This, in turn, required that she write another letter to the Soviet embassy in Washington, D.C., to request financial aid for her return. Before he mailed her letter, Oswald appended a note asking the embassy to expedite Marina's request so that their baby could be born in the Soviet Union and to consider his entrance visa separately—he still had other travel plans.

The same day, Oswald borrowed a new book from the library, William Manchester's *Portrait of a President*—the story of John F. Kennedy. Oswald soon had plenty of time for reading, for he was once again fired from his job, effective July 18. He'd been playing hooky from work, often visiting next door at the Crescent City garage, where he would talk with owner Adrian Alba, a gun buff, about firearms. He picked up Kennedy's *Profiles in Courage*, a collection of stories about Americans who bravely swam against the political currents of their day. As a leftist revolutionary, Oswald knew what it was like to be always bucking the trend.

Very much at loose ends, the itchy political warrior cast about for ways to make some fantasy or another come true. He fired off another letter to Vincent Lee at the Fair Play committee in New York, claiming that he'd opened a Fair Play office in New Orleans. With typical disregard for the truth, he fabricated a whole schedule of imaginary dues and assured Lee that he wouldn't cheat the head office out of any money. He also advised Lee that one of his attempts to distribute flyers had been disrupted by anti-Castro agitators and that he had been cautioned by the police about his activities. Lee never replied, but Oswald didn't seem to care. He kept sending periodic advisories to New York about his progress, possibly assuming that the information was somehow getting back to Cuba. Then he set out, it seems, to make the imaginary confrontation come true.

On August 5 Oswald walked into the clothing store of Carlos Bringuier, New Orleans spokesman for the Cuban Student Directorate, an anti-Castro exile group. He broke into a conversation between Bringuier and a couple of teenagers to announce that he'd like to train some volunteers to fight against Fidel Castro. He cited his Marine credentials and said that he'd received training in guerrilla warfare—he'd be happy to teach the arts of sabotage and explosives. Bringuier, justifiably suspicious, put him off. As he left, Oswald offered to contribute money to the anti-Castro cause. He came back the next day to drop off a copy of his Guidebook for Marines as a way of further establishing his bona fides.

But Oswald was quickly seen to be working both sides of the Cuban issue. Only a few days after his offer to Bringuier, Oswald was handing out Fair Play for Cuba leaflets on downtown Canal Street. Word got back to

A perfect shot if only he hadn't moved.

Bringuier, who arrived with two friends to discover that the demonstrator was none other than the ex-Marine who'd offered to train men to fight Castro. A scuffle broke out, in which Oswald waited passively to be hit. They were all arrested for disturbing the peace. Oswald spent the night in jail and the next morning regaled a skeptical cop with stories about the size of his fictional pro-Castro chapter.

No one has fully explained Oswald's contrary actions. Some conspiracists take his anti-Castro posturing as a feint to improve his communist credentials. Others say that it could equally have been an expression of his real, anti-Castro sentiments, leaking suddenly into the light. The mystery was deepened by a further Oswald antic: From jail, he demanded, and got, an interview with a local FBI agent—an interview in which he detailed his largely invented Fair Play for Cuba activities. Again, conspiracists point to that meeting as one laden with significance, suggesting that Oswald, the presumed spy, had felt a compelling need to summon his handlers. But he may have been pulling levers merely for the sake of producing an effect. It could have given him a moment's intoxicating power, being the summoner of the FBI instead of the summoned. In any case, he was soon back on the street.

The incident brought a few minutes' local fame, however. Eight days after the incident, Oswald was invited to appear on local radio station WDSU to explain his views for the show Latin Listening Post. He delivered himself of a 40-minute interview that was edited down to four and a half minutes. The interview went well enough that he was invited back on August 21 to take part in a debate with Carlos Bringuier and a representative of another Cuban exile support group. Oswald agreed. But the reporter who invited him did some checking with the FBI and learned about Oswald's defection. Bringuier too had been doing some checking. The radio show soon turned into an exploration of Oswald's Marxist background, Soviet residence, and rumored attempt to renounce his U.S. citizenship.

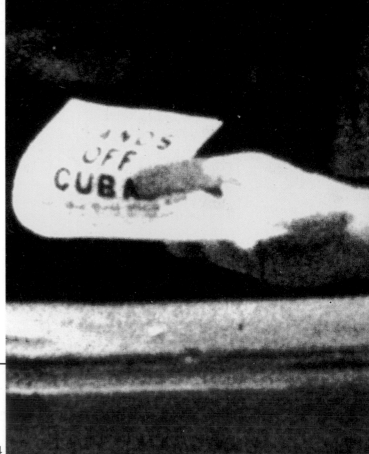

Oswald was crestfallen but pumped up his deflated psyche in typical fashion. He fired off a letter to the Central Committee of the Communist Party in the United States, outlining what had happened in highly colored terms and asking that body for advice. Since he'd been exposed, he wondered, should he go underground? The letter clanged with Oswald's grandiose political illusions and with his wish that someone be aware of the important role he'd taken in the global struggle.

But Oswald never really listened to anyone's advice. He knew what he wanted: Cuba, whose closest embassy was in Mexico City. He urged Marina to write to her friend Ruth Paine, explaining that he was out of work and looking for a job and accepting Paine's earlier invitation to spend the last weeks of her pregnancy in Irving, Texas. Paine said she would pick Marina up in New Orleans on September 20. While they waited for that day to arrive, Oswald began laying down a false paper trail, perhaps to confuse the FBI. He wrote a series of letters to the *Worker* saying that he planned to relocate to New York City and asking about employment. Then he wrote the Socialist Workers Party and the Communist Party to say that he and his family would be moving to the Baltimore-Washington area and asking for the names of contacts. On September 20, true to her word, Ruth Paine arrived. Lee packed his rifle among Marina's belongings, to be stored in Paine's garage.

On September 25, 1963, Oswald took off by bus for Mexico via Houston, where he briefly attempted to contact a member of the Socialist Labor Party. On September 26 he crossed the border and hopped a Mexican bus at Nuevo Laredo for the capital city some 550 miles away. He was going to see Fidel, he told his puzzled fellow passengers. Arriving in Mexico City the next day he began to bounce between the Soviet and Cuban embassies, to little effect.

Since travel to Cuba was illegal for Americans, Oswald had to adopt the subterfuge of obtaining a Soviet visa that would allow him to apply for a "transit" visa to Havana as part of that trip. That made the Soviet embassy his first stop. Oswald spoke with Valery Vladimirovich Kostikov, a consular officer—later identified by American counterintelligence as a KGB spymaster operating undercover—and asked about his wife's and his own requests for a Soviet reentry visa. He also

displayed his Fair Play for Cuba membership card. Then he walked the several blocks to the Cuban embassy and spoke with Sylvia Duran, a Mexican national working in the consulate, who heard him out sympathetically and made some calls on his behalf. He was told that it would not be difficult to get the Cuban visa, but the prerequisite Soviet visa could take as long as four months— an eternity, given Oswald's scant resources.

Unhappy with that news, Oswald came back the next day to try again and got the same answer. His anger so alarmed Duran that she summoned the Cuban consul, Eusebio Asque, who confirmed the bad news. Oswald was outraged: Someone of his clear dedication, who had already made sacrifices for the Cuban revolution, deserved better. Asque lost his temper and declared that people like Oswald harmed the revolution more than they helped it. Sylvia Duran, more sympathetic, handed Oswald her name and telephone number and processed his Cuban visa application. He was told that the precious slip of paper would be provided in 15 to 30 days but would not be valid for travel without his Soviet visa. Once again, Oswald tried at the Soviet embassy—without much success.

On the face of it, Oswald's trip appears to have been a disaster, consuming such little money as he'd saved in New Orleans but taking him nowhere. Conspiracists view it differently. To some, his interview with KGB agent Valery Kostikov evoked Soviet instruction of a mole and their involvement in the assassination to come; to others, his visits to the Cuban embassy seemed an ominous prelude to political murder. Still others believe that the man in Mexico City was not Lee Harvey Oswald at all, but a ringer. To those who do not subscribe to a conspiracy theory, however, an impoverished, anxious Lee Harvey Oswald futilely beating his head on the diplomatic doors of Mexico City has a factual ring—futility, after all, was the fuel that his rising anger had always fed upon.

The thwarted, embittered Oswald returned to the United States by bus on October 2 and by the following day was back in Dallas. His grand plan lay in splinters; he was jobless; he needed money. After spending the night at the YMCA, he called Marina to let her know that he was back in town and looking for work. Almost immediately he ran into a new problem—as usual, one of his own creation. He was turned down for a job he had applied for at a printing plant after the owner had talked to people at Jaggars-Chiles-Stovall, who related Oswald's troublemaking and "communist tendencies." He hitchhiked to Irving to spend some time with his family and reviled the Cuban bureaucracy, which he said was the same as that in Russia.

The following week Oswald began looking for a job again, without success. Marina remained with Ruth Paine in Irving while he sought accommodations. In his first rooming house, the landlady asked him to leave after five days—she didn't like him eating in his room. He thought she was motivated by a visit from the FBI. Thus, when he took another room, at 1026 North Beckley Street, he adopted an alias, O. H. Lee. Conspiracists have found his recurring use of aliases significant, suggesting an agent in motion. More likely, the aliases were a symptom of Oswald's distorted sense of his own importance—famous communist revolutionaries would find it hard to find a place to stay in Dallas. They certainly found it hard to get a job.

During his second week in Dallas, Oswald got a rare break. Linnie Mae Randle, a neighbor of Ruth Paine's, had heard that there might be a temporary position at the company where her brother worked: the Texas School Book Depository in Dallas.

The depository is an unremarkable seven-story red-brick structure that stands by itself on the north side of Dallas's Dealey Plaza, a small park of sculpted lawn and plantings, and is flanked to the east by a line of county and state public buildings. Oswald started work there bright and early on October 16, 1963. Ruth Paine had telephoned the superintendent, Roy Truly, and Oswald had made a favorable enough impression to be hired temporarily at $1.25 per hour. He later told Marina that the work was "interesting and clean." It was also not very demanding: Oswald filled orders and brought down books from the upper floors of the depository. In the mornings, with characteristic frugality, he would read the previous day's newspapers his coworkers left in a first-floor rest area called the domino room.

Employed at last, Oswald may have been happy, in his fashion. Four days after he started at the book depository, his second daughter—Audrey Marina Rachel Os-

wald—was born. Still, he lived alone in Dallas and left his family to Ruth Paine's generous reflexes. For days at a time he kept to himself in his rooming house; the landlord, Arthur Johnson, remarked that he "never talked." Still, by October 23 his political instincts had begun to stir. That night he attended a political rally and heard a speech by General Edwin Walker. The next day, stirred up by Walker, the crowd spat on Adlai Stevenson, the Illinois liberal then serving as Kennedy's ambassador to the United Nations. The placards the mob carried had been stored at Walker's home.

On October 25 Oswald attended a meeting of the American Civil Liberties Union. The meeting left Oswald unimpressed, he said, but a few days later he filled out an ACLU membership application. The same day he rented a post box for two months. Then he wrote another letter to the U.S. Communist Party, asking their assessment of the civil liberties organization. "Could you advise me," he wrote, "as to the general view we had on the ACLU and to what degree, if any, I should attempt to highten its progressive tendencies?" Once again, the misty architecture of Oswald's imagined role in the world revolutionary movement coalesced in his mind.

But Oswald's roamings had not gone unnoticed. On November 1 Marina Oswald and Ruth Paine received a visit from FBI special agent James P. Hosty, who had a few questions about Lee. The FBI had learned of Oswald's visit to the Soviet embassy in Mexico City, reviving fears that he might be a communist agent. Marina kept mum. On the weekend she told Oswald of the visit. Hosty returned the following Tuesday, looking for Oswald's address; Paine said they didn't have it.

Visibly shaken by this official attention, Oswald fled into the security of his fantasized nationwide revolutionary network: He typed a letter at Ruth Paine's desk addressed to the Soviet embassy telling of the FBI inquiry, which he claimed was the result of his Fair Play for Cuba activities. He added portentously that if he had "been able to reach Havana as planned the Soviet Embassy there would have had time to assist me." Oswald then left the letter on the desk, where Paine discovered it in the morning. It startled her, she said later, for it was her first look into Oswald's secret revolutionary soul. She made a copy and left the original where she found it.

The following Tuesday, November 12, Oswald report-

The red-brick facade of the Texas School Book
Depository looms over Dallas's Elm Street
and Dealey Plaza, along the route of President
John F. Kennedy's November motorcade.

ed for work after the Veterans Day holiday. On his lunch break he walked over to the nearby FBI office in Dallas and left an envelope for James Hosty. Inside, on a single sheet of paper, he'd cautioned the agent: Quit bothering my wife. If Hosty did not comply, Oswald said, he would be compelled to "take action." The note was unsigned. Oswald was only one of a number of people that Hosty thought might have sent such a message.

As it happened, Hosty's entire office was preoccupied with the impending visit of the president of the United States. The date of John F. Kennedy's Dallas trip, a fence-mending exercise with conservative Democrats intended to show that the president was not just another left-leaning liberal, had been announced on November 8. The advance Secret Service detail arrived the same day that Oswald passed on his warning to Hosty. Concerns about Kennedy's safety were high in the wake of the reception accorded Adlai Stevenson. At the insistence of newly elected governor John Connally, the president had agreed to address a businessmen's luncheon at the Dallas Trade Mart as part of the one-day venture. It would be preceded by a motorcade from the airport in the open presidential Lincoln limousine.

On Tuesday, November 19, the Dallas newspapers bannered the president's planned route through the city, an itinerary that would take him through Dealey Plaza. Oswald himself may not have learned of the motorcade route until Wednesday, November 20, when he read the day-old papers in the domino room. If the news moved him, he evidently gave none of the usual signs—no stepped up wife-beating, no drop in job performance, no secret planning sessions, no manifestoes.

On November 21, after a normal day at work, Oswald asked Linnie Mae Randle's brother, Wesley Frazier, for a lift out to Ruth Paine's house. It was a Thursday; Oswald did not normally visit his family until Saturday. He explained that he wanted to pick up some curtain rods. Sometime during the day he fabricated a paper bag about 27 inches long from brown paper and tape. At Paine's home, Oswald greeted Marina and later went to spend a few minutes in the garage. Then he played with the children. That night Ruth Paine also went to the garage, to paint some blocks for her children; she noticed that some things had been disturbed and the light left on, and she thought it was Lee's usual carelessness.

Oswald went to bed around 10 p.m. but, according to Marina, was sleepless and tense until about three in the morning. The next day, he slept briefly through the alarm but was ready to leave the house around 7:15. On the way out, he kissed the children, then returned briefly to say that he'd left some money on the bedroom dresser. "Take it and buy everything you and Junie and Rachel need," he said. It was a completely uncharacteristic gesture for this miserly man. Unbeknownst to Marina, he'd left her the entire Oswald estate—$170. Later she discovered his wedding ring in a small demitasse cup. He had not planned to return.

Next door, Linnie Mae Randle saw Oswald coming from the Paines' house with a long brown package that he put in the back seat of her brother's car. As the two men left Oswald explained that it contained the curtain rods he'd mentioned the day before. Less than 45 minutes later they arrived at the depository; Oswald picked up his package and walked on ahead of Frazier. Superintendent Roy Truly arrived at 8 a.m. to discover Oswald already at work. Sometime between 9:30 and 10, the ex-Marine casually asked another order filler to point out the direction that the president's motorcade would take on its way through the city from Love Field.

On the sixth floor that Friday, five workmen were laying a new plywood floor. At 11:40, one of them, Bonnie Ray Williams, saw Oswald on the east side of the sixth floor. There was nothing unusual about that; order fillers often drew from stocks kept on that level. Five or ten minutes later the workers got on freight elevators at the rear of the building and spotted Oswald again, this time on the fifth floor. Yet another witness remembered seeing him on the second floor at about 12:15. Charles Douglas Givens, one of the workers, had forgotten his jacket; he went back to the sixth floor and found Oswald there, walking from the southeast corner of the building toward the elevators with a clipboard in his hand. That corner of the room was filled with book cartons that the workmen had moved to carry out their flooring job, and the southeast corner window was partially shielded by them. Givens asked whether the order filler was going downstairs. Oswald said no.

At 12:20 p.m. Bonnie Ray Williams and two other men went to the southeast corner of the fifth floor to watch the motorcade pass by. The Lincoln convertible

Smiling for the cheering Dallas crowds, President and Mrs. Kennedy enjoy an unexpectedly warm reception from Texans. Moments later their Lincoln entered Dealey Plaza.

approached from the east on Main Street. A driver and Secret Service agent occupied the front seat. Texas governor John Connally sat on a jump seat on the passenger side, facing forward; his wife Nellie sat on his left. First Lady Jacqueline Kennedy sat behind Nellie Connally, and the president had taken the right rear seat, behind the governor. The day was fine, and Kennedy had elected to leave the limo's transparent bubble behind. The crowd was heartening—Dallas was a lot friendlier than he had expected.

The Lincoln made a right turn onto Houston Street. A block later, the driver pulled through the 120-degree left turn onto Elm, slowing almost to a stop directly in front of the southeast corner of the depository; then the limousine crept away downhill through Dealey Plaza, where a meager crowd had gathered to catch a glimpse of the president.

In a nest of book cartons six stories above Elm Street, the assassin watched the limousine through an open depository window. Then he brought the Mannlicher-Carcano carbine to bear, using book boxes and an improvised leather sling to steady the muzzle. He let the cross hairs of his telescopic sight hover upon the tiny figure in the right rear seat not 200 feet away, took a shallow breath, exhaled, and began to squeeze the trigger.

The people who were in Dealey Plaza on that day described events there very differently. Some believed the shots had come from a now-famous grassy knoll just beyond the depository building on the same side of Elm Street. Some reported seeing puffs of smoke from the knoll, even men fleeing with guns. Some heard as many as eight shots, while others heard two, or none. Some of those present added strata of conflicting minutiae with every retelling of their experience. The one objective witness to the assassination was a strip of 8-mm. color film, exposed by Dallas dressmaker Abraham Zapruder, who resolutely kept his camera going as he watched his president horribly cut down.

The Zapruder film has been studied as intensively as scripture because it is more than just a view of the assassination—it is a precise clock. With the film moving through the camera at 18.3 frames per second, each frame is about fifty-five thousandths of a second apart. The investigation that followed the assassination *(page 51)* concluded that Lee Harvey Oswald had fired three times from the sixth floor, southeast corner window of the school book depository but that only two of the bullets found their mark. This scenario required one leap of faith, however: It assumed that one bullet followed a tortured path, entering Kennedy's upper right back and exiting the front of his neck, then passing through John Connally's chest, shattering his wrist, and penetrating his thigh, without much deformation of the slug itself. Conspiracists have derided this as the Magic Bullet theory. Others note that the high-velocity copper-jacketed bullet did exactly what it was designed to do—penetrate without deforming—and they further point out that bullets, with their enormous charge of energy, can do all kinds of unlikely things.

As the scene unfolded, the Lincoln's driver, alarmed by gunfire, virtually stopped the car. At that instant, as the wounded John Kennedy raised his hands to his neck, another shot hit him, in the right rear quadrant of his head, exploding the right front of his skull as the bullet exited with a gory jet of blood, brain matter, and bone fragments. Dazed Secret Service men suddenly realized they were under assault. The Lincoln lurched as an agent behind the car ran forward and Jackie Kennedy clambered onto the limousine's rear deck—to recover a portion of her husband's skull, she later testified. Then the president's car quickly roared away in the direction of Parkland Memorial Hospital.

When Dallas motorcycle policeman Marrion Baker heard the first shot, he looked up and saw pigeons scattering from the depository. He roared over and ran to the entrance, where supervisor Truly ran with him to the elevators. Because the elevator cars were both at the fifth floor of the building, Baker rushed up the stairs. On the second floor, he spotted someone through a window in the domino room door. Waving his pistol, Baker told the man to walk toward him; he obeyed. "He never did say a word or nothing," Baker later testified. "In fact, he didn't change his expression one bit. He didn't seem to be excited or overly afraid or anything. He might have been a bit startled, like I might have been if somebody confronted me. But I cannot recall any change in expression of any kind on his face." It was Lee Harvey Oswald, unarmed. Truly identified him as an employee, and Baker rushed on.

Frame 237 of Abraham Zapruder's 8-mm. film catches the instant that a sniper's bullet strikes the president in his upper back and wounds Governor Connally.

Although almost intact, this so-called magic bullet (actual size) evidently passed through both men.

Less than five seconds later, in Zapruder frame 313, the assassin's third shot fatally wounds the president, hitting him in the right rear quadrant of the skull.

Seconds later, a clerical worker on the second floor spotted Oswald walking slowly, carrying a bottle of Coca-Cola. He crossed the floor, walked down the stairs, and left through the depository's main entrance. Oswald walked, or ran, seven blocks east on Elm Street and boarded a bus heading back toward the depository en route to his rooming house neighborhood. But traffic was in bedlam. After two blocks, Oswald walked to the front door; always frugal, he asked for a transfer. Four blocks away, he politely hailed a cab at the Greyhound Station. He asked the driver, William Whaley, to take him to 500 North Beckley Street, which was about five blocks beyond his boardinghouse at number 1026—

presumably to see if the police had arrived there before him. It would have taken about six minutes to walk back to his room, where the housekeeper noticed him arrive near 1 p.m.

In a hurry, Oswald donned a light windbreaker and stuck his snub-nosed .38 revolver in his waistband, then emerged from his room, zipping up his jacket over the pistol. He began walking rapidly south. By now, doctors at Parkland Memorial had pronounced John F. Kennedy dead of massive head wounds, and police dispatchers were broadcasting a description of the suspected assassin—white male, approximately 30, slender build, height five feet ten inches, weight 165—which had been

In Zapruder frame 389, Secret Service agent Clint Hill clambers aboard the accelerating Lincoln to help Jacqueline Kennedy back into the car.

supplied by an eyewitness, a man sitting on a concrete wall across the street from the book depository. The man, Howard L. Brennan, told investigators that he looked up to see a man fitting that description "aiming for his last shot" from the sixth floor, southeast corner window of the building.

Just after 1 p.m., patrolman J. D. Tippit spotted someone who matched the suspect's description nearly a mile from the North Beckley Street rooming house. The policeman pulled his car alongside the walking man, who eventually stopped. After a brief conversation through an open window, the man stepped back. Tippit got out and walked toward the front of the car, his gun still hol-

stered. As the officer reached the left front wheel the man pulled a revolver and opened fire. Tippit was hit four times. The man began to reload as he ran, and he threw the cartridge cases into some nearby bushes. A dozen bystanders—a number of whom would later disagree about exactly what they saw—witnessed the shooting. One of them called for help on Tippit's police radio at 1:16.

Eight blocks away, shoe store manager Johnny Brewer heard police sirens and looked up. He saw a man duck into the recessed entrance of his store and turn his back to the street. A police car U-turned outside. The man quickly glanced over his shoulder, then walked toward

JEFFERSON DAVIS TIPPIT

the nearby Texas Theatre. Brewer followed and asked a cashier whether the man had bought a ticket. The answer was no. Brewer and an usher checked the exits and the darkened cinema, then called the police.

At 1:45 p.m. a small horde of police took up positions inside the theater. When the lights went up, Brewer pointed to a man sitting by himself near the back. A patrolman approached and asked him to stand up. He rose, put up his hands, and said, "Well, it's all over now." Then he tried to punch the cop and drew his gun, which he jammed against the officer's body. Before he could fire police grabbed him and yanked the gun away. "I protest this police brutality," the man shouted. As he was being led away, he turned and yelled, "I am not resisting arrest." At 2 p.m. he arrived at the basement of the Dallas Police Department. He was asked if he wanted to conceal his face as he went inside the building. "Why should I cover my face? I haven't done anything to be ashamed of."

At 2:15 p.m. the head of the Dallas homicide bureau arrived and told his men to "pick up a man named Lee Oswald." He was a suspect in the assassination. One of the cops pointed a finger. "There he sits."

Lee Harvey Oswald's interrogation was conducted in bedlam, with seven or eight men doing the questioning and no one keeping a verbatim record of the questions and answers. Over 12 hours, only sporadic notes and memos were written down. "We were violating every principle of interrogation," Dallas police chief Jesse Curry admitted later. One of the questioners was FBI agent James Hosty, who drew the only emotional attack from the suspect; Oswald accused the agent of accosting his wife and generally abusing her. Oswald denied any wrongdoing, but by evening five witnesses had identified him in a lineup as the man who shot Officer Tippit. Conspiracists and critics of police handling of the case contend, however, that the lineup was stacked against Oswald—the other men participating were markedly dissimilar in dress, age, and physical appearance from Oswald. However, police were able to identify the discarded cartridge cases that were found near the Tippit crime scene as having come from Oswald's gun.

That evening Oswald was arraigned for the murder of J. D. Tippit. During a crowded, jostling midnight press conference, he was asked a shouted question: Did he kill the president? "Nobody has said that to me yet," he replied. When the question was put to him by police, he once again denied everything.

That might have struck some sophisticated interrogators as unusual, since a political assassin who carried out such a staggering crime might be expected to have a manifesto near at hand. Oswald, however, claimed that he'd had no reason to shoot John Kennedy; in fact, he and his family were "interesting people." Oswald had been eating lunch on the first floor of the depository when the shooting occurred, he maintained. Why had he left the building? "I didn't think there would be any work done that afternoon," was his reply. He even denied owning the Mannlicher-Carcano carbine that police had found stashed in the northwest corner of the sixth floor. A handmade paper bag had been found alongside the window from which the shots were believed to have been fired.

One of the spectators eddying through the Dallas police station that night was Jack Ruby, the 52-year-old owner of the Carousel Club, a low-class nightspot on Commerce Street. Ruby had become a familiar, sycophantic figure to some of the city's lawmen, always hanging around the station, foraging for favor. The for-

Clamping his cigar while trying to restrain the struggling assassin, Dallas detective Paul Bentley, aided by officer C. T. Walker, wrestles with Oswald outside the Texas Theatre immediately after the arrest.

Flourishing the Mannlicher-
Carcano rifle used to kill
President Kennedy, a Dallas
police officer wades through a
crush of journalists waiting at
police headquarters.

mer street brawler from Chicago was reputed to be linked to fringes of the Mob, although it had not made him rich. By 1963, in fact, Ruby had come almost to the end of his financial tether and was about to crack. Ruby had cried at the news of John Kennedy's death and had closed the Carousel Club in mourning. Seeing the alleged assassin, across a room teeming with reporters and police, Ruby may have been tempted to use the .38 revolver he always carried. But he simply watched the smirking suspect.

The evidence against Oswald built rapidly. Fingerprint experts had discovered his palm print on a carton that had been pushed to the window. Firearms identification matched the bullets at the assassination scene with the gun. Back at Ruth Paine's house, police had discovered the photo of Oswald brandishing his weapons, proof that the gun had been in his possession for some time. Oswald's response to that piece of evidence was to claim that someone had transposed a photo of his face onto someone else's body—an idea since promulgated by conspiracists, despite Marina Oswald's insistence that she'd taken the photos at Oswald's request.

At 1:36 a.m. on Saturday, November 23, Lee Harvey Oswald was formally arraigned for the murder of John F. Kennedy. Oswald demanded as his lawyer John J. Abt of New York City—a well-known leftist lawyer who had defended people charged under the Smith Act, a 1940 statute that made it a criminal offense to advocate the overthrow of the United States government. No one could reach Abt, however. He was spending the weekend in the country.

That afternoon, Oswald had his first meeting with Marina—and Marguerite. Along with the children, they had been sequestered by *Life* magazine in a Dallas hotel. "Why did you bring that fool with you?" Oswald asked Marina when he saw his mother. "I don't want to talk to her." Then he added: "It's a mistake. I'm not guilty. There are people who will help me." Whom he meant by that is unclear. He may have been referring to Abt, assuming that the attorney would rally to his cause in the same way he had succored revolutionaries in the 1940s. Oswald's romantic view of himself as a daring revolutionary echoed throughout his interrogation. He made much of his contacts with the Soviet embassy in Washington, D.C., his residence in the Soviet Union, his Fair

Play for Cuba Committee chapter, his Marxist beliefs. On that night, his world of political fantasy had finally become important to somebody else.

Oswald's intermittent interrogations lasted into Sunday morning, November 24, when he was supposed to be moved to the county jail, in keeping with Dallas police practice for handling accused felons. At 11:10 a.m., he was ready to be transferred. He refused to wear a hat or anything that would cover his face. He wanted to be seen. At 11:20 Oswald was brought downstairs in the police station to the basement, where a car was waiting to ferry him away. More than 100 policemen were present, but so were scores of reporters, photographers, and three television camera crews—and Jack Ruby. He'd stopped at a nearby Western Union office in order to send a former Carousel Club girl a $25 money order. Seeing the flurry of activity at the station, he'd left his beloved dachshund, Sheba, locked in his automobile and strolled into the basement. As usual, Ruby was wearing his .38.

Flanked by five police detectives, Oswald walked to-

Wearing his trademark smirk, a confident Oswald displays his handcuffs to the police headquarters crowd.

ward the car, preceded by the shout "Here he comes!" Later, Jack Ruby told his brother Earl that he'd seen a smirk on Oswald's face and thought, "Why, you little S. O. B." A minute later, Ruby stepped forward and fired a single shot into the accused assassin's abdomen. The wounded man was rushed to Parkland Memorial Hospital, where he was pronounced dead. "Well, you guys couldn't do it," Ruby later explained to a Dallas assistant district attorney. "Someone had to do it."

On Monday, November 25, 1963, the day that John F. Kennedy's funeral procession crossed from Washington to the hallowed high ground of Arlington National Cemetery, Lee Harvey Oswald was buried at the Rose Hill cemetery in Fort Worth. Others had refused to accept his body. Four ministers declined to perform the service before the Dallas office of the National Council of Churches prevailed on a Lutheran volunteer. At the last minute he too dropped out, leaving Reverend Louis Saunders of the Fort Worth Council of Churches to bless the outcast. There was only a perfunctory graveside service, and there were no pallbearers until a handful of journalists covering the interment volunteered. And there was no peace.

The death of John Kennedy had created a kind of political watershed, beyond which lay more assassination, decades of racial strife, and a ruinously divisive war in Vietnam; his murder had foreclosed on what many Americans believed was the opening of a Golden Age. To many, such a feat was beyond the abilities of Lee Harvey Oswald. To many, he had to have been a small cog on a great gear of conspiracy—a nobody forever. How he would hate it.◆

Stepping suddenly from the eddying reporters and police, nightclub operator Jack Ruby thrusts a .38 revolver toward Oswald and fires a fatal shot into his abdomen.

Except for the reporters who served as pallbearers, Lee Harvey Oswald's wife, brother, mother, and children are the only mourners at his Dallas grave.

Eternal Web

Of the four American presidents murdered in office, none has provoked the brooding controversy of John F. Kennedy. Since 1963 his assassination has been tangled in a vast web of hypothesized conspiracy, which, by its nature, pivots on coincidence. And this tragedy has more than its share of coincidence.

For example, within 90 minutes of Kennedy's murder, Lee Harvey Oswald was arrested—to conspiracists, a suspiciously short interval suggesting that Oswald, as he himself protested, was framed, either by coconspirators or by the government. Then, less than 48 hours after his arrest, while still vociferously maintaining his innocence, Oswald was himself shot to death on live national television by Jack Ruby, a nightclub operator with links to organized crime. Ruby claimed that his act had been a grieving impulse, committed to spare the president's widow from the agony of a trial. Few people believed him, however.

Kennedy's successor, Lyndon Baines Johnson, moved quickly to allay fears of a wide conspiracy to assassinate the president. On November 29, 1963, he appointed Earl Warren, chief justice of the Supreme Court, to chair a commission to probe the murder. The 888-page *Report of the President's Commission on the Assassination of President Kennedy*, issued 10 months later, incorporated more than 26,500 interviews by the FBI and the Secret Service and the testimony of 552 witnesses questioned or deposed by the commission itself; the evidence filled 26 volumes.

It concluded that only three shots had been fired that day in Dealey Plaza and that Lee Harvey Oswald had fired all of them, killing the president and wounding John Connally. The commission believed that Oswald had acted alone and that Jack Ruby's stated motive for killing Oswald was his true motive. These conclusions have been under attack ever since.

More than a decade later, a new wave of skepticism led Congress to establish the House Select Committee on Assassinations. By that time the country had learned, among other things, of CIA complicity with the Mob to assassinate Fidel Castro and had witnessed, during the Watergate scandal, the tentacular reach of right-wing Cuban groups, former CIA officials, and the FBI into the Nixon White House. What had been unthinkable in 1963 seemed plausible in the 1970s.

The House committee spent two and a half years researching the Kennedy assassination, as well as that of civil rights leader Martin Luther King Jr. *(page 167)*. In the end it reported that "acoustical evidence"—sounds heard by witnesses as well as scientifically analyzed sound recordings—pointed to the possibility of a second shooter, and thus to a wider conspiracy. If that were

true, the committee concluded, Oswald must have been killed to silence him. But its report absolved the governments of Cuba and the Soviet Union, as well as the American CIA, FBI, and Secret Service. It also absolved anti-Castro and organized-crime groups but did not rule out the the possibility that individuals within such groups may have played a role.

Still, theories abound, among them:

The Mafia Did It. Organized crime and corrupt representatives in the labor movement retaliated against their prosecution by John Kennedy's younger brother and attorney general, Robert F. Kennedy. Major players, both deceased: New Orleans crime boss Carlos Marcello and Santos Trafficante Jr., former head of the Mafia in Cuba and the Tampa Bay area, forced out by Castro's revolution. This plays on Ruby's Mob ties and on Oswald's time in New Orleans.

Castro Did It. Using Oswald as its instrument, the Cuban government retaliated for CIA involvement in attempts to kill Fidel Castro. In September 1963 Castro had told an Associated Press reporter in Brazil that Cuba was prepared to "answer in kind" any attempts on the lives of Cuban leaders. In this interpretation Oswald's trip to Mexico City becomes sinister: He wasn't seeking a visa; he was being primed by the Cubans to kill JFK.

The KGB Did It. Oswald returned from the Soviet Union as a KGB agent, run by Soviet spymasters posing as consular officials in Washington and Mexico City. The motive: vengeance for the humiliating outcome of the Cuban missile crisis.

The CIA Did It. Still smarting from the Bay of Pigs fiasco and fearing that Kennedy would disenfranchise them by ending the Cold War, rogue agents plotted revenge, duping Oswald into pulling the trigger.

Right-wingers Did It. A band of die-hard segregationists, oilmen, and Cuban exiles with CIA ties were convinced that Kennedy would take advantage of the civil rights movement and of détente with the Soviet Union to destroy the American way of life. They used revolutionary arguments to dupe Oswald into participating, but only as a fall guy. New Orleans District Attorney Jim Garrison, who first proposed this scenario, named New Orleans entrepreneur Clay Shaw as the mastermind, with such lieutenants as the bizarre pilot-adventurer David Ferrie, who'd known Oswald in the Civil Air Patrol. Shaw was acquitted of conspiracy to assassinate Kennedy in 1969.

Preying on Presidents

During the first 217 years of its history, the United States lost four sitting presidents to an assassin's bullet—Abraham Lincoln, James Garfield, William McKinley, and John Kennedy. But seven other presidents have been stalked, some narrowly surviving their encounter with a murderer or madman. Andrew Jackson was saved by misfiring pistols, Teddy Roosevelt by the draft of a speech, Gerald Ford by pure luck—*twice* in one month.

Among the 11 assassins that follow, only three successfully completed their lethal plan. Yet all had much in common. All were obsessively charged by some real or imagined grievance, or some maddening political or romantic idea—they were hot-blooded, not cold-blooded, killers. All stalked their prey, some for weeks at a time. And successful or not, all were in deadly earnest. This evident seriousness of purpose was rewarded by execution, by life imprisonment, or by lifelong commitment to a mental institution. Such punishment makes clear the point that assassination, for all its psychological and social undertones, is just another term for premeditated murder.

Richard Lawrence made his living as a house painter in Washington, D.C., although his true wish was to be a landscape artist. During his early thirties, Lawrence became combative and deluded—fellow painters were afraid to share a scaffold with him.

Worse, he decided he was King Richard III, rightful ruler of England and the American colonies—and children took to calling him King Dick. But this self-proclaimed monarch also believed that the United States Congress, and President Andrew Jackson in particular, had deprived him of his vast inheritance. Brooding over the injustice done to him, King Dick had burst into the White House several times to plead his case, once to Jackson himself.

On the morning of January 30, 1835, a frail 67-year-old Jackson went to the Capitol for the funeral of Warren R. Davis, a South Carolina congressman. As the procession filed out of the chamber, the president abruptly came face to face with Richard Lawrence, who was lurking near a column.

Lawrence carried with him two finely made percussion-cap pistols. Now he pulled them from his overcoat pockets and fired one. The cap detonated, but it failed to ignite the powder. President Jackson lunged at the assassin with his cane, and Lawrence dropped the empty pistol. But he passed the second one to his right hand, aimed, and pulled the trigger. Again there was a misfire. By this time a naval aide had wrestled Lawrence to the floor.

At his trial in April 1835, Richard Lawrence, alternately laughing and cursing, pleaded not guilty by reason of insanity. The jury assigned to the case took just five minutes to agree with him. The failed assassin passed away in 1861, still confined to the federal asylum, St. Elizabeth's Hospital in Washington, D.C.

John Wilkes Booth was the ninth of 10 children in America's first family of the stage. Born in Bel Air, Maryland, in 1838, Booth from an early age sought out fame, and his brooding good looks and energetic presence made him a popular matinée idol. When the Civil War erupted in 1861, the actor chose not to fight, but his sympathies lay with the South—and against Abraham Lincoln.

As the Confederacy began to lose, Booth's disdain for Lincoln curdled into obsessive hatred, and he began to hatch a plot against the president. On April 11, 1865, the day after the Confederate surrender, Booth attended a White House celebration where the president spoke of enfranchising blacks in the conquered South. Booth swore this speech would be Lincoln's last, and the actor put his plan into action.

Visiting Ford's Theatre on April 14, Booth learned that the Lincolns would be attending the evening performance of *Our American Cousin*, a British comedy. That night, as the audience laughed at the antics onstage, Booth crept into the presidential box and fired a single-shot .44-caliber derringer into Lincoln's head, behind the left ear.

Fending off a guest with his dagger, Booth leaped for the stage. One of his spurs caught in a flag, however, and the actor broke his left leg when he landed. Getting to his feet, he brandished his knife and shouted, "*Sic semper tyrannis!*"—Thus always to tyrants!—and hobbled off. He heaved himself onto his horse and galloped into the night.

By April 24 Booth had holed up in a tobacco barn on a farm near Bowling Green, Virginia. Two days later, surrounded by Union soldiers, Booth apparently shot himself.

Charles Guiteau believed it was his endorsement that had propelled conservative Republican James A. Garfield to his divided party's nomination in 1880 and into the White House in 1881. But when the Illinois-born Guiteau—who described himself as a lawyer, politician, and theologian—went to Washington and pestered the new leader for his reward, he got the cold shoulder. On May 18, 1881, Guiteau said later, "an impression came over my mind like a flash that if the President was out of the way, this whole thing would be solved and everything would go well."

On June 8 Guiteau borrowed $15 and bought a powerful pearl-handled .44-caliber British revolver—he thought it would display well in a museum. Ten days later he watched as President Garfield and his wife said goodbye at the Baltimore and Potomac railroad depot, but he was too touched by the tender scene to pull the trigger.

Garfield was again at the depot on July 2. Guiteau stole up close behind him, drew his revolver, and shot the president in the back. Immediately seized by police, Guiteau said, "It's all right. I wish to go to the jail."

It took three months for the bullet, lodged near Garfield's pancreas, to kill him. The murder trial began on November 14, 1881, and on January 25, 1882, a jury took an hour and five minutes to decide that Guiteau, 40, was both sane and guilty. Cried the assassin, "God will avenge this outrage."

On June 30, 1882, Guiteau walked to the gallows. As the noose was adjusted and a black hood drawn tight, he chanted, "Glory, glory." When the trapdoor fell, the crowd outside the jail cheered.

Leon Czolgosz was the brooding son of eastern European immigrants to Michigan. Because he worked in turn-of-the-century factories, Czolgosz knew firsthand the plight of such workers, and the brutal suppression of strikes led him to join the growing anarchist movement. To Leon Czolgosz, the 1896 election of arch-capitalist William McKinley was a victory for evil.

In 1898 the 25-year-old Czolgosz suffered a nervous breakdown, which forced him to leave his job at a Cleveland wire factory. He became reclusive and peculiar, and his fellow anarchists lost interest in him. He soon developed a plan that evidently coalesced sometime in 1901. By September 1 Czolgosz had purchased a .32-caliber Iver-Johnson revolver and rented a room in Buffalo, New York, where President McKinley was expected to visit.

On September 6 the assassin joined the crowd for a McKinley reception at the Pan-American Exposition. Inside, police and soldiers formed a gauntlet to the receiving line, where McKinley stood smiling, surrounded by plain-clothesmen. But the diminutive Czolgosz, with the humble aura of a working man, seems to have been invisible.

As he approached McKinley, Czolgosz held the gun in his right hand, wrapped in a handkerchief. When the president extended his hand, the anarchist knocked it aside and fired twice at close range. McKinley stiffened but stayed on his feet, gasping, "Be easy with him, boys."

McKinley lingered, rallied, and then died on September 14. Czolgosz was convicted in a two-day trial. But as the assassin was strapped into the electric chair on October 29, he had the last word: "I am not sorry for my crime."

John Schrank dreamed on September 15, 1901, that the late William McKinley pointed at his vice president, Theodore Roosevelt, and said, "This is my murderer. Avenge my death."

The compact, German-born saloon keeper and self-styled poet-philosopher pondered the dead president's words but deferred action. In 1906, the 30-year-old sold his New York bar and roamed the city, evolving principles that he loftily dubbed the Four Pillars of the Republic. One of those pillars was that presidents should serve two terms at most.

But in 1912 Teddy Roosevelt, having served out McKinley's term and one of his own, was back as the Progressive, or Bull Moose, candidate. Schrank was outraged. The reappearance to him of McKinley's ghost on September 14 of that year, the 11th anniversary of the president's death, sealed the matter. Armed with a .38-caliber Colt revolver, Schrank set out to hunt Roosevelt.

On October 14 the stalker was outside Milwaukee's Hotel Gilpatrick, where the candidate, having dined, was preparing to motor to the municipal auditorium. In two earlier chances at Roosevelt, in Chattanooga and Chicago, Schrank had lost his nerve. This time, when his prey came out, he drew his gun and fired. Roosevelt staggered, but did not drop: Slowed by a folded copy of his 50-page speech and a metal spectacle case, the bullet hadn't gone far into his chest. "It takes more than one bullet," crowed TR, "to kill a Bull Moose." Doctors left the bullet in his rib cage.

Hoping to avoid a circuslike trial, the judge encouraged a panel of experts to find Schrank insane. Instead of jail, he was confined to an insane asylum for life.

Giuseppe Zangara bought a .32-caliber revolver in a Miami pawnshop in February 1933, not long after he decided it was time to kill a president. The slight, Italian-born bricklayer, driven half-mad by chronic stomachache, had planned to shoot Herbert Hoover in Washington. Then he read that newly elected Franklin Delano Roosevelt was coming to Miami on a fishing trip with millionaire sportsman Vincent Astor, whose yacht would dock there on February 15. FDR was scheduled to make a speech at Bay Front Park that evening, and Zangara, following the path of least resistance, planned to attend.

On February 15 Zangara arrived at the park's amphitheater an hour and a half early, only to find the seats filled and the aisles jammed. The new president arrived at 9:30 in a touring car and delivered a brief speech from the car. But Zangara couldn't see to shoot.

Chicago mayor Anton Cermak was in the audience, and he went forward to shake hands with the president. The crowd around Zangara dispersed, freeing some nearby seats. Seeing his chance, Zangara jumped up on a chair, drew his revolver, and started shooting. Cermak and four bystanders were hit, but FDR was untouched. Roosevelt had Cermak placed in the car with him and held the fatally wounded mayor in his arms on the way to the hospital.

Pleading guilty to four counts of assault, Zangara was sentenced to 80 years in prison. "Oh, Judge," he responded, "don't be so stingy—give me a hundred." When Cermak died on March 6, Zangara was tried again, for murder, to which he pleaded guilty. The 32-year-old was executed on March 20—barely five weeks after his attempt.

Oscar Collazo and Griselio Torresola arrived in Washington, D.C., from New York on October 31 in 1950, armed with two 9-mm. semiautomatic pistols—a Luger and a Walther P-38. They came to strike a blow for Puerto Rican independence and had traveled on one-way train tickets—neither thought they would see New York, or Puerto Rico, again.

November 1 was the hottest November day Washington could remember. President Harry S Truman was resting in his upstairs bedroom in Blair House —White House renovations had forced the first family into temporary quarters across the street. Just after 2 p.m., Collazo (above) and Torresola approached from different angles; 37-year-old Collazo carried the P-38—the first time he'd ever held a weapon, beyond a short course given him by Torresola, just 24.

Collazo aimed the Walther at a uniformed guard standing under the canopied entrance and tried to shoot. Nothing happened—he'd forgotten to release the safety. He fumbled with the pistol; it went off, wounding the guard in the leg.

Now other guards poured out of Blair House, guns blazing. Collazo crouched and fired wildly eight more times, hitting no one. He was wounded in the nose and ear; finally a bullet in the chest knocked him to the sidewalk. Torresola fired eight rounds, wounding two guards, one fatally. When he stopped to reload, he was killed by a shot in the ear.

On March 7, 1951, a convalescing Collazo was found guilty of homicide and related crimes and sentenced to die. Truman commuted his sentence to life in prison, and in 1979 President Jimmy Carter set him free.

Samuel Byck blamed the rising tides of inflation and political corruption for his considerable marital and financial woes. By 1974 the 44-year-old unemployed tire salesman from Philadelphia had concluded that the source of his problems was the current incumbent, Richard M. Nixon.

Very early on Friday, February 22, 1974, Byck sent newspaper columnist Jack Anderson, among others, a tape describing what he called Operation Pandora's Box. "I will try to get the plane aloft and fly it toward the target area, which will be Washington, D.C.," Byck said. "I will shoot the pilot, and then in the last few minutes try to steer the plane into the target, which is the White House."

The DC-9 assigned to Delta's flight 523 to Atlanta that Friday was being readied for a 7:15 a.m. departure from Baltimore-Washington International when Byck arrived. He shot and killed an airport guard at the gate; then, carrying a gasoline bomb in a suitcase, he ran down the Jetway and into the cockpit. "Fly this plane out of here," he ordered the pilots, brandishing the bomb. When the captain said he could not move the plane with the wheels chocked, Byck started shooting. Both pilots were wounded, the copilot fatally. Byck seized a passenger as a shield.

By now, a local policeman, drawn by the gunfire, had reached the gate. Taking the fallen officer's .357 Magnum he hurried down the Jetway. Using his own .38, he fired once as the fuselage door swung shut. Still able to see Byck through a window, the officer fired the borrowed Magnum, this time hitting Byck in the chest. The hostage broke free. Then Byck, his fate sealed, put his pistol to his temple and fired a final shot.

Lynette Fromme was a consort to cult leader Charles Manson, who'd masterminded the vicious 1969 murder  of actress Sharon Tate and six others in a Beverly Hills estate. Fromme had met him on the boardwalk in Venice Beach in 1967, the year she was graduated from high school and banished from her parents' comfortable Santa Monica home. She joined Manson's family—a clutch of young women devoted to him—and he affectionately called her Squeaky for her high-pitched, reedy voice.

When Manson and three of his followers went on trial for the Tate murders, Squeaky Fromme and other Mansonites stood vigil on the Los Angeles courthouse steps. When Manson was transferred to San Quentin, Fromme made veiled threats against the judge's children and blamed political leaders for the loss of Manson. On the morning of September 5, 1975, she was among the well-wishers lining the route that President Gerald Ford would take from his Sacramento hotel to the state capitol, where he was to speak against crime.

As Ford strolled past, she stepped up to him, a Colt .45 automatic pointed at his stomach. "The country is in a mess," she said. "This man is not your president." She squeezed the trigger, but an alert Secret Service agent interceded—the webbing between his thumb and forefinger blocked the hammer. "It didn't go off, fellas, it didn't go off," she chirped as agents knocked her down and handcuffed her. "Can you believe it? It didn't go off."

Fromme explained, "I just wanted to get some attention for Charlie and the girls." Upon hearing the guilty verdict and of her life sentence, she threw herself on the floor and screamed, "You animals!"

Sara Jane Moore was arrested on Sunday afternoon, September 21, 1975, the day President Gerald Ford started a  Bay Area visit. She was cited for packing a .44-caliber revolver in her purse. The gun was taken, but she wasn't detained because, police said, the Secret Service felt she "was not of sufficient protection interest to warrant surveillance"—this just over two weeks after Squeaky Fromme's attempt at Ford.

Moore's whole life had been of insufficient interest to others. By 1975 the 45-year-old West Virginian, known as Sally to family and friends, had suffered five broken marriages and borne four children, three of whom had been adopted by her parents. Living in San Francisco's Mission District, where working-class families mingled warily with young radicals, she'd informed for both the FBI and the local police, then shared her secret with the leftists she spied upon. Now she feared for her life and wanted to be taken into protective custody.

On Monday, September 22, Moore took her son to school, then drove to Danville, where she paid $145 for a .38-caliber Smith & Wesson. She loaded the gun as she crossed the San Francisco-Oakland Bay Bridge on her way back to town. When President Ford emerged from the St. Francis Hotel at 3:29 p.m., Moore was waiting 40 feet away. But as she took aim, a bystander spotted her and grabbed her arm, deflecting the shot. The bullet missed Ford, whined off a wall, and wounded a nearby cabdriver.

Moore was taken to jail, handcuffed and bleeding. "There comes a point," she told a reporter, "when the only way you can make a statement is to pick up a gun." She pleaded guilty to attempted murder and received a life sentence.

John W. Hinckley Jr. fell in love with actress Jodie Foster in 1976, when he saw her play a 12-year-old prostitute in  *Taxi Driver*—a movie he saw 15 times. The obsessed fan followed her to Yale University in September 1980, left notes at her dormitory, phoned her, and trailed her at a distance. She ignored him.

On December 8, 1980, 25-year-old Hinckley's already fragile hold on reality suffered a crucial shock: Musician John Lennon, his idol, was gunned down by a stalking fan in New York. In early March of 1981, Hinckley received another jolt. On one of his stops at his oil-wealthy parents' home near Denver, his disappointed father told him he was on his own. Hinckley decided it was time to get Jodie Foster's attention.

On March 29 Hinckley checked into a Washington, D.C., hotel, bearing two .22-caliber pistols and a .38 of the type used by Lennon's killer. The next morning he loaded one of the .22s and wrote a note to Foster. "Jodie, I would abandon this idea of getting Reagan in a second if I could only win your heart." He left the note in his suitcase.

As President Ronald Reagan emerged from a speech at the Washington Hilton, Hinckley crouched in the crowd and fired six times, hitting the press secretary, a police officer, and a Secret Service agent. The president was struck by a bullet that caromed off his limousine's fender. The wound was serious but not fatal.

Hinckley went on trial in May 1982. Psychiatrists testified convincingly that the young man had gradually lost the ability to distinguish between reality and fantasy. The jury acquitted Hinckley, who was committed for an indefinite period to St. Elizabeth's Hospital.

I *can explain, I did it for my country.*

SIRHAN SIRHA

2

The Exploited One

For Robert Francis Kennedy, the moment of undoing came in a hotel serving pantry, a narrow, dimly lighted passageway smelling of stale food and lined with warming tables and ice machines. It was an unlikely chamber of execution, this cramped space behind the Embassy Ballroom of the Ambassador Hotel in Los Angeles. But death is not selective. And Kennedy knew, as few others, how doom can arrive at any time, any place. "If anyone wants to kill me, it won't be difficult," he once told a reporter, and he often quoted a line from a favorite historian: "Men are not made for safe havens."

All through the spring of 1968, he had moved fearlessly through the crowds, demanding to be close to the public, convinced he could, as he said that night in the Embassy Ballroom, "end the divisions within the United States." The Democratic nomination for the 1968 presidential race was very much up for grabs. In March, Lyndon B. Johnson, the harried incumbent, had announced that he would not seek reelection; Vice President Hubert H. Humphrey was burdened by the administration's prosecution of an unpopular war in Vietnam; and the likely Republican opponent was Richard M. Nixon, a former vice president under Dwight D. Eisenhower who had lost to John F. Kennedy in 1960.

This younger Kennedy—whom the press called Bobby or RFK—was not without liabilities as a candidate: He was only 42, a former U.S. attorney general who had just once pursued and won elective office, in 1964 as U.S. senator from New York. He had been hardened by years of political battle in the service of his brother Jack and had a reputation for ruthlessness. But he possessed one inestimable asset. He was a Kennedy, a man from Camelot. He could win it all.

The critical test, Kennedy and his advisers believed, would be the California primary election held on June 4. He had won three earlier primaries but had experienced his first loss—in Oregon—the week before. With 174 delegate votes at stake in California, he wanted badly to win. Kennedy campaigned at a furious pace, caught a wave of sentiment, and that day rode it to victory over Minnesota senator Eugene McCarthy and Vice President Humphrey. California's votes at the upcoming Democratic National Convention were now RFK's. Momentum was building.

In the early minutes of June 5, Robert Kennedy delivered a short speech of thanks to the estimated 1,800 supporters gathered in the Embassy Ballroom of the Ambassador, where the campaign's victory celebration was scheduled to take place. "We are a great country, an unselfish country and a compassionate country," he told the jubilant crowd. "I intend to make that the basis for my running." Ending his speech with "On to Chicago!"—site of the Democratic convention—Kennedy left the podium, headed for a press conference in the nearby Colonial Room. Uncharacteristically, he decided to avoid the crush of well-wishers that swarmed between him and the ballroom's main doors and instead took a shortcut through the kitchen pantry, retracing the route he had taken earlier to enter the room. "This way, Senator," said one of his aides, and Kennedy exited through a door at the back of the stage. He walked down an incline and through an anteroom into the pantry.

It was a fatal choice for Bobby Kennedy. Off to one side of the pantry, among the kitchen workers, stood a slight, dark-complexioned young man dressed in faded jeans, a white shirt, and a loose-fitting sweater. Someone later remembered that he had an odd smile on his face and was holding his right hand against his stomach.

The senator's bodyguard and his campaign coordinator were usually right by his side, but this night they had gotten separated from their charge as he left the stage. An armed security guard was at Kennedy's elbow, but he detected no threat amid the 70 or so reporters, photographers, aides, and kitchen helpers squeezed into the narrow service area.

Suddenly, the young man in the baggy sweater ap-

Mortally wounded by an assassin's bullets, Senator Robert F. Kennedy sprawls on the floor of a Los Angeles hotel pantry, as busboy Juan Romero attempts in vain to comfort him.

peared in front of Kennedy. He reached out to the candidate, as if in congratulation, as if to shake hands. But in his right hand, he held a snub-nosed revolver. Robert Kennedy didn't see him. At that moment, the candidate had turned to greet a well-wisher. The revolver spat flame and then spat again and again. It looked and sounded like a starter pistol used at a racetrack; in truth, it was not much of a weapon—a small .22-caliber Iver-Johnson Cadet revolver that retailed for $31.95. But it found its mark.

Kennedy fell back, spinning and slumping to the floor as the assassin continued to fire as fast as he could pull the trigger. One round from the eight-shot revolver penetrated Kennedy's skull one inch behind his right ear. Both the hollow-point bullet and the bone shattered, and a spray of lead particles and bone fragments flew into Kennedy's brain, shredding cells, ripping blood vessels. The brainstem, which controls breathing and heartbeat, was in the path of the fragments and sustained most of their tearing action. Damage from the bullet also extended to the areas of the brain that regulate muscle action and balance, memory, and higher thought processes. Another three bullets hit the senator: Two slugs entered his right armpit, but they inflicted only minor injuries; a fourth passed through a shoulder pad of his jacket.

By now, aides and bystanders had leaped on the swarthy young man. He was strong for his size—five-feet-four-inches tall and 120 pounds—and managed to empty the gun before he was pinned back against one of the stainless-steel warming tables. Five more people were hit, but none seriously.

Bobby Kennedy lay on his back, a pool of blood spreading out from his head. His right hand reached out, as if he were trying to grasp something. His lips moved. His left eyelid opened and closed. Someone pressed a rosary into his hand; he brought it up to his chest. A busboy stooped to cradle his head and heard him say, "Is everybody all right?"

Seventeen minutes later, when ambulance attendants put him on a stretcher, he spoke again, in terrible pain: "No, please don't." But that was all. With the aid of life-support equipment, he hung on for 25 hours at Los Angeles's Good Samaritan Hospital. His heart finally stopped beating at 1:44 a.m. on June 6, 1968.

As with the assassination of President John F. Kennedy, the killing of Robert Kennedy immediately spawned a multitude of conspiracy theories. In a relatively brief public life, RFK had made his full share of intractable enemies. As chief counsel for the U.S. Senate Select Committee investigating improper labor practices, Kennedy had been instrumental in jailing for mail fraud and mishandling pension funds the most powerful union leader in America: Jimmy Hoffa, president of the mammoth International Brotherhood of Teamsters. Hoffa had every reason to wish Kennedy dead, and had said so on a number of occasions. The Mafia, whose links to the Teamsters were under intense scrutiny, surely prayed—and, some believe, might well have paid—for Kennedy's demise.

Various terrorist groups, of which there were many in the 1960s, could easily have been looking for a sensational score. Other suspicions involved the CIA, that all-purpose scapegoat for certain segments of American society. Some theorists insisted that the assailant had not acted alone—that more than one assassin had been in the pantry that night, and that the wiry young man may not have fired the fatal bullet. Still others said that while the assassin might have been working on his own, he had been brainwashed to do the job, an idea inspired by a best-selling novel, *The Manchurian Candidate*.

Anything seemed possible. At the time of the shooting, the police had no idea who their suspect was or what affiliations he might have. One man who had grappled with the killer was Jesse Unruh, a prominent California politician and Kennedy's state campaign manager. Unruh thought the young man might be Mexican and remembered that during their struggle the assassin claimed, "I did it for my country."

In jail, the young man refused to answer questions about the assassination or himself. "I wish to remain incommunicado," he said repeatedly. To one of his interrogators, he seemed "very cool, very calm, very stable and quite lucid."

He had brown eyes, full lips, and a tangle of black hair, and he spoke with a slight accent that was hard to place. His fingerprints were not on file with any law-enforcement agency. Nor did he carry any papers that revealed his name. The contents of his pockets consisted of four $100 bills along with some smaller bills and

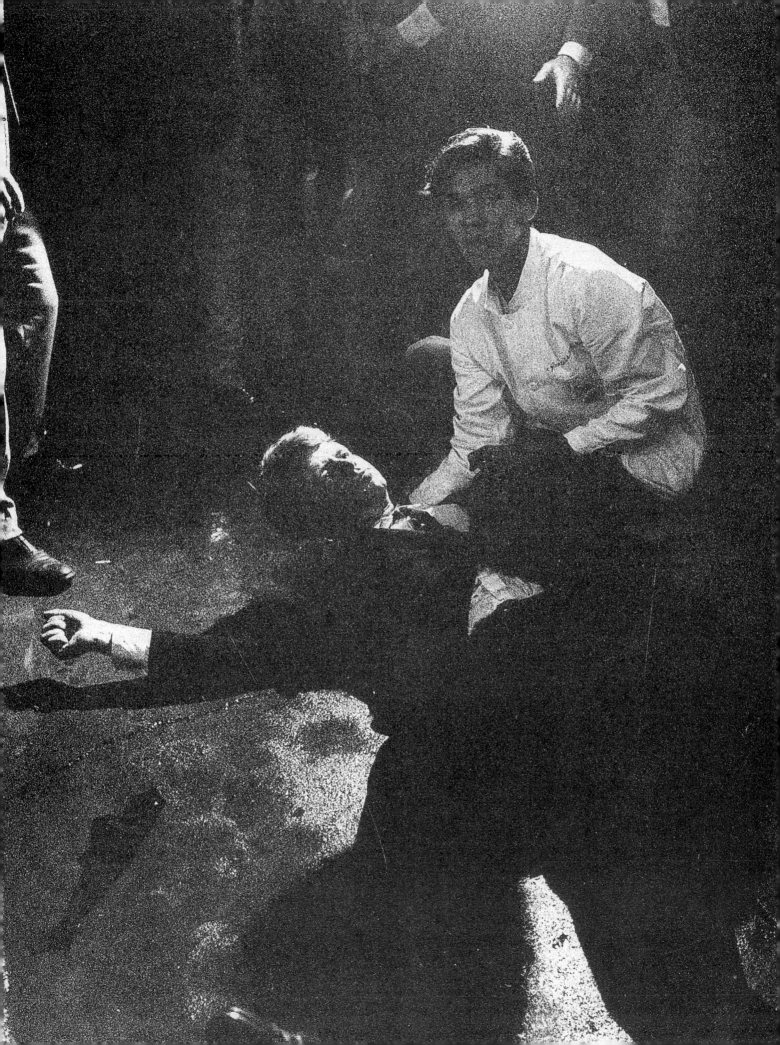

In a 1947 family portrait, three-year-old
Sirhan sits between his father, Bishara Sirhan,
and brother Adel; mother Mary holds Munir
on her lap. In the back row are, from left to
right, Saidallah, Aida, and Sharif.

change, a car key, and some items that linked him with his victim—two unexpended .22 cartridges, a newspaper column discussing Kennedy's dovish position on the war in Vietnam, and a flier announcing a Kennedy rally at the Ambassador Hotel on June 2.

The mystery was solved later that morning. Two men, 29-year-old Adel Sirhan and 21-year-old Munir Sirhan of suburban Pasadena, presented themselves at their local police station and said that the person whose picture filled every TV screen was their 24-year-old brother, Sirhan Bishara Sirhan.

Within days, investigators had learned much of Sirhan's life story—and the conspiracy theories began to fade. He was Palestinian—an immigrant who had lived in America for a dozen years without seeking citizenship. But Sirhan Sirhan was not a sacrificial hero of the Palestine Liberation Organization or a jihad-bent holy warrior allied to some competing band. Nor was he a Teamster hired gun or a Mafia rubout artist or a terror-

ist. No one had brainwashed him to do the deed.

For Sirhan Sirhan, like so many assassins, was merely a pathetic loner, a loser, intelligent enough, but drifting bitterly from defeat to defeat in his adult life, endeavoring less and less, and succeeding not at all. Only in his livid fantasies did he find any feeling of worth, of power and purpose. His name—Sirhan—translates as "one who is abstracted, lost in thought." In the end, he did become lost in his thoughts, and those bitter, angry, vengeful daydreams led him to his fatal encounter with Robert F. Kennedy.

If violence is learned, Sirhan Bishara Sirhan had some very early teaching. He was born on March 19, 1944, in Jerusalem, Palestine, the sixth child of seven children and the fifth son of Bishara and Mary Sirhan. His parents both were Christians, a distinct minority among the primarily Muslim population of Palestine, and had lived in modest but comfortable circumstances since their marriage in 1930. The father was a master mechanic employed by the government's Public Works Department; he was sufficiently good at his job to rise to the level of foreman, and the couple rented a ground-floor apartment in a mixed neighborhood of Arabs and Jews outside the walls of the Old City.

For much of their married life, the Sirhans had coexisted more or less at peace with the relatively few Jews living in Palestine. The country had been under British mandate since World War I, when it was seized from the Ottoman Empire, and Britain, eager to keep oil supplies flowing from the Arab nation, had strictly controlled Jewish immigration into what the Jews regarded as their national homeland.

The coming of Adolf Hitler and the Second World War changed all that. In the mid-1930s, European Jews started entering Palestine in larger numbers—many illegally—and the exodus resumed in even greater earnest immediately after the defeat of Nazi Germany in 1945. Between the war's end and 1948, more than 600,000 immigrants had arrived in Palestine, grimly determined to establish a Jewish state. The 1,200,000 Palestinian Arabs reacted violently, and the Jews responded in kind.

In late 1947 the United Nations voted to divide Palestine into separate Jewish and Arab states—and the British announced that they would depart by May 14, 1948. The partition would take effect on that date. Instantly, Palestine became a war zone as each side battled to grab as much territory as possible before the division of land occurred.

Sirhan Sirhan was not quite four years old when snipers took to the rooftops of his neighborhood, barbed wire blocked off streets, and machine guns rattled in the night. One particularly vicious tactic was to dynamite crowds of people. This happened near the Sirhan home on December 13, 1947, when Jews retaliating against earlier acts of violence tossed sticks of dynamite into a group of Palestinians waiting at a bus stop. Seven people were killed and 54 injured. Two weeks later, on December 29, a Jewish group speeding past the same spot in a taxi hurled a bomb at another throng of Palestinians; 11 people were killed and more than 30 wounded. Sirhan Sirhan and his father were just a short distance away when it happened. "There was blood on the road and people with wounds and broken limbs," related the father. "I saw flesh and bones. Everybody was shouting and crying. Sirhan said, 'I don't want to see this, Daddy.' So I took my handkerchief and tied it around his eyes." When they reached home, the little boy went to bed for two days.

About that same time, in late 1947, violence claimed a member of the Sirhan family. It was an accident, a quirk of fate. The British had strung barbed wire across a street near the Sirhan home so that vehicles could be stopped for inspection. One day, gunfire erupted as Sirhan was playing outside with his brother Munir, who was four years older. A British army truck, trying to evade the sniper fire, hit the barricade, then struck Sirhan's brother and killed him instantly. Sirhan ran home screaming, "Munir is dead. Munir is dead." But for years afterward he would uncomprehendingly ask his mother, "Mamma, why is Munir taking so long to come back? Can't he come home so I can play with him?" (The Sirhans would name their youngest son Munir in honor of his slain brother.)

Other horrors burned themselves into the young mind: a neighbor's corpse lying against barbed wire; a Jewish soldier blasted to bits by dynamite. Sirhan's mother described this last scene: "I don't know how many pieces you could count of his body. His leg was hanging up on the tower of one church," she remembered. "In the morning, after the curfew when everybody was allowed to move a little bit, we found a finger of that soldier right in our own back yard. Sirhan when he saw that thing got really pale."

Even through these violent days, the family tried to adhere to their daily routine: Little Sirhan went to a kindergarten class in his neighborhood. But the last semblance of normalcy was shattered when the remaining British forces left on May 14. All-out combat raged through Jerusalem. The Sirhan children huddled on the floor of their house quivering in fright at the rip of machine-gun fire and the concussive slam of mortars and artillery rounds. At 4 a.m. on the second day of fighting, the family fled, leaving everything they owned and taking refuge inside the walls of the Old City.

By January 1949 an uneasy truce was worked out between the warring factions, and the partition of the country went forward. But it proved a dismal bargain for the Palestinians: Israel now claimed much of the

Arab lands, forcing more than half the population of Palestine—700,000—out of their homes and condemning them to a bleak, blighted life in refugee camps.

The Sirhans chose to stay in Jerusalem, where the family was allotted one 15-by-30-foot room in a two-story house. This room, lighted by a single kerosene lamp, would be their home until Sirhan Sirhan reached the age of 12. Nine other families occupied the house, bringing the total to about 50 people. They all shared one small toilet off the stairway.

With the vanishing British government went Bishara Sirhan's job, and he was unable to find another one. He retreated into himself, brooding, occasionally venting his anger by breaking furniture or lashing out ferociously at the children. If one of the boys disobeyed, Bishara might beat him with his fists or a stick. Once, he pressed a hot iron against young Sirhan's heel; the boy went to school barefoot until the blisters healed.

Mary Sirhan managed to get work from time to time

in a nursery sponsored by the Lutheran Church. Although the Sirhans were not members of the congregation, the Lutherans provided them with secondhand clothing, food, and free schooling. Sirhan Sirhan, who attended classes at the church, appeared to the pastor to be "very quick, but unstable and very unhappy. I remember thinking that he would have a very difficult time later in life because the family he grew up in lacked the basic things a boy needs to understand life."

The others in the house considered the Sirhans decent people but perplexingly aloof. They were "honest, correct, polite," said one, "but they were different. They came home and locked the door and stayed by themselves inside"—in that one small room. Sirhan was the least sociable of the children. He was small for his age, with a quiet, withdrawn temperament. "He preferred reading to playing," his father later said. Mostly, the boy read religious tracts.

Like other Palestinians, the Sirhans nursed hopes that

their Arab brethren in neighboring countries would someday launch a crushing blow against Israel. They listened expectantly, adults and children alike, to the ubiquitous transistor radios that crackled in nearly every home and public place, bringing the latest word on Arab politics to the masses. But their hopes were dashed in October 1956, when Israeli forces swept through Egypt's Sinai Peninsula with an ease that astonished and appalled the Arab world. The conquered territory was turned over to a U.N. force, but Israel's military potency was clear. Dreams of an Arab reconquest of Palestine evaporated.

At that point, the Sirhans opted to leave their homeland. The United States Congress had authorized special immigrant visas

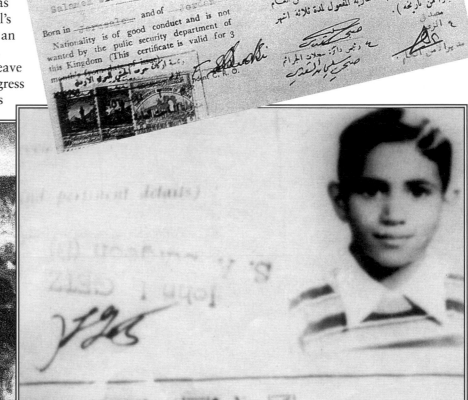

Sirhan *(left, circled)* plays at Jerusalem's Martin Luther School in about 1950. In 1956, in preparation for the family's move to the United States, he appears with his mother on a Jordanian Good Conduct Certificate *(top)*, then on an Alien Registration Form *(above)* marking his 1957 arrival in America.

allowing 2,000 Palestinian "refugee" families to enter America—a small gesture considering the amount of money and military aid it was supplying to Israel. The Sirhans qualified for one of the coveted slots and made the necessary arrangements to leave with the help of a United Nations relief agency and two sponsoring families who belonged to the First Nazarene Church of Pasadena, California. The plans for emigration did not include the Sirhans' two oldest sons, however. Bishara had quarreled with Saidallah, then 24 years old, and Sharif, 23, for frittering away the family's meager funds on self-indulgent pleasures.

Twelve-year-old Sirhan Sirhan almost missed the boat himself. The day before the family was scheduled to depart, he ran away, going to a town about 15 miles north of Jerusalem. He spent the day in a public park, brooding. Finally, as night approached, he returned home. He would later say that "I wanted to stay in my own country with my own people. I knew that the U.S. was against the Arabs and was friendly with Israel, and a friend of my enemy is my enemy." Ideology of that sort might sound improbable in a preadolescent, but Palestinians were steeped in politics, adults and children alike. Another, minor reason for Sirhan's behavior may have been that the lonely, insecure youngster was simply terrified at the prospect of the unknown.

The next day, the Sirhans traveled to Beirut, then embarked on a long voyage that took them, via Naples, Italy, to New York. A train carried them across the continent to California, where they moved into a small apartment in Pasadena and tried to make their way in America. All except for Bishara Sirhan. The one-time public works foreman could not find a position worthy of his skills and experience. He toiled at a succession of odd jobs for about six months. And then one day, after quarreling with his wife over disciplining the children, he took all of the family savings—about $500—and walked out the door. For some years, he held down a job as a maintenance mechanic in New York, but eventually he returned to that part of Palestine now called Jordan and the village where he was born. Neither his wife nor his children saw him again.

Mary Sirhan found employment as a housekeeper for a Presbyterian church nursery in Pasadena, earning about $200 a month. Two of her children contributed to the family income as well. Daughter Aida, 20 years old when she arrived in America, did secretarial work, and son Adel, 18, did odd jobs and had some carpentry skills. He also earned a bit singing Arabic songs and playing a guitarlike instrument called an oud at restaurants and supper clubs catering to Arab-Americans.

The Sirhans' circumstances improved enough that in 1962 the family bought a small home. Located at 696 East Howard Street in Pasadena, it was a three-bedroom house in a pleasant, lower-middle-class neighborhood of tall shade trees and neatly tended gardens. By then, with the help of the local Baptist church, the two older boys, Saidallah and Sharif, had been able to emigrate and join the family in Pasadena.

Mary Sirhan might have expected further help with the finances from her eldest sons, but they did not fare well in America. When they got jobs, they couldn't seem to keep them, and both had brushes with the law.

Sirhan was 17 years old when his family moved to the Pasadena house on the right.

Actually, the son who seemed to hold the most promise—at least for a few years—was Sirhan. In both junior high and high school, he was bright enough to compile a C+ average and took the toughest courses even when easier ones would have meant better grades. Yet he did not easily fit in with the other students. During Sirhan's last year at Eliot Junior High, one of his teachers remembered, the boy was the only dark-skinned student in the school. The other children thought him odd, and either teased him about his nationality or ignored him altogether. At John Muir High School, which he attended from 1960 through 1963, Sirhan graduated in the lowest third of his class, 558th out of 829. Teachers and fellow students there remembered him as obedient and polite yet distant and formal. "He was so dark and scrawny but always so neat," said one classmate. "The other kids came to school in sweat shirts and jeans, but Sirhan always had a clean shirt." Possibly because he was so different, he seems never to have had a girlfriend. At the one school dance he described attending, he watched from the sidelines.

One thing that interested Sirhan greatly was the California Cadet Corps, a kind of high-school version of R.O.T.C. The youth spent three years drilling and learning about weapons and military history. To some, that later seemed significant—and chilling—especially since Sirhan in one of his high-school history books had underlined a passage about the 1901 assassination of President William McKinley. The 25th president had been touring an exposition in Buffalo, New York, when he was slain by an anarchist named Leon Czolgosz, the 28-year-old son of a Polish immigrant laborer. The history book noted that McKinley was "the third victim of an assassin's bullet since the Civil War."

Sirhan (highlighted above) appears in the 1959 Eliot Junior High School yearbook. A 1963 discharge (below) from the California Cadet Corps at John Muir High School marks one of the young Palestinian's rare successes.

State of California

To all whom it may concern:

This is to Certify, That _____ of _____ Company, California Cadet Corps, who was enrolled in the _____ day of _____ one thousand nine hundred and _____ is hereby Honorably Discharged from the

California Cadet Corps

by reason of _____

Service _____

Given under my hand at _____ California, this _____ day of _____ one thousand nine hundred and _____

Just below the underlined passage, Sirhan had scribbled, "And many more will come."

Yet whatever dark fantasies may have been rising in Sirhan Sirhan's adolescent brain, the polite citizen at school remained the model son at home. He did not smoke or drink. He worked after school selling papers, mowed the lawn, acted as the family handyman, and sometimes even cooked meals.

The neighbors liked him. Indeed, they liked the whole family, although no one knew them very well. As they had done in the Old City of Jerusalem, the Sirhans held themselves apart. While they all learned to speak English, conversation at home was always in Arabic. They preferred to eat and drink the same foods and beverages they had known in Jerusalem, and Arabic music was always playing on a tape recorder in the house. Sirhan was particularly fond of a popular Arab singer named Umm Kulthoum; some of her songs were religious, some had a patriotic theme, but mainly she sang of love and its pains—love lost, love unrequited. Many of the tapes were sent to the Sirhans by relatives and friends still living in Jerusalem or on the West Bank, remnants of Palestine now incorporated into Jordan. The Sirhan family often spoke of going home someday. They stayed in touch with events there by subscribing to a weekly Arabic newspaper, *Al Bayan,* that was published in New York.

By the time Sirhan graduated from high school in June 1963, he had been in the United States six years. Yet the powerful Arab environment maintained at home and the ostracism he endured at school left him feeling as much a stranger in his new home as when he arrived. Fueled by a need to succeed at something but hindered by the lack of a desire to assimilate himself into Ameri-

Drawn to horse racing, Sirhan was photographed in 1965 for his application to be a track hot walker—the trainer who walks the horses until they cool.

na City College. However, his attempt at higher education also sputtered. The respectable grades of his high-school years now became mostly Fs, and his attendance was haphazard. Sirhan blamed his failure in part on his need to work. He was dismissed in May 1965—and that made him very bitter.

"The way they did things at PCC," he would later say as he awaited trial, "helped detach me from society, or at least campus society. I majored in political science, foreign languages. Diplomacy was my main interest. But I soon gave up on the idea of being a diplomat. When I figured the score, I saw the odds were stacked against me. You gotta be rich to be a diplomat. You have to give big parties. You could blow your entire year's salary in three months."

Sirhan's Palestinian background was another obstacle to his success, he believed: "Being an Arab is worse than being a Negro." He particularly remembered an argument with a professor on the issue of Palestine. "I really wanted to clobber this fellow, this blond son of a bitch, and I did. I put him where he really belonged. I talked for one solid hour. There were two or three colored people in the class. They had to applaud: I went on their side when they got up to tell about their grievances. My argument? Well, I said that if the U.S. was really as benevolent as it claimed to be, why did it send Hitler's Jews to Palestine? Why not to the Mojave Desert? Then see how much milk and honey they could produce!"

The last in Sirhan's string of excuses for his dismal attendance at college was the illness of his sister, Aida. In February of 1965, the 29-year-old woman, married and living in Palm Springs, was diagnosed with leukemia.

Alone among the family members, Aida had made a move toward a new life, leaving home and taking a job as an accountant in a candy store in Palm Springs in 1962. She had also married a much older man named Herbert Mennell without getting her family's permission. The Sirhans refused to meet him. Her mother, Mary, told some Syrian friends, "Aida went to Jordan to take care of her father."

But Aida was the one who needed care. Not long after her marriage, she became ill. The cancer sapped her strength, and she often came back to Pasadena to rest. Her younger brother Sirhan, the only family member not working full-time, assumed much of the burden of

can culture, Sirhan embarked on a life of mediocrity.

In his last year of high school, Sirhan had worked part-time as a gardener's assistant, and he continued with the job after graduation. Later that summer, following a scuffle with his brother Saidallah, Sirhan moved into a vacant camper owned by his Pasadena employer. Sirhan's experiment with personal independence didn't last long, however—by the following spring, he had returned to his mother's house. A few months later, in August 1964, he was fired from the gardening job for neglecting his duties.

But Sirhan had another part-time job to fall back on, as a waiter and short-order cook at a local hamburger joint. And in the fall of 1963 he had enrolled at Pasade-

Although Sirhan worked briefly as an exercise boy at this track—Hollywood Park—he spent most of his time betting on the horses, to little effect.

looking after her when she was at home; sometimes blood would gush from her nose, and Sirhan, with his childhood horror of blood, came near to fainting.

Sirhan was fiercely angry when Pasadena City College officials dismissed him, rejecting his explanation of the family's crisis. "I gave up my scholastic ambition completely at that time," he later said. But books remained important to him. He spent many hours reading books that he borrowed—and sometimes stole—from the Pasadena Public Library. Most of them were about Middle Eastern affairs.

The young Arab also passed his time playing the horses. During the racing season, he often went to the track at nearby Santa Anita and bet whatever money he had—not much, although he was now working at a service station in downtown Pasadena, pumping gas, washing cars, and cleaning the rest rooms. His weekly earnings were around $60. But after an argument with his supervisor in June 1965, the 21-year-old moved to another service station close-by. The new job lasted just a few weeks. One day Sirhan announced that he had scored heavily at the track and was quitting.

The racing world loomed larger and larger. It was the one place he felt he had a chance to be somebody; he had flunked out of college and lost a string of jobs, but here, at the track, he sensed possibilities. Sirhan now had visions of being a jockey. He was about the right size and wiry enough; excitement, fame, riches would be his. While he was learning to ride—and when his money ran out—he applied for a job as a stable hand and "hot walker" at Santa Anita. A hot walker simply had to lead racehorses around after they had run, cooling them slowly, but a license was required. So in December 1965, Sirhan applied for and a month later received a license from the California State Racing Board.

He soon became an exercise boy—allowed to ride the horses but not race them—and Sirhan recalled that riding came easily to him. But John Shear, his foreman at Santa Anita at that time, remembered that he was constantly being thrown or falling from the horses he was working. Some coworkers felt that he was frightened of the high-strung thoroughbreds.

The work took him to other tracks, including Hollywood Park, and in the summer of 1966, to the Granja Vista del Rio horse ranch in Corona, 50 miles southeast of Los Angeles. At the Corona horse ranch, he took two minor falls while exercising animals. Then, on September 25, a more serious mishap occurred. That morning, patches of fog had settled on the exercise track. The horses were scheduled to get a good workout, and their owners were on hand to see them run. Everyone knew that fog was a danger: If the horses could not see, they might panic. The fog seemed to be lifting, however, and the workout proceeded as planned. Sirhan was assigned to ride a chestnut filly named Hy-vera.

Just as the horses hit their stride, heavy fog again settled over the track. As the owners strained to see through the gray veil, the measured pounding of hooves suddenly gave way to the sound of disaster—thudding bodies, squealing animals, a man screaming in pain and fright. The onlookers ran to the scene. There, amid the swirling mist, they found one exercise boy standing dazed but unhurt. Another—Sirhan—was crumpled against the outer rail, his face covered with mud and blood. "My face, my eyes, I'm blind!" he howled.

An ambulance rushed Sirhan to the hospital, where doctors assured him that his eyes were undamaged. X-rays revealed no concussions, fractures, or internal injuries. He was treated for bruises, cuts, and abrasions, kept overnight, and released. The attending physician remembered him as a decidedly troublesome patient. "He questioned all of the medical applications and all the medicines administered to him and appeared unduly frightened of the various treatments," said the doctor. "He was one of the most reluctant patients I ever had."

Sirhan returned to the horse ranch, but he took several more falls. Finally, he was told that he would never make it as a jockey. Another corrosive defeat. He quit his job in December 1966. "The kid had a lot of ambition," the ranch owner later remarked, but "he sort of lost his nerve." Sirhan would remain unemployed for the next nine months.

The jockey episode seemed to accelerate the young Palestinian's descent into inertia and anger. He complained often of blurred vision, motion in his eyes, and pain—all as a consequence of that frightful fall in the fog. Twice in the months after the accident, he was examined by a Corona ophthalmologist. The doctor could find nothing wrong and told Sirhan that "he seemed to be exaggerating." But Sirhan insisted that he had been seriously injured, and in July 1967 he filed a disability claim for workmen's compensation. As part of the adjudication of the claim, physicians again examined his eyes and again stated that his vision was fine. However, a neurosurgeon who was consulted in the matter refused to rule out the possibility of head injury: It was impossible to know, he said. The case continued to inch along through insurance company channels; it would be April of the following year before a small settlement—Sirhan received $1,705—was reached.

Sirhan's mother later spoke of his fall as a turning point. "He didn't seem to be hurt too bad after the accident physically," she said. "But he changed somehow. After the accident we seemed not so close any more. I couldn't get through to him when we talked." Still, she remained sympathetic, and she evidently did not press him hard to get another job, even though she felt that unemployment had a debilitating effect on him. "He became nervous. He used to go often to the library. Sometimes he used to take me to work himself and he used to tell me one day he's going to let me rest when he got a good job," she continued. "He used to be really upset very much to see me go to work and he has no job."

But Sirhan's efforts to find work were halfhearted at best. He told his younger brother, Munir, that he wanted a "professional position"; he did not want to be a "clerk," he said. Not surprisingly, a professional position failed to materialize during the endless days spent at the library, hanging out at the track, puttering around the house at 696 East Howard Street, or—when time hung especially heavy—playing Chinese checkers with a pair of elderly ladies who lived down the block.

After several months of watching her son drifting aimlessly, Mary Sirhan decided to take matters into her own hands, and in September she beseeched John Weidner, the owner of a health-food store the family frequented, to hire her son. The job was part-time at first, then became full-time in November, with a salary of $90 a week. Weidner found Sirhan to be courteous to customers and neat in his dress, but out of pride the young man stubbornly refused to wear an apron. Occasionally he became aggressive and ill-tempered with his boss—although according to another employee he quickly cooled off—and his opinions were forceful when the talk turned to religion or politics. One day Weidner asked him why he had not yet become an American citizen. Sirhan replied that the United States was Israel's ally and stood against the Arabs. "I am an Arab," he asserted, "so how can I become an American?"

Sirhan lasted only six months in the job, in part because, as Weidner observed, his new clerk "found it hard to take my orders and he didn't like to have things explained to him." Perhaps that was because in the private recesses of his mind, the outwardly polite, withdrawn Sirhan was feeling his own power build.

Back in the days when he was working as a hot walker, Sirhan had begun to entertain the notion that he possessed unusual mental abilities—psychic gifts. The idea was evidently planted by a fellow employee at Santa Anita, a groom who lived alone in the stables and was interested in the occult. One day the groom said, "Kid, you've got a way with horses," then went on to explain that he believed Sirhan was able to communicate with the animals by means of thought waves. Sirhan considered the possibility. It might well be so, he decided.

Not long after that conversation, in June 1966, he took a step toward sharpening those powers. In response to a magazine advertisement, he applied for membership in the Ancient Mystic Order Rosae Crucis, commonly known as the Rosicrucian Order. His friend the groom had given him some Rosicrucian literature on techniques of meditation, and Sirhan was impressed enough to want more.

**After losing his clerking job in
this Pasadena health-food store,
Sirhan tried in vain to sue
owner John Weidner.**

The Rosicrucians were made to measure for Sirhan Sirhan. Styling themselves "the oldest fraternal or secret order known to man," they had sprung into existence in Europe during the upheavals of the 16th and 17th centuries. They claimed to have won the trust of Middle Eastern sages and to have learned from them the ancient secrets of mathematics, medicine, and alchemy. In time, they evolved a large body of ritual practice that supposedly enabled members to create gold, devise medicines that could cure any disease, and tame various spirits that inhabited the elements of air, water, earth, and fire. As the movement spread, the Rosicrucians shifted with the cultural winds, discarding some of their quasi-medieval magic in favor of more modern ideas of empowerment—expanding the mind, mainly.

In the early 1900s, an occultist named H. Spencer Lewis founded a Rosicrucian order in San Jose, California. For a modest initiation fee and monthly dues, an applicant would get a membership card, the secret password, instructions on how to execute a secret handshake, a magazine published by the brotherhood, and twice-monthly lessons in Rosicrucian lore. Faithful adherence to the program would produce dramatic results, assured Lewis. The practitioner would develop greater will power, a more retentive memory, good health, and the ability to influence other people. A member would also learn about reincarnation and build up a kind of cosmic consciousness. In time, said Lewis, the member would reach an exalted plane of accomplishment shared by such figures as the pharaoh Akhenaton, Aristotle, Jesus, and Ben Franklin. It was a compelling pitch, and the San Jose order propagated rapidly, establishing more than a hundred lodges in the United States.

On the application form Sirhan Sirhan sent in with his $20 initiation fee, he claimed that he had been a student of psychology, philosophy, and metaphysics for three years. "I have discovered how much I do not know about myself despite all the philosophical worked that I have been reading," he wrote. "I sincerely want to better myself, and on that basis I submit my application." The Rosicrucians evidently overlooked his misspelling and scrambled grammar and accepted him as a member.

The betterment coveted by Sirhan centered on using his mind to control people and events. In a magazine he received from the order, he read an article entitled "Put It in Writing," which stressed the importance of making written commitments to whatever was desired: "Pick a goal. Set a target date. Now start working to make it come true." Sirhan would take that advice to heart.

He was convinced that he would be an apt student in psychic matters. "I have this propensity," he would later tell an investigator. "There are many things about me which cannot be explained by laboratory science." The only requirement was diligence, and for the first time since high school Sirhan worked hard. For hours, he honed his powers by staring at a candle flame in his bedroom or gazing in a small mirror or concentrating on a pendulum. He felt his mental strength growing and confided some of his small triumphs to a woman he knew. Out of the corner of his eye, Sirhan said, he could see "mystical bodies," and he could summon up an image of his guardian angel when he wished. He told the friend that one night he tried a telepathic experiment on his mother. She was sleeping in the bedroom next to his. He concentrated his mind on her and transmitted a wordless message that she was to get up and go to the bathroom. She did.

Whatever else they might or might not be, the Rosicrucians were peaceable. Not Sirhan Sirhan. He had various scores to settle. In the spring of 1967 he went to Hollywood Park and applied his mind-magic to a thoroughbred that was running that day. The horse was owned by Bert Altfillisch, proprietor of the horse ranch in Corona where Sirhan had failed to become a jockey. Altfillisch had become the focus of Sirhan's frustration and rage, and Sirhan meant to take it out on the horse. He focused intently on the animal as it broke from the starting gate. After only a few strides, the horse hit the rail and dropped back, out of the race almost as soon as it had begun. Even Sirhan was surprised. Following the advice of the Rosicrucian magazine article, he began keeping diaries—spiral notebooks left over from school—in which he revealed his innermost thoughts, his goals, his plans, his actions—words that would come back to haunt him later. On this day he wrote: "I believe that I can effect the death of Bert C. Altfillisch."

Already Sirhan was contemplating death for his ene-mies. But now there were more important things to occupy his rapidly expanding mind. In the late spring of 1967, the Middle East cauldron began to boil again. Egypt's President Gamal Abdel Nasser had struck an alliance with Syria and demanded that the United Nations withdraw troops from the borders shared by Egypt and Israel, which had been worked out in the earlier wars in 1948 and 1956. The United Nations obliged. Nasser next blockaded the Strait of Tiran at the head of the Red Sea, effectively shutting off the Israeli port of Eilat. By then, all the Arab powers in the region—Saudi Arabia, Iraq, Jordan, Kuwait, and Sudan as well as Egypt and Syria—were preparing for armed conflict against the detested Israelis.

Sirhan Sirhan sat riveted before the TV news shows and pored over the newspapers and magazines in the Pasadena Library; he even started reading the Jewish B'nai B'rith *Messenger* to "know what the Zionists are up to." The media seemed to him disgracefully biased in favor of Israel and willfully blind to Arab grievances. It drove him to fury. As tensions in the Middle East tightened, he sat in his room and composed a barely coherent manifesto, writing it in one of his diaries:

"2 June 67 12:30 pm

"A Declaration of war against American Humanity

"when in the course of human events it has become necessary for me to equalize and seek revenge for all the inhuman treatments committed against me by the American people."

The words were coming faster now, the ideas starting to coalesce, the emotions spilling out.

"The manifestation of this Declaration will be executed by its supporter(s) as soon as he is able to command a sum of money ($2,000) and to acquire some firearms the specifications of which have not been established yet."

Then his anger and frustration started to close in on a target.

"The victims of the party in favor of this declaration will be or are *now*—the President, vice, etc—down the ladder.

"The time will be chosen by the author at the convenience of the accused."

Sirhan Sirhan ranted in this manner for several paragraphs, alternating between self-importance and self-pity and ending with a passage of apocalyptic emotion.

"The conflict and violence in the world subsequent to the enforcement of the decree, shall not be considered lightly by the author of this memoranda, rather he hopes that the initiatory military steps for WWIII—the author expresses his wishes very bluntly that he wants to be recorded by historians as the *man* who triggered off the last war—

life is ambivalence

life is a struggle

life is wicked

If life is in anyway otherwise, I have honestly never seen it

I always seem to be on the losing end, always the one exploited to the fullest."

On June 5, 1967, just three days after Sirhan composed his manifesto declaring war against American Humanity, the shooting began in the Middle East. The results, for the Arab nations, were calamitous. The Egyptian air force was obliterated at the outset when Israeli jets made a preemptive strike at dawn, catching the enemy's aircraft on the ground. Israeli armored columns then lanced deep into the Sinai, driving the Egyptians back toward the Suez Canal and occupying the Gaza Strip. Simultaneously, Israeli forces in the north and east slammed into the gathering Syrians and Jordanians. Jordan speedily lost Jerusalem and the West Bank of the River Jordan; the Syrians were swept from the plateau called the Golan Heights.

The war lasted only six days. Dismayed by the performance of its Arab surrogates, the Soviet Union started making apoplectic noises—and the United States persuaded the Israelis to accept a cease-fire rather than pursuing a longer war. Nevertheless, any hope that the Palestinians might soon regain their homeland was shattered. In fact, an additional 400,000 Palestinians had lost their homes.

That the Israelis had struck first, no matter the provocation, no matter Arab intentions, lodged in Sirhan's mind as the ultimate Zionist offense. He would not forget the date of the attack—June 5. Its events required revenge—killing, he sensed, although it was not yet clear whom he must eliminate. Pick a goal. Set a date. Start working to make it come true. That's what the Rosicrucian magazine had advised. Sirhan brooded about it for

a number of months, and then he identified the person that he might kill in retaliation for what America was doing to his people.

Many Americans thought Robert Kennedy to be a champion of the poor and downtrodden, and Sirhan Sirhan was no exception. At one time he had considered RFK "a saint" and had evidently expected that Kennedy would be sympathetic to the plight of the displaced Palestinians. But even though Kennedy's pro-Israel view had always been firm, it was not until he caught the spotlight as his party's likely nominee for the 1968 presidential election that his positions on political issues—including his support of Israel—began receiving wide attention.

In January of 1968, Kennedy stated publicly a number of times that he favored the sale of 50 F-4 Phantom jets to the Israeli Air Force. The sophisticated Phantom was a premier U.S. fighter, far superior to anything the Soviets could sell the Arabs; it would ensure Israeli control of the air. For Sirhan, that was an unforgivable betrayal, and on January 31 he spewed fury across the pages of his notebook:

"RFK RFK RFK RFK RFK

Robert F Kennedy Robert F Kennedy

RFK RFK RFK RFK RFK must die RFK must die . . ."

Sirhan continued to write out the death sentence many more times. Then, however, a small voice of doubt made itself heard:

"Who killed Kennedy? I don't know I don't know I don't know . . ."

The psychic battle seesawed back and forth:

"yes yes yes yes yes yes yes yes

no no no"

In mid-February 1968, Sirhan's younger brother, Munir, bought a snub-nosed .22-caliber Iver-Johnson revolver from a coworker for $25. Sirhan gave Munir $6 toward the purchase price and afterward treated the gun as at least partly his. Around this time, Sirhan also began to focus exclusively on Kennedy as his candidate for extermination. On March 16, the junior senator from New York announced for the Democratic presidential nomination, and that fanned the flames of Sirhan's hate. He had trouble containing himself, and he once declared his deadly intentions out loud. On April 10, a few days after civil rights leader Martin Luther King Jr. was assassinated, Sirhan was chatting with a city sanitation worker whose trash-collection rounds brought him to East Howard Street. They had talked before, usually about politics. Sirhan now asked the man whom he planned to vote for in the upcoming California primary. When the sanitation worker said that his choice was Kennedy, Sirhan responded, "Well I don't agree. I'm planning on shooting the son of a bitch."

The sanitation worker did not take him seriously, of course. But Sirhan was very serious indeed. Pick a goal. Set a target date. Now start working to make it happen. On the morning of May 18, Sirhan scrawled haphazardly in his notebook:

"My determination to eliminate RFK is becoming more the more of an unshakable obsession . . . Robert F. Kennedy must be assassinated R.F.K. must be assassinated R.F.K. must be assassinated . . . R.F.K. must be assassinated before 5 June 68 . . . "

There never was any mystery about why Sirhan chose that date for a deadline. It would be the anniversary of the Six Day War. "June 5 stood out for me," Sirhan later told an investigator, "more than my own birth date."

Sirhan's resolve was hardened by reading about a number of pro-Israel statements from Kennedy during the Oregon and California primary campaigns. On May 20, the senator visited a Los Angeles synagogue and, wearing a yarmulke in the sanctuary, spoke of the need for a U.S.-Soviet agreement to stop the shipment of arms to the Middle East. Until such an agreement was reached, he said, the United States "must fully assist Israel—with arms if necessary." A week later, in Oregon, Kennedy gave another speech in a synagogue, declaring that the United States must defend Israel against aggression "from whatever source." Israel's request for 50 Phantom fighters should be granted without delay. Moreover, Kennedy recommended that the United States cut off any economic aid to Arab countries if that aid was used "in support of aggression against Israel."

At about this time, Sirhan saw a half-hour television documentary suggesting to him that Kennedy had been a lifelong enemy of the Palestinians. The film, titled "The Story of Robert Kennedy," explained how, in 1948, Kennedy had visited war-torn Palestine as a Harvard senior and had written up his observations for a

Emblazoned with Sirhan's emphatic signature *(above)*, excerpts from the assassin's diaries *(right)* testify to his growing obsession with Robert Kennedy and, perhaps, money—among the repeated phrases is "Pay to the order of . . ." The two pages at top are part of Sirhan's rambling manifesto, a bizarre parody of the Declaration of Independence. But as his obsession focused, the refrain became, "RFK must die." On the fragment of a U.S. Treasury envelope at lower right, Sirhan notes, "RFK must be disposed of the way his brother was."

Boston newspaper. His articles, while sympathetic toward the Jews, had stressed the need to find a peaceful settlement—but the film did not go into the subtleties.

The documentary also suggested that one of the purposes in the young man's trip was to "celebrate" Israel's independence. Said the narrator, "Bob Kennedy decided his future lay in the affairs of men and nations." An Israeli flag was flying in the background as the narrator spoke these words, leaving Sirhan in no doubt as to which men and what nation Kennedy favored.

The vision of himself avenging the wrongs heaped on his fellow Palestinians grew stronger and purer. He readied himself in his room. "I concentrated on RFK in the mirror: I had to stop him," he later said. "Finally, his face was in the mirror instead of my own."

He began to circle his quarry. On the evening of Sunday, May 24, Sirhan attended a rally for Kennedy held in the Los Angeles Sports Arena, joining an enthusiastic throng that waited in the parking lot to see the senator as he departed. A clinical psychologist in the group noticed Sirhan because he seemed "so completely out of character" among the others who had come to cheer Kennedy. The psychologist later said that Sirhan "appeared very intense and sinister."

Two days later, on May 26, it was reported that Kennedy again urged the sale of fighter jets to Israel. That same day, an editorial titled "Paradoxical Bob," which criticized Kennedy's seesawing position on the Vietnam War and questioned his suitability as the country's president, appeared in the *Pasadena Independent State News*. Sirhan clipped the piece and kept it with him, like a talisman.

Sirhan Sirhan now looked to his marksmanship. On June 1, he spent two hours practicing at the Corona police shooting range. Later that afternoon, he bought two boxes of .22-caliber ammunition at the Lock, Stock 'N Barrel gun shop in San Gabriel, a suburb south of Pasadena. The next evening, he turned up at a Kennedy campaign rally held at the Ambassador Hotel in Los Angeles, but he did not get close to the senator.

June 4 was the day of the primary, a beautiful day, a good day for shooting—a necessary day for killing, if Sirhan was to meet his deadline. At about 11 a.m., he arrived at the San Gabriel Valley Gun Club and bought some .22-caliber Super-X "Long Rifle" ammunition.

For the next six hours, Sirhan practiced with his short-barreled pistol. He was intent on volume fire and blazed away more rapidly than range regulations allowed—removing the spent shells from the revolver cylinder with a small screwdriver, loading up again, emptying the gun again. The rangemaster decided to ignore the rule violation; the man was a good shot, and by the time he was finished the center had been completely torn out of the target.

At one point, after firing about 100 shells, Sirhan complained to the rangemaster that some of the Super-X bullets were duds; he asked for ammunition that absolutely would not misfire. The rangemaster sold him Mini-Mag hollow-point bullets. Sirhan practiced with the Mini-Mags and seemed pleased. He remarked to another shooter that hollow points inflict more damage than ordinary slugs. "They spread a lot more on impact," said Sirhan. All told, he expended more than 400 rounds during the practice session.

After leaving the range, Sirhan Sirhan drove to a Bob's Big Boy restaurant in Pasadena for a hamburger and coffee. There, he met an Indian exchange student he knew and the two of them went to the Pasadena City College cafeteria, where they spent half an hour chatting about summer courses with some Arab students.

Sirhan later returned to the restaurant and, leafing through a newspaper, spotted a story that interested him: "Tonight," it reported, a Zionist organization would stage a parade in downtown Los Angeles to celebrate the anniversary of the Six Day War. About 7:30 p.m., Sirhan left the restaurant and drove into the city in search of this "Jew parade," as he called it. But there was no parade. The newspaper was an early edition of the next day's issue and "tonight" meant the evening of June 5, another 24 hours away.

Just before 9 p.m., Sirhan arrived at the Ambassador Hotel on Wiltshire Boulevard. Kennedy supporters were already there in large numbers, getting ready to celebrate their candidate's anticipated victory in the primary vote held that day. But the computers used in vote counting were not functioning well, and there was no definitive word on the outcome of the election. It seemed clear that Kennedy would not make an appearance for several hours.

Sirhan ventured into a party for a U.S. senatorial can-

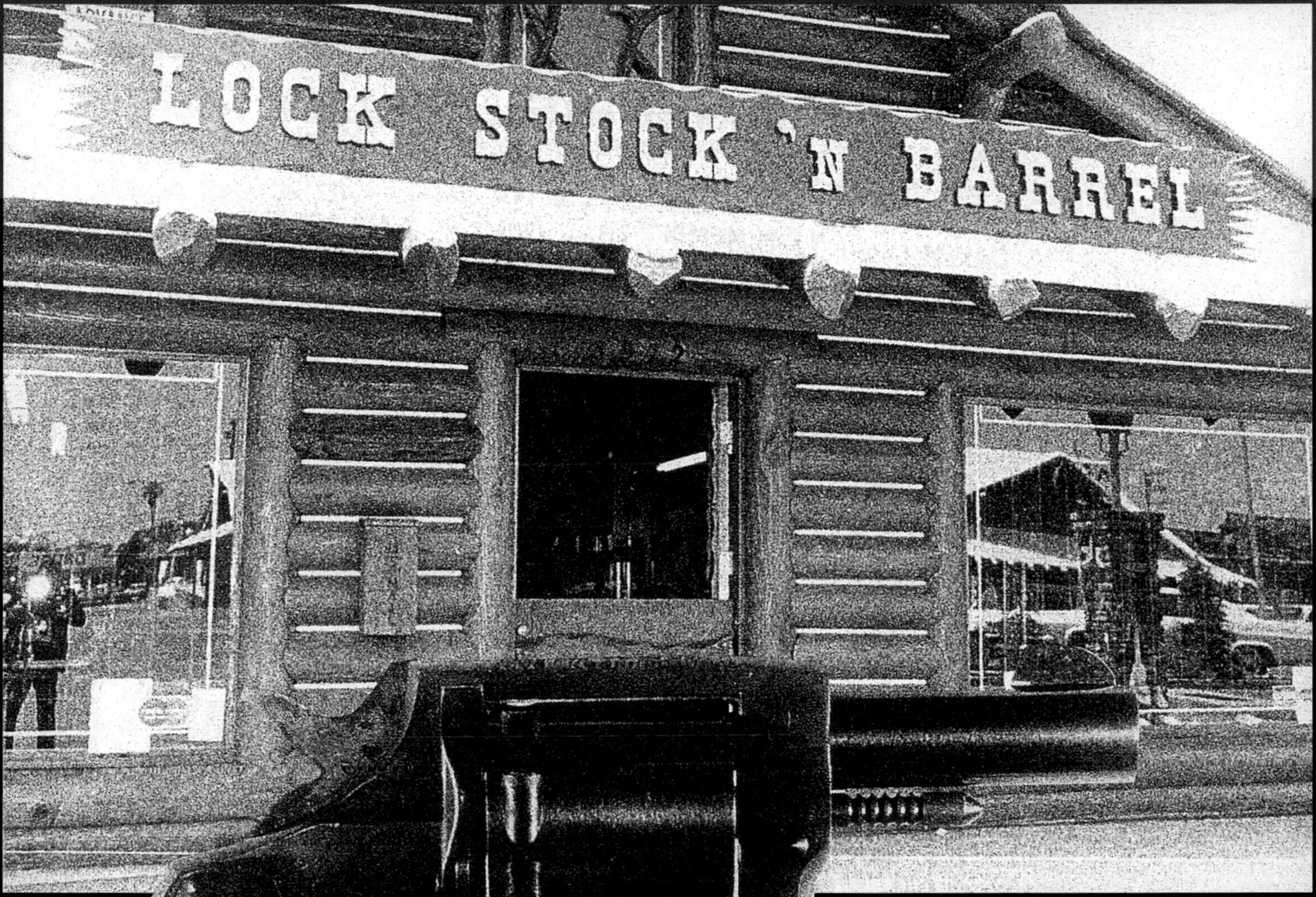

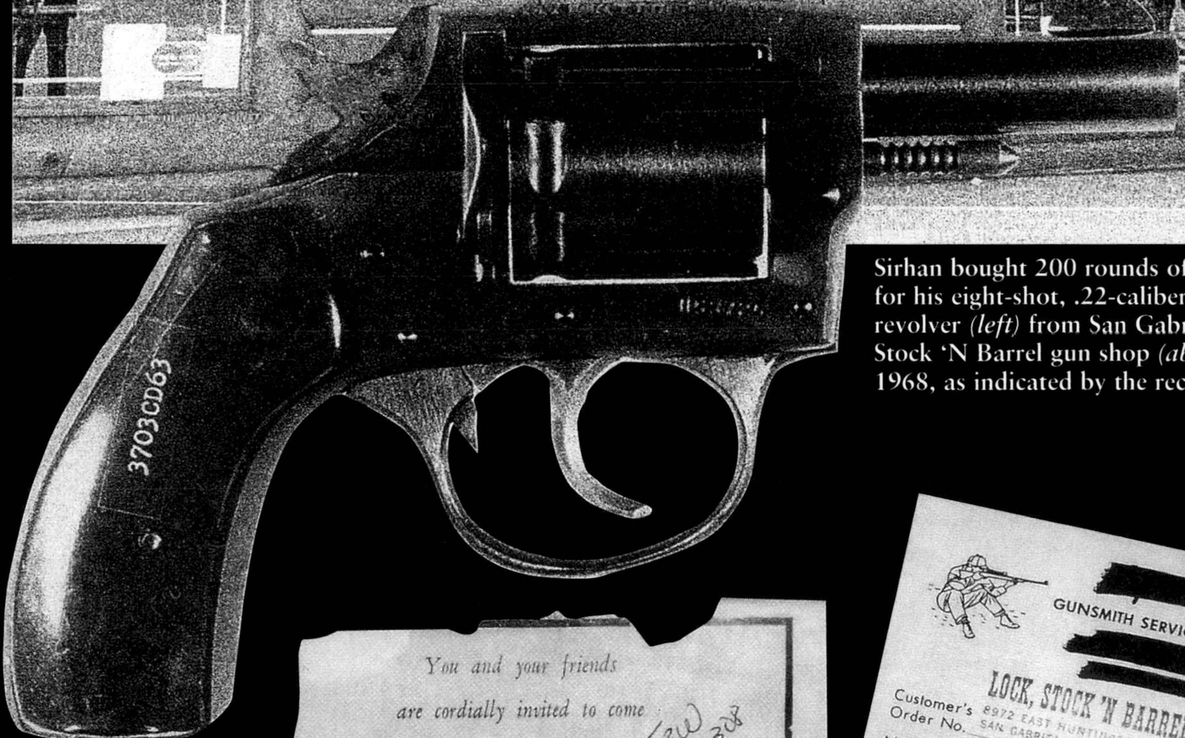

Sirhan bought 200 rounds of ammunition for his eight-shot, .22-caliber Iver-Johnson revolver *(left)* from San Gabriel's Lock, Stock 'N Barrel gun shop *(above)* on June 1, 1968, as indicated by the receipt below.

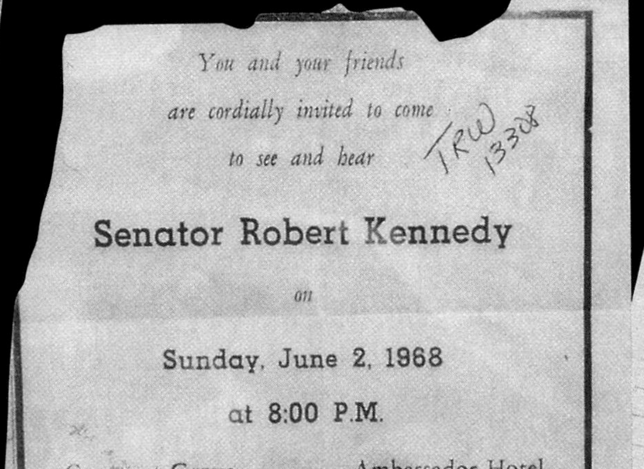

A notice for a Kennedy rally *(right)* found in Sirhan's pocket attests to the fact that the killer had stalked his quarry a full two days before the murder.

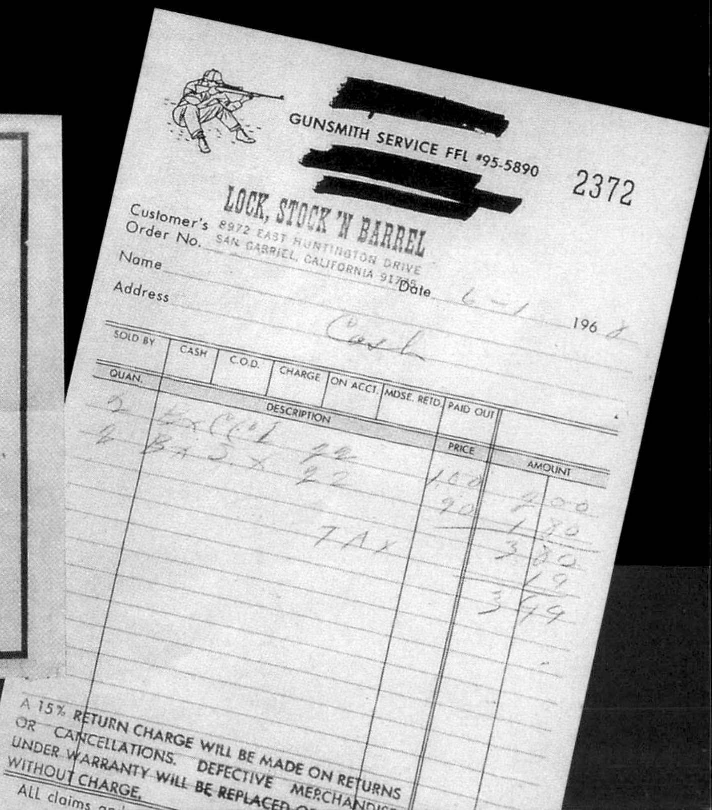

You and your friends
are cordially invited to come
to see and hear

Senator Robert Kennedy

on

Sunday, June 2, 1968

at 8:00 P.M.

Cocoanut Grove   Ambassador Hotel

Los Angeles

75

On June 4, the day before he assassinated Robert Kennedy, Sirhan Sirhan spent about six hours at this San Gabriel valley shooting range *(top)*, firing high-velocity .22-caliber bullets from this box of Mini-Mag long rifle rounds.

didate named Max Rafferty, who was also having his victory celebration at the Ambassador. Sirhan later testified that he drank two Tom Collinses, a lemony, punch-like gin concoction, the first one quickly, the next more slowly. He was apparently asked to leave the party he had crashed, and outside the room he met two men who had arrived for the Kennedy victory celebration. The three chatted, with one expressing concern about whether RFK would garner enough votes to win the primary. Sirhan replied, "Don't worry about him if he doesn't win, that son of a bitch. He's a millionaire and he doesn't need to win. He just wants to go to the White House, but even if he wins he's not going to do anything for you or for any of the poor people." Sirhan then wandered around the hotel. By 11 p.m., he said, he had downed two more Tom Collinses.

That much booze that fast would be enough to give an ordinary man a pretty good buzz and perhaps make a slight man drunk. Sirhan Sirhan, in fact, later claimed that his last conscious memory of what happened that night was going out to his car and deciding he was too drunk to drive home. After that point, he said, everything was a blank.

In fact, when he went out to his car he got his gun. He left his wallet in the vehicle and returned to the Ambassador Hotel. A number of people spotted him in the time leading up to the shooting. In the Colonial Room, where the press was set up, a Western Union telex operator talked to Sirhan between 9:30 and 10 p.m. Judy Royer, a Kennedy staffer, was trying to clear unauthorized persons out of the pantry and kitchen area behind the ballroom where RFK would greet his supporters. She recalled asking Sirhan to leave the area twice that evening. Despite her efforts, shortly after 11 p.m. Sirhan was in the serving pantry. It was one likely route to the ballroom podium and he hovered in the vicinity, his .22 pistol tucked into the waistband of his trousers.

Upstairs in his fifth-floor suite, Kennedy waited and worried as the vote counting dragged on. But by 11:45, the anxieties had evaporated—it was clear that he would defeat Eugene McCarthy in California. He gave the word that he was ready to go downstairs to the Embassy Ballroom.

The senator made his way to the ballroom podium by way of the serving pantry—just as Sirhan had hoped. If the killer was in the pantry as Kennedy passed through, however, he made no move. Sirhan may have been outside and missed him. But he was back in the pantry when Kennedy was addressing the crowd and wanted to know if RFK might pass through again. Several times he asked the kitchen workers, "Is Mr. Kennedy coming this way?" They said they did not know.

In the ballroom, the crowd responded to the victory speech with exultant yells and applause. A chant began: "WE WANT BOBBY, WE WANT BOBBY." Kennedy acknowledged their cheers, and then he stepped off the podium—and hurried away to his rendezvous with a bullet in the brain.

Police led Sirhan Sirhan through the dazed and hostile group crowding the kitchen. According to the officers who interrogated him, Sirhan showed no overt signs of intoxication or drug use, and other than a few incoherent mumbles, he was silent. His temper flashed once when he asked if he could have a sip from a drink one officer was holding. When the officer declined, Sirhan asked if the liquid was hot. Told that it was, Sirhan suddenly kicked out, splashing hot chocolate on himself and the officer.

The self-anointed Palestinian warrior was first booked as John Doe and charged with assault with intent to murder. Within 24 hours RFK was dead and Sirhan's identity was known; he was charged with first-degree murder on June 7. That day his mother sent a telegram to the Kennedy family: "It hurt us very bad what has happened and we express our feelings with them and especially with the children and with Mrs. Kennedy. . . . We pray that God will make peace, really peace, in the hearts of the people." Bishara Sirhan, then living in a West Bank village, sent a letter to his son: "I am very angry with you for the deed you have committed and I don't encourage you or any other persons to kill another. Son, you forget all the bad acts committed against the Arab people. Learn to forgive and forget what happened in the Palestine wars . . . Pray God and Jesus Christ."

Meanwhile, millions mourned, not just in America but around the world. On June 8, funeral services for the slain senator were held in Saint Patrick's Cathedral in Manhattan. Then a special train slowly conveyed the casket south to Washington. All along the route, thou-

His presidential campaign invigorated by his triumph in California's 1968 Democratic primary election, Senator Robert F. Kennedy gives a rousing victory speech to supporters in the Embassy Ballroom of the Ambassador Hotel in Los Angeles.

Moments after acknowledging his victory in the California primary and exhorting his followers to carry him into the White House, Robert Kennedy lies fatally wounded on the pantry floor, as bystander Dr. Stanley Abo tries to keep the senator alive.

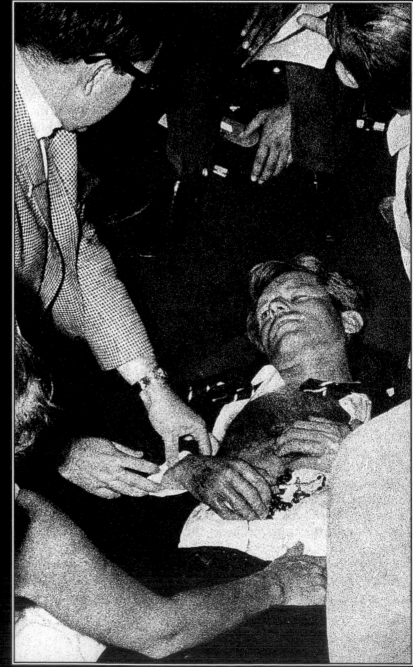

Aided by former L.A. Rams tackle Roosevelt Grier (foreground), author George Plimpton (with arm raised) and Kennedy bodyguards wrestle Sirhan Sirhan (center) to the floor—too late, however, to save the candidate.

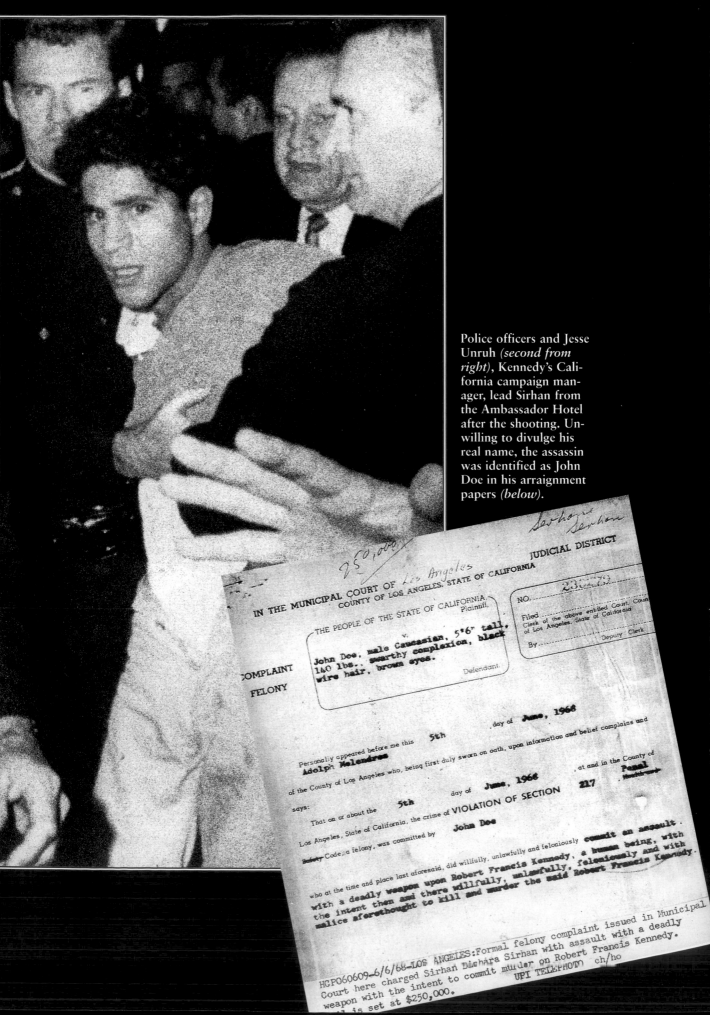

Police officers and Jesse Unruh *(second from right)*, Kennedy's California campaign manager, lead Sirhan from the Ambassador Hotel after the shooting. Unwilling to divulge his real name, the assassin was identified as John Doe in his arraignment papers *(below)*.

IN THE MUNICIPAL COURT OF *Los Angeles* JUDICIAL DISTRICT
COUNTY OF LOS ANGELES, STATE OF CALIFORNIA

THE PEOPLE OF THE STATE OF CALIFORNIA, Plaintiff,

NO. 236479

v.

John Doe, male Caucasian, 5'6" tall, 140 lbs., swarthy complexion, black wire hair, brown eyes.

Defendant.

Filed ....
Clerk of the above entitled Court, County of Los Angeles, State of California

By .... Deputy Clerk

COMPLAINT

FELONY

Personally appeared before me this 5th day of June, 1968

Adolph Melendres

of the County of Los Angeles who, being first duly sworn on oath, upon information and belief complains and

says: That on or about the 5th day of June, 1968 at and in the County of

Los Angeles, State of California, the crime of VIOLATION OF SECTION 217 Penal

~~Safety~~ Code, a felony, was committed by John Doe

who at the time and place last aforesaid, did willfully, unlawfully and feloniously commit an assault

with a deadly weapon upon Robert Francis Kennedy, a human being, with

the intent then and there willfully, unlawfully, feloniously and with

malice aforethought to kill and murder the said Robert Francis Kennedy.

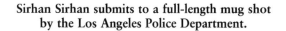

sands of people stood by the tracks to pay their last respects. As the funeral train rolled slowly past, many supporters held up signs saying, "We love you, Bobby" and "We'll miss you."

That evening, Robert Kennedy was buried in Arlington National Cemetery a few yards away from the grave of his brother. The NBC television reporter who covered the somber, candlelit ceremony, Sander Vanocur, chose to simply be a witness. For 17 minutes, he said nothing—the longest silence in the history of television news. "I didn't know what to say," the journalist declared. "I think it spoke for itself."

In the days, weeks, and months that followed, Sirhan Sirhan never wavered in his contention that he remembered nothing of the shooting. Obviously, he was aware that he might receive the death penalty if premeditation was proved. And he knew that rock-solid proof of his plot against Kennedy existed in the notebooks he kept in his bedroom. When a representative of the American Civil Liberties Union met with him the day after his arrest to arrange legal counsel, Sirhan made a sly suggestion: "Tell my mother to clean up my room. It's a mess." But it was too late. The police had already searched his bedroom and confiscated the notebooks.

As he worked with lawyers to devise a defense, Sirhan portrayed himself as a political prisoner and expressed the fatuous hope that he would be exchanged for some valuable captive the Arabs held—just like the swap for U-2 pilot Gary Powers after his spy plane had been shot down over the Soviet Union in 1960. When Richard Nixon won the presidency in

November 1968, Sirhan had an even brighter idea. "Hell, I gave him the election," he said—in return for which, Sirhan reasoned, a grateful Nixon should allow him to go free, supply him with a passport to Jordan, and even award him a nice, neat $1,000,000. He was completely serious. He printed out his demands on a sheet of paper.

The trial of Sirhan Sirhan began in January 1969. His lawyers had but one aim: to avoid the death penalty. If they succeeded in showing that Sirhan could not recognize the gravity of his act because of diminished mental capacity, they might get a verdict of second-degree murder or even manslaughter under California law.

A stream of psychiatrists and psychologists mounted the witness stand. On the basis of various tests and their study of the notebooks, most of them judged that Sirhan's mind was severely disordered. He was a "borderline psychotic," concluded one expert. "A schizophrenic of the paranoid type," testified another. "He started showing signs of mental illness no later than the time when he fell from the horse," advised yet another.

The star witness for the defense was Dr. Bernard L. Diamond, a professor of law, criminology, and psychiatry at the University of California at Berkeley. This triple-barreled expert concurred with most of his colleagues in assessing Sirhan as schizophrenic. And he went further, spinning out an elaborate scenario of Sirhan's "dissociated" mental state on the night of the shooting. Supposing that the defendant had conditioned himself for self-hypnosis by his psychic exercises with the candles

Sirhan Sirhan submits to a full-length mug shot by the Los Angeles Police Department.

This Palestine Liberation Organization poster, distributed in the Middle East at the time of Sirhan's 1969 trial, portrays the assassin as a hero.

and mirrors in his bedroom, the professor then speculated that Sirhan had inadvertently lapsed into a trance at the Ambassador Hotel—a hypnotized state that was brought on by the four Tom Collinses and the mirrors and lights at the hotel.

"I see Sirhan as small and helpless, pitifully ill with a demented, psychotic rage, out of control of his own consciousness and his own actions, subject to bizarre dissociated trances, in some of which he programmed himself to be the instrument of assassination, and then in an almost accidentally induced twilight state, he actually executed the crime, knowing next to nothing about what was happening," offered Diamond.

Did the professor feel certain of this explanation? the prosecution asked. In a burst of dazzling candor, Diamond confessed that the scenario he had just outlined sounded like "an absurd and preposterous story, unlikely and incredible." The prosecutors grinned; the defense groaned inwardly.

For the most part, Sirhan remained calm during the proceedings, and when he took the witness stand, he spoke with passion about Palestinian grievances and what he saw as Western indifference: "Where is the justice involved, sir? Where is the love, sir, for fighting for the underdog? Israel is not underdog in the Middle East, sir. It's those refugees that are underdogs. And because they have no way of fighting back, sir, the Jews, sir, the Zionists, just keep beating away at them. That burned the hell out of me."

But he lost control of himself when the judge placed his notebooks in evidence—an invasion of his innermost thoughts, Sirhan believed. He informed the judge that he wanted to change his plea to guilty and would ask to be put to death. The judge turned him down, but it was just academic.

Thoroughly unimpressed by the parade of psychiatrists and psychologists, the jury of seven men and five women reached their verdict easily. They found Sirhan guilty of first-degree murder; they did not recommend clemency. Sentencing took place a few days later, on April 23, 1969. The prosecuting attorney had asked for the death penalty—"the only proper penalty for political assassination in the United States of America." Despite a written plea for mercy by Robert Kennedy's brother, Senator Edward Kennedy, the jury sentenced 25-year-old Sirhan Sirhan to die in the gas chamber. On May 23, 1969, he took up residence on death row in San Quentin.

The legal road to execution turned out to be a long one, however, and Sirhan Sirhan never quite reached the end of his journey. In 1972 the United States Supreme Court outlawed the death penalty, thereby changing his sentence to life imprisonment.

To this day Sirhan Sirhan remains behind bars in the Protective Housing Unit of Corcoran State Prison in Corcoran, California. From time to time, the convict has given interviews in prison, professing remorse, insisting that he did not know what he was doing and that he would give anything if Robert Kennedy could somehow be brought back to life. Although he has repeatedly applied for parole, he has always been denied. That makes him bitter. "There are guys who have committed multiple murders and guys who have hacked people up or tortured them to death who have gotten shorter sentences," Sirhan says. "That is not fair to me. That is all I'm asking for, fairness."

This complaint is an old refrain, an echo of what he wrote in his notebook a year before he drilled a bullet into Robert Kennedy's skull:

"Life is ambivalence
life is a struggle
life is wicked
If life is in anyway otherwise, I have honestly never seen it
I always seem to be on the losing end, always the one exploited to the fullest." ◆

Sixteen years after
killing Kennedy, Sirhan
waits to hear if his
1984 parole request—
one of many—will be
granted. Thus far, none
has been approved.

The Man Who Would Be Sirhan

When police searched the Milwaukee, Wisconsin, apartment of Arthur Herman Bremer in May of 1972, they found plentiful evidence of a murderous state of mind. Among the items in the three messy rooms were boxes of bullets, a booklet entitled *101 Things to Do in Jail*, and a newspaper article about the difficulty of providing protection for politicians. Bremer's car, a decrepit 1967 Rambler Rebel, contained another suggestive trove: binoculars; a radio that could listen in on police frequencies; a Browning 9-mm. semiautomatic pistol; and two books about someone Bremer wanted to emulate, a lone gun who had stepped forward and killed a famous man—Senator Robert Kennedy's assassin, Sirhan Sirhan.

In fact, Bremer and Sirhan had much in common. Both men were loners, acutely withdrawn, steeped in feelings of frustration and failure, and bent on gaining revenge for the world's injustices by killing a national leader. In Bremer's case, it hardly mattered who. He had never had much of a life himself. Born on August 21, 1950, the fourth of five children, he grew up in a grimy working-class neighborhood in Milwaukee. His father, a truckdriver, was a passive man who sought relief from his troubles in drink; his mother, raised in an orphanage, viewed the world with mistrust and often lashed out at her husband and children. Some of Arthur Bremer's siblings ran afoul of the law early, and the family was well known to Milwaukee social workers, who described the Bremers as dysfunctional.

Outwardly, Bremer seemed normal enough. Although he stood only five-feet-seven-inches tall, he was a husky young man. His attendance record was good in high school and in the technical school where he studied photography afterward. His intelligence was about average, and he was able to get through his courses. But Arthur Bremer had no friends, and girls avoided him, thinking him strange, angry, and erratic.

At the age of 21, by then employed part-time as a busboy at an athletic club and as a janitor at an elementary school, Bremer left home and rented his own apartment. He somehow managed to attract the attention of a 15-year-old girl who served as a monitor at the elementary school, and they briefly dated. But she was disturbed by his interest in pornography, his prying questions, and his bizarre public behavior—such as the time he kissed an unknown girl at a rock concert and applauded and yelled at all the wrong moments. Concluding that he was "childish" and "weird," she dumped Bremer in January 1972.

Without meaning to, the girl had given Bremer's empty life a turning point, and it veered toward violence. He shaved his head, purchased a .38-caliber revolver, and began keeping a diary, which he filled with bloody thoughts. Before long, he'd stopped working and was holed up in his apartment, his mind alive with fantasies of assassination. As he put it to his diary, "I am one sick assissin." By April he was ready to act. He traveled to Canada and made a half-dozen attempts to get close to President Richard Nixon during a state visit, but the tight security thwarted him. He wrote in his diary:

"My fuse about bernt. There's gona be an explosion soon. I had it. I want something to happen. I was sopposed to be dead a week & a day ago. Or at least in a few hours. F——— tens-of-1,000's of people & tens-of-millions of $. I'd just like to take some of them with me & Nixy."

Next, he considered going after Democratic presidential candidate George McGovern, but finally, as he confided to his diary, "I've decided Wallace will have the honor." The governor of Alabama, a long shot running primarily on a law-and-order platform, would be more accessible, he figured. In fact, the murder of Robert Kennedy four years earlier had given candidates Secret Service protection.

Bremer stalked Wallace for weeks, tagging along through Michigan and Maryland—again and again, Bremer appeared in photographs taken along the Wallace campaign trail. On May 15, 1972, as Wallace was shaking hands during an afternoon rally at a shopping center in Laurel, Maryland, Bremer—wearing Wallace buttons and red, white, and blue clothes—caught the candidate's attention. Shouting, "Hey, George! Hey, George! Over here!" he pushed close to Wallace, managing to squeeze through the ring of bodyguards. He fired five times, hitting his target repeatedly and wounding three other people, including a Secret Service agent. One bullet lodged in Wallace's spinal canal. Although the governor survived, he was paralyzed from the waist down; the shots also ended his political career.

At the trial, defense lawyers argued that Bremer was insane and thus not culpable. As in Sirhan's case, a jury disagreed; he was found guilty of assault with intent to murder and given 63 years in prison. At sentencing, the judge asked him if he wanted to make a statement. "Looking back on my life," Bremer said, "I would have liked it if society had protected me from myself."

A Wallace campaign photo captures Arthur Bremer just before he shot the candidate.

My son was too happy to think of doing what he is accused of trying.

CARL ADAM WEISS

3

Killing the Kingfish

ear the end of its course to the Gulf of Mexico, the
Mississippi River runs wide and deep past Baton
Rouge, moving sluggishly through the swampy flatlands
as though exhausted by its long southward journey. On
the night of Sunday, September 8, 1935, the river wore a
silver sheen from a quarter moon whose light filtered
down through the sweltering late-summer night. The
shimmer seemed to heighten the great river's lofty indifference to the petty, fleeting passions of the humans
along its banks. Yet just beside the Mississippi, from a
building that rose in a garish hive of light, those passions
were about to crest in a flood tide as destructive as the
mighty river at its worst.

The new Louisiana capitol, towering 34 stories above
the levee, was then the tallest building in the South. The
bold edifice had been ordered into existence four years
earlier during the single term of Governor Huey Pierce
Long—the man who called himself the Kingfish, after a
wily character on the popular radio show, *Amos 'n
Andy*. Some said the $5 million skyscraper was a grand
memorial to himself.

Elected to the U.S. Senate in 1930, Long did not go to
Washington until 1932, after he'd bequeathed his previous office to a pliable puppet governor named Oscar K.
Allen—familiarly, and fittingly, "O. K." Allen. But the
senator was often back in the capitol he'd created: It was
his base for maintaining and extending his control over
the state. Whether his title was governor or senator,
Huey Long remained *the* power in Louisiana. Now, as
always, he aspired to greater things—he'd said he would
make a run for the presidency of the United States.

Long had every reason to believe that he could prance
to good effect on the nation's political stage. By 1935
America had settled into the economic paralysis of the
Great Depression, and millions of people across the land
were now no better off than the poor whites of Winn
Parish, Long's hill-country county in northern Louisiana. "There wants to be a revolution," his father had

told him years earlier. Huey's ambitious Share Our
Wealth program, a radical plan to redistribute America's
riches, sounded like one.

Certainly, Long's populist tactics had played well in
his home state—few men have commanded such love
from their followers. To them, Huey was the savior who
through sheer force of will had dragged Louisiana from
an almost medieval mire into the 20th century. At 42 he
was the leader who'd called on the legions of the poor in
his state to lift their eyes from the dirt and envision the
possibility of a better future, following his own example—he'd passed the Louisiana Bar exam on grit and
brilliance, after all; he'd become Louisiana's youngest
governor; and now, from the U.S. Senate, his colorful
voice rang forth across America. "Every Man a King,
but No Man Wears a Crown." He'd run on that, and
people had believed him.

In only one term as governor Long had built 1,583
miles of concrete highways and more than 3,500 miles
of asphalt or gravel roads and 111 new bridges; the tim-
bermen and hardscrabble farmers in the north and the
fishermen and trappers in the south could get their
goods to market—and, of course, themselves to the
polls. He'd made good medical care available to them,
and he'd provided their children with free schoolbooks.
No man had ever done nearly so much, and Huey
promised to do even more.

If Long seemed sometimes to trample on democracy, it
could be argued that there'd never been much of it to
trample in the first place. The old-line planter aristocracy, in league with big business interests and a political
machine in New Orleans—the state's only big city—had
ruled Louisiana like a feudal fiefdom for as long as anyone could remember. Huey, his friends said, merely
shook up the system and gave the poor folks a chance. In
return, they forgave him his sins of flesh, alcohol, and
venality and offered him their unalloyed loyalty, the true
source of his power.

An Art Deco steel and stone monument to power completed in 1932, the $5 million Louisiana capitol towers above the Mississippi at Baton Rouge.

Long's detractors pointed out that his improvements had increased the state's debt tenfold, to $125 million, and that Louisiana had paid top dollar and more for its roads and bridges and hospitals—charges flew of graft, bid rigging, and kickbacks. And there was all that heavy-handed restructuring along lines of patronage. When he'd taken office as governor, Long fired state employees who weren't loyal to him and grabbed control of state boards and agencies.

By wielding his influence in the elections of judges, he'd grasped the levers of judicial power in the state as well. He'd even brought the hiring and firing of teachers into his political grip, using loyalty to him as a litmus test for educators. He extracted a political tithe from state employees before elections and used the state police and National Guard as a private army; he had once declared martial law in Baton Rouge and in New Orleans to quell dissent against him. He manipulated the state legislature as if it were a rubber stamp. For ex-

With New Orleans under martial law, Huey Long travels surrounded by guardsmen.

ample, when advised that a certain measure was unconstitutional, Huey had snapped, "*I'm* the constitution around here now."

Only one serious counterattack had been mounted by Long's growing legion of foes. It had come in 1929, when Long, governor for less than a year, tried to slap a burdensome tax on Standard Oil, at the risk of driving away the state's biggest employer. Enraged, the Louisiana House of Representatives had impeached Long on a variety of charges, ranging from plotting political assassination to engaging in nightclub pranks. Long wriggled free of that, however, and left Standard Oil alone—at least for the time being.

But as Long traveled the state, he began to smell the acrid odor of disaffection. In 1933 the Kingfish found his usually worshipful audiences cold, even hostile. There were sneers and taunts. In one town he was pelted with eggs, in another with garbage; in another he was hanged in effigy. And still he steamrollered on. In

Long moved his wife, Rose, and children into this Audubon Boulevard mansion in New Orleans.

December 1934 Huey had finally managed to push through his tax on industry in general, and Standard Oil in particular. The company responded to this by reducing its work force. In Baton Rouge, a city of 30,000, a third of Standard's 3,000 refinery employees were dismissed, bringing hard times to everyone in town and creating an angry regiment of unemployed.

Such ploys had won Huey a multitude of mortal enemies. He traveled in an entourage of armed thugs who called themselves his Cossacks, often flanked by a squad of National Guard soldiers. Brash on the stump and on the parliamentary floor, Long was something of a physical coward; the Cossacks, with their penchant for roughing up people at the Kingfish's behest, were proof of that, according to Huey's foes.

By 1935, however, Long had good reason to fear for his life. The state's democracy-minded citizens were outraged by his authoritarian tactics. Even without his national aspirations, Long was regarded as a dangerous man, even a mentally disturbed one, by those who hated him. An upstart backwoods bumpkin who'd bullied, bludgeoned, bribed, bought, and blackmailed his way to a stranglehold on the state, he was seen as a demagogue and a fascist, an American echo of the dictators the Depression was spawning in Europe.

The very thought of a President Huey Long—or even a candidate Long manipulating the balance of power—was enough to stir his many enemies to frenzy. So egregious had his behavior become that the federal government's Bureau of Internal Revenue had begun to scrutinize Long; he alleged that the Roosevelt administration was out to kill him. But his deadliest enemies were closer to home, where a commonly voiced opinion, often uttered with chilling relish, was that the only way to stop Huey was to kill him. In fact, nightriders had fired half a dozen bullets into the door of the elegant home on New Orleans's Audubon Boulevard where his wife, Rose, and three children resided—Long spent most of his time at the Roosevelt Hotel or at the Heidelberg Hotel in Baton Rouge.

Although the specter of his death rode with him everywhere those days, power must have been foremost in Huey Long's mind the night of September 8 as he strode to and fro in his capitol, personally overseeing one of the frequent special sessions of his pliant state legislature. Intent as he was on business, geniality beamed from his pudgy, earnest face, the face of the traveling salesman he once had been, a face whose country-boy homeliness effectively masked both his genius and his arrogant ambition.

Long had reason to feel genial that night; his lawmakers were dutifully churning out a set of bills that would put the finishing touch to his absolute control of state government. Still, he left nothing to chance, scurrying between the house and the governor's office to shore up strategy or merely swap jokes. He moved in a trademark gait that was almost a run, as though impelled by an urgency that he alone could perceive. As usual, he tended to outpace his ever-present phalanx of bodyguards, but only by a few steps. Jittery and watchful, the Cossacks were out in strength on this night, drawn by rumors that someone would try to assassinate the Kingfish during the special session.

About 9:20 p.m. Huey hurried out of the governor's office and into a marble hallway that ran along the rear of the capitol's first floor between the house and the senate chambers. A small crowd of bodyguards and political cronies eddied nervously, struggling to assemble themselves around him. Long paused momentarily to have a word with one of them. At that instant, a thin, bespectacled young man in a white linen suit stepped forward. He'd been waiting by a marble pillar in the hallway just opposite the double doors of the governor's office. For a moment, Senator Huey Pierce Long and the man history has named as his assassin, Dr. Carl Austin

Extending his hold on southern hearts and minds during the 1932 election campaign, Huey Long expertly stumps for senatorial candidate Hattie Caraway in neighboring Arkansas.

Weiss, stood face to face. Seconds later, a frightened Huey fled down the marble hall, his right hand clutching an abdominal bullet wound, as Weiss shuddered in a fusillade of Cossack gunfire. It was the first time the two had met; then they were linked forever.

Just as history presents conflicting portraits of Huey Long—messiah to some, bayou Mussolini to others—so does it preserve starkly different versions of Carl Weiss. According to one, Weiss was an intense and darkly brooding young intellectual who, driven by family honor or by a martyr's impulse to rid the world of evil, killed Huey Long, giving up his own life for that privilege. But almost everything known about Weiss before that September night in Baton Rouge points to someone for whom such an act would have been unthinkable: a gifted, caring physician, a devoted husband and father—a man who, greatly loved and loving, looked forward to a long and sunny future. Almost every scrap of anecdote or evidence insists that Carl Weiss would have been deterred by his religion, his profession, and his own gentle nature from killing anyone. Thus, although Weiss endures in the official accounts as the assassin, no one is entirely certain—and many doubt—that he killed Huey Long.

Certainly, the profile of an assassin as a loner, loser, lowlife, and misfit in no way fits Carl Weiss, who was none of those things. He was born in Baton Rouge on December 18, 1905, to a family that, while it was not a part of the Louisiana aristocracy, fit easily into the gentry. Weiss's father, Carl Adam Weiss, was himself the son of a Bavarian Catholic choirmaster and organist who'd left Germany for New Orleans in 1870. A teacher of music in his adopted

A one-year-old Carl Austin Weiss cheerfully contemplates a rose in this formal photograph taken December 16, 1906.

country, he had deftly guided his reluctant son, who felt no vocational call to medicine, into a medical career.

After attending Jesuit College in New Orleans, Carl Adam had apprenticed as a pharmacist, then entered Tulane Medical School, where he was graduated in 1900. Like many young physicians, he began his practice in a small country town—Lobdell, across the Mississippi from Baton Rouge. In 1905 he married Viola Maine, a gentle Baton Rouge woman of French-Irish descent, and late in the year they had their first son, Carl Austin Weiss. He was followed by a sister, Olga Marie, in 1907, the year that the father, anxious to specialize, moved his family to New Orleans, where he trained as an eye, ear, nose, and throat man at Tulane Medical School, earning his living as a pharmacist. For several years the family lived above his brother-in-law's pharmacy, then moved to a nearby house. In 1916 they returned to Baton Rouge, where Weiss established one of the few eye, ear, nose, and throat practices in the state, and where a third child, Thomas Edward—known as Tom Ed to the family—was born.

Hard work and mental agility gained Weiss a large practice and a fine reputation. By all accounts the bald, upright physician had three passions in life—his faith, his family, and his patients. But he was also something of a political man, although he never sought office. "Dad was a very rigid German," recalled the younger son, now a rheumatologist in New Orleans, "and white was white and black was black and right was right and wrong was wrong. No grey areas in his moral convictions." The senior Weiss counted among his close associates New Orleans cotton broker John M. Parker, who would be Louisiana's governor from 1920 to 1924 and who would urge Vice President James

Nance Garner in 1933 to lock Huey Long away as a "dangerous paranoiac." From his vantage point in Baton Rouge, Weiss was keenly—often vocally—aware of the irregularities of Louisiana politics and would be doubly so when Long came to power.

The years in New Orleans had been quiet—some would say too quiet—for young Carl. An inquisitive, unusually bright little boy, he loved to tinker with things. When he was only eight, he disassembled an antique grandfather's clock that didn't run and reassembled it in working order. He loved playing with blocks or with his Erector Set, and he enjoyed examining playground equipment more than playing on it. He was a solitary child, bookish, rather shy, and myopic—he wore glasses from an early age.

The boy was 11 when the family left New Orleans, and no longer socially aloof. He liked to hang out at a shop near his home that specialized in electrical gadgets, and his inquisitive mind derived much from this hobby. When he and some other boys built a clubhouse behind a garage, Carl diverted electricity from a nearby streetcar line to the building's galvanized roof, and the clubhouse sported electric lighting. From that triumph he went on to wire a five-room house for his grandaunt. He was then around 12 or 13 years old.

Young Weiss's agile mind ran to many interests, among them drawing and photography. Though slight of build, he took pleasure in several physical pursuits, including tennis, fishing, fencing, and wrestling. He never lost his love of tinkering; according to Tom Ed he

Boy Scout Carl Weiss (*second from left*) clowns in a camporee chow line with his Baton Rouge troop.

built one of the first radios in Baton Rouge and a screened porch for his family. He joined the Boy Scouts. A major passion in his young life was music. He evidently inherited talent from his choirmaster grandfather, for Carl learned to play the piano and the saxophone. Oddly, however, he didn't like playing tunes so much as he delighted in the rote drills of practice exercises. It seemed it was the mechanics of the music, not the beauty, that touched his heart, at least at first.

Like many southern men of his day, the elder Weiss liked hunting and owned a few firearms, and he saw no harm in indulging his son's interest in them with a rifle— a .22-caliber Remington pump gun. Carl liked target shooting, but he didn't care for killing animals. It was just as well; with his bad eyesight, he wasn't much of a shot. With guns as with music, his primary pleasure seemed to rest with the mechanics; he liked to take the closely machined, precisely fitted weapons apart and put them back together.

Weiss graduated from St. Vincent's Academy as valedictorian, first in his class of four, when he was only 15. In 1921 he entered Louisiana State University in Baton Rouge and set out to become an engineer. It seemed a logical choice, given his orderly turn of mind; besides, his father had counseled against a career in medicine. Carl Adam felt that his own practice took too much of his time from his family. Still, young Carl eventually decided that he wanted to be a doctor after all. In his junior year he transferred from LSU to Tulane in New Orleans, which then had the state's only medical school.

For much of his time at Tulane, Carl Weiss stayed with the family of his uncle, Norbert Weiss, in New Orleans. "He was strictly a family-oriented young man," recalled Norbert Weiss Jr., Carl's first cousin, who was about 13 years old at the time. "He kept taking the piano all apart because one of the keys was stuck on the baby grand. He said, 'I know all about Steinway pianos.' He had it from one end of the house to the other." But it was a musical household, a musical time. Weiss learned to play the clarinet in order to fill the only open chair in the Tulane band. "That's when he and grandfather got together," recalled Tom Weiss. "We were all quite shocked that grandfather taught somebody a reed instrument." On weekends the family played together. "Mother and dad would play on the violin and fiddle," said Norbert

Weiss. "Carl would be playing his clarinet—he called it a licorice stick—and I played the drums. We'd have a jam session. We more or less played New Orleans jazz— they called it ragtime back in those days. He was just a regular fine fellow. We really enjoyed having him here."

Weiss remembered driving with his mother in the family's 1927 Studebaker: "Carl'd be having his licorice stick, sitting there in the back just tooting away, and Ma would be speeding down St. Charles Avenue with two boys." But most of the time, Carl walked or cycled.

By the time he finished college, Carl Weiss was no longer an introverted boy; he'd become an engaging and unusually self-contained young man. Though not conventionally handsome—his long face and glasses gave him a rather owlish cast—he was pleasant looking. He had smooth olive skin, dark hair, and solemn gray eyes. He played in the school bands and at Tulane he joined a medical fraternity and was elected secretary-treasurer of his class. He made friends; he was generally liked and admired. After two years of premed, two of medical school, and two more interning at Touro Infirmary in New Orleans, Weiss received his medical degree in 1927. He was only 21 and still as methodically creative as he had been as a child. "Carl had a tendency to thoroughly investigate what he was doing," recalled Tom Ed Weiss. "He would start talking to me about anything from building a piece of furniture to planning a house, or some of his work in medicine, and it was obvious he had thought it all out step by step."

Educator Mercedes Garig, who'd taught him freshman English at LSU and had known him when he was a young doctor, recalled, after his death, how exceptional he had been. "One's dominant impression of him was of the singular quietness which enveloped his personality," Garig wrote in a touching eulogy, "as though somewhere along his pathway he had discovered a secret zone of calm in which he moved serenely and cheerfully through a turbulent world."

But inside that secret zone of calm, Weiss cared passionately about others. Although not physically combative, he detested bullying behavior and was quick to point it out, no matter who the offender might be. According to Tom Ed, Carl once scolded their priest after Mass for rudely ordering a woman standing at the back of the church to take a seat. "He told Father Gassler that he didn't think that was the way to behave and that was an insult to this lady."

In another incident, the younger brother recalled, Weiss had dressed down a senior physician while a student at Tulane Medical School. He had insulted a female technician, Weiss told the professor. "You owe her an apology." According to his son, Carl, an angry Weiss later dumped a bowl of porridge on the head of a colleague in Bellevue Hospital after some defamatory remark. As Tom Ed said to one biographer, Carl seemed not to have any strong political opinions, "just right and wrong, and that was it." He was his father's son, after all.

For both of the men destined to meet on that fatal September night, 1928 was a pivotal year. It was the year that Huey Pierce Long made his second bid to be elected governor of Louisiana; his first, in 1924, had foundered on his inexperience, and he'd spent the next four years roaming the state, talking and listening. He was one of the greatest stump speakers the South had ever seen. He usually talked in the backwoods dialect of his listeners, arms flailing, a shock of wiry, rust-red hair jutting over his forehead. He spoke without notes and sometimes rambled, but he could move a crowd to tears or laughter almost at will.

"Evangeline is not the only one who has waited here in disappointment," Long told a gathering near the town of St. Martinville, the final resting place of Emmeline Labiché, a Cajun girl immortalized as Evangeline by a Henry Wadsworth Longfellow poem. She had wept beneath a moss-hung oak for Gabriel, the lover who never returned to her. Huey continued: "Where are the schools that you have waited for your children to have, that have never come? Where are the roads and the highways that you send your money to build that are no nearer now than ever before? Where are the institutions to care for the sick and the disabled? Evangeline wept bitter tears in her disappointment, but it lasted only through one lifetime. Your tears in this country, around this oak, have lasted for generations." He paused to seek the eyes of the farmers and trappers and hunters listening to him. "Give me the chance," he said, "to dry the tears of those who still weep here."

Having moved them, Long added a final, crude touch reflecting his hatred of federal interference. The combination of eloquence and crudity won the day. In January the 34-year-old Long became the youngest man ever to be elected governor of Louisiana.

Weiss stayed on for a third year at Touro, where he was highly regarded for his medical abilities as well as for being generous with his time. "Right across the street was the old folks home," recalled Tom Weiss, "and he used to play the organ over there and lead singing. That was the Little Sisters of the Poor." At about the time Huey was stumping St. Martinville, Weiss learned that he'd won a prestigious internship at the American Hospital in Paris—the distinguished medical facility that had developed the expatriate American Field Service to provide ambulances to the Allies during World War I. Only two other New Orleans doctors had ever been so honored. Typically, Weiss decided to make as much of the opportunity as he could. On September 19, 1928, he sailed to France from Hoboken, New Jersey, aboard the USS George Washington.

In Europe the Carl Weiss who had been bright and promising also became polished and refined. After checking in at the American Hospital in Paris, Weiss, who spoke a fluent German taught him by his grandfather, headed east to take some postgraduate medical courses in Vienna, then the center of the medical world. He reveled in the baroque architecture, the excellent opera, the vineyard cafés and coffee shops of the beautiful, timeless city as it slipped into a winter of such depth that the Danube froze. He attended Mass at St. Stephens and Vienna's other grand cathedrals and skied in the Austrian Alps. "It was a magnificent experience," observed Tom Weiss, who followed Carl's accounts in letters. "He just ate it up."

When the Vienna classes ended, Weiss returned to Paris and the American Hospital, located in Neuilly, a western suburb of Paris. Then, with a Paris friend, John Archinard, he toured Hungary, Yugoslavia, and Italy. It was a fascinating time to be abroad, a time of sweeping social and political change that would produce a new Europe—a largely Fascist one. Adolf Hitler was beginning his ascent in Germany, and up and down the length of Italy, Weiss saw images of jut-jawed dictator Benito Mussolini and encountered his strutting Black Shirts. In a letter to his parents, Weiss wrote that he and his companion had been pushed off the sidewalk by Fascists.

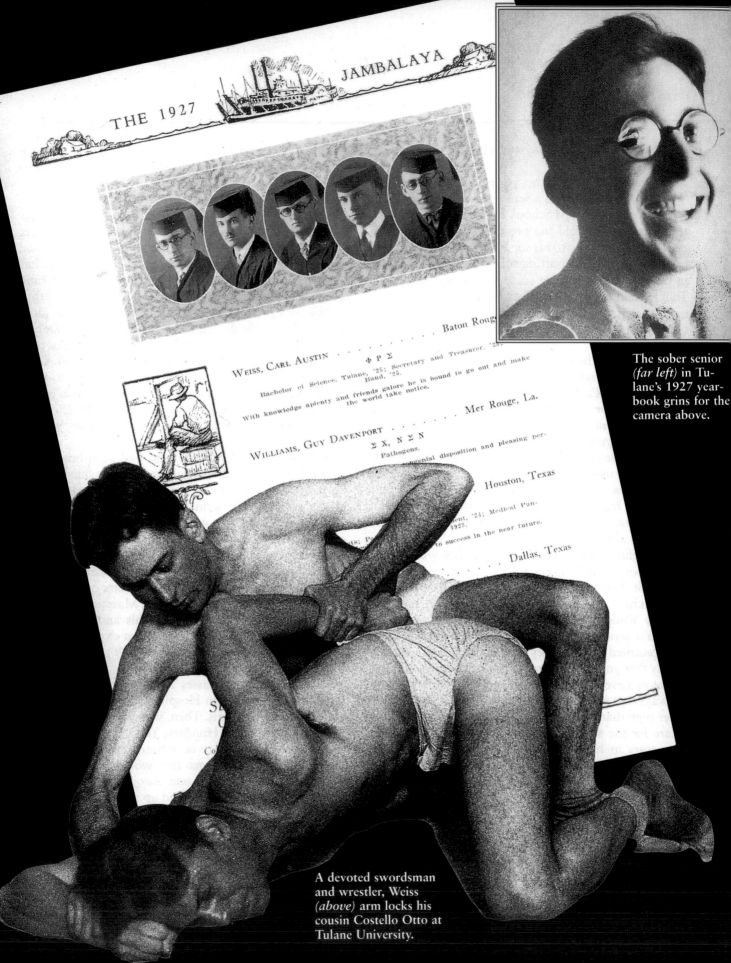

THE 1927 — JAMBALAYA

WEISS, CARL AUSTIN . . . . Φ P Σ . . . . Baton Roug[e]
Bachelor of Science, Tulane, '25; Secretary and Treasurer, '2[8];
Band, '25.
With knowledge aplenty and friends galore he is bound to go out and make
the world take notice.

WILLIAMS, GUY DAVENPORT . . . . Mer Rouge, La.
Σ X, N Σ N
Pathogens.
. . . . . . renial disposition and pleasing per-

. . . . . . Houston, Texas
[n]ent, '24; Medical Pan-
1925.
. . . to success in the near future.

. . . . Dallas, Texas

The sober senior *(far left)* in Tulane's 1927 yearbook grins for the camera above.

A devoted swordsman and wrestler, Weiss *(above)* arm locks his cousin Costello Otto at Tulane University.

Tulane intern Weiss cavorts with Teddy, a friend's dog, in New
Orleans in 1926, just two years before the promising new doctor set
out for his European odyssey and a prestigious Paris internship.

"He described how well they were groomed and how puffed up they were," remembered his younger brother, "and John wanted to get into a fight, and Carl said, 'No, don't do that, they're just peacocks.' " If he saw in these dangerous peacocks any resemblance to his incumbent governor, he evidently said nothing.

By the time Weiss reached Paris in the summer of 1929, Huey Long had been in power just over a year and was fighting off impeachment in Louisiana—a threat he narrowly escaped. The year at the American Hospital, an institution whose clientele consisted mainly of American expatriates, was a fruitful one for the young physician. He worked under the hospital's chief surgeon, Count Thierry de Martel, one of the top doctors in France. His sister Olga joined him in Paris, and they ran with a happy crowd of colleagues and American women in town to learn to be models. "When they weren't working or traveling," Tom Ed said, "they fre-

quently had parties and they would ice the champagne down in the bathtubs."

Along with all his other activities, Weiss managed to work in a visit to Belgium's famed arms company, Fabrique Nationale d'Armes. According to Tom Weiss, this side trip was inspired by a query from his father. "Dad did a lot of bird hunting," he said, "he lived in a flat area in the plantation region, and quail shooting was the primary sport among particular business people. Dad used a double-barrel shotgun. He read about this automatic gun that Browning had produced, gas powered, and I think he wrote Carl about this and if he had an opportunity to buy one and send it to him he'd appreciate it."

According to the younger brother, Weiss traveled to Belgium and bought his father the Browning shotgun, which Fabrique Nationale manufactured. It may have been on the same trip that he saw a handgun that intrigued him: A .32-caliber semiautomatic pistol, a less

powerful variant of the more famous Browning 9-mm. When he returned to the United States, he had one of his own, serial number 319446, apparently purchased from the Cartoucherie Francaise, on the rue Bertin Poiree in the center of Paris.

En route to Europe, Weiss had visited Bellevue Hospital in New York, hopeful of landing an internship there after his Paris sojourn. Bellevue was famed for the excellent training that it afforded gifted young doctors. On his return from France, he interned there from the summer of 1930 until July of 1932, working mostly as an ear, nose, and throat man—the eye had become a separate specialty. He gained a reputation as a perfectionist, and he performed so superbly that he was appointed house surgeon. Such leisure time as his busy schedule allowed he spent at operas or the theater or visiting with his sister, Olga, who by then was living in Greenwich Village. When his father and Tom Ed came to town, he took them to see *Ziegfeld's Follies* and, with Prohibition still in force, to a speakeasy near Bellevue. "He always felt he could extend himself," Tom Weiss said of his brother, "if he went beyond the borders of medicine. His immediate world was medicine but he always felt there was an awful lot out there other than medicine."

Colleagues at Bellevue remembered well Weiss's talent and dedication, but their accounts of his feelings about politics in his far-off home were less precise. According to some reports he disliked what Huey Long was doing in Louisiana, but his life was far too full to dwell on the matter. By other accounts, however, the young doctor brooded about Long. "It was curious," one colleague reportedly said, "here was Dr. Weiss, handsome, lovable, with as brilliant a mind as I have ever met, and rapidly rising in his field. Sociable as anybody could be, in his pleasant southern way. But mention Huey Long and he became moody, bitter. He hated Long vehemently. He had the belief fixed in his mind that Louisiana politics were the worst of any state's. He was always a strong-willed and determined man, and on this point he could not be shaken."

Whatever Weiss's feelings about Louisiana, he was being drawn back to his roots, perhaps by his highly developed sense of filial obligation. "He apparently noticed on one of his visits back to Baton Rouge," recalled Tom Weiss, "that Dad's practice had increased a great deal. I

think he recognized then that possibly he would have been called on. He made no commitments at the time." But later, his father's doctor friends, sensing that the elder Weiss needed assistance and that the community needed a man with Carl's level of training, prevailed upon him to return.

Too, it may have seemed a good time to go home to Louisiana. That year, 1932, Huey Long had gone to Washington as a U.S. senator.

Having gone from triumph to triumph in his brief career, Weiss, at 27, had credentials that established him as one of the most accomplished young men in his field, certainly in his home state. With limitless horizons, he nevertheless seemed to settle down tranquilly into the sleepy little river town where he was born. His brother has suggested that, in returning, Carl had resolved to make the best of life in what was then just a "main-street town." In their offices on the seventh floor of the Reymond Building, he and his father squabbled from time to time, as sons and fathers do, but their love for each other was bedrock in both of their lives, and for the most part, they got on comfortably in their shared practice.

"That was sort of a pleasant atmosphere there in the office," recalled Tom Weiss. "I made it a point to get down to the office any afternoon I could because their discussions mostly were around medical features. Carl was an intense reader and Dad was sort of a practical guy, and they would get into a discussion—which is good, which is bad." These discussions generally ended, according to Weiss, when Carl said, "Okay, Chief, you win." The elder Weiss handled the eye patients, while his son took care of ears, noses, and throats.

As he always had been, young Weiss was viewed by his peers as brilliant, dedicated—a doctor's doctor, a serious man. At the same time, he could joke with a reporter that a few gray hairs would aid him immeasurably; asked how the girls of Europe compared with those of Baton Rouge, he replied, "Well, I could hardly be called an authority on that subject, but you see I didn't bring any back with me."

Along with medicine and music, an abiding interest in Weiss's life was the Catholic Church. He went to Mass regularly. Once he seemed to have a small crisis of faith,

His beret jauntily in place on a family fishing trip, Carl helps Tom Ed, his adoring younger brother, show off the day's catch.

Senior Yvonne Pavy (*circled*)
beams for a 1925 class photograph at Opelousas High School.

and he reexamined his religion in his characteristically deliberate fashion, ending with a reaffirmation of his beliefs. Along with his skill, his piety became part of his reputation. On an occasion when parents thanked him for saving their child's life, he answered, "I did nothing. God did that. He gave me the power."

Weiss's life seemed almost—but not quite—complete. The remaining void began to fill, however, one November day in 1932 when a lovely young brunette complaining of eyestrain came to visit his father. Her name was Yvonne Louise Pavy and, recently returned from studying at the Sorbonne in Paris, she was teaching French at LSU. Chatting during her examination by the elder Weiss, she mentioned her sojourn in France, and he asked if she'd known his son there. When she said she hadn't, Weiss asked his son to join them.

As the young people talked, they found that they'd barely missed each other on a number of occasions. Yvonne had attended Sophie Newcomb College, the women's adjunct of Tulane, while Carl was at Tulane. Moreover, she'd lived near the American Hospital in Paris. And their hometowns weren't far apart. Yvonne was from Opelousas in St. Landry Parish, about 50 miles from Baton Rouge. Three days after they met, Yvonne returned to the office to pick up her glasses, and she ran into Carl in the elevator. After they parted she turned to a friend and announced, "I've met the man I'm going to marry."

And so it was, although for a time it looked as if nothing were going to happen. "He waited months before he called her for a date," recalled Ida Pavy Boudreaux, Yvonne's younger sister. "She always teased him, told him he didn't have the courage to fool with a woman like her." Carl and Yvonne began dating in April of 1933; by June of that same year he had asked her to marry him and she had accepted.

Her family had some reservations about the match; the Weisses were German, after all, while the Pavys were from old French Louisiana stock. Yvonne's father was Judge Benjamin Henry Pavy, a man of great substance in his community. In 1910 he'd been elected district judge of St. Landry and Evangeline Parishes, and his constituents had returned him to office continuously for the next 26 years.

Pavy had refused a ride on the Long bandwagon,

judging Huey to be a dangerous fraud who deceitfully manipulated the masses for his own evil ends. He compared the Kingfish with Hitler and even sentenced five of Long's election officials to jail; Governor Allen duly okayed a pardon for them. According to a story the judge told his family, Long paid him a visit in the Ville Platte courthouse and asked Pavy what it would take to get him on board. The judge had cursed him, he said, and told him to leave, establishing himself as that thing Huey Long could not abide: a man he could neither defeat nor control.

The Pavy family home was an antebellum house set at the end of a long walkway lined with ancient oaks. It was there in June of 1933 that Carl Weiss met his in-laws-to-be. Tall and massively built, his looks set off by flowing silver hair and a bristling mustache, Judge Pavy was an imposing presence. "I don't think they ever talked politics," Ida Boudreaux recalled. "They hit it off beautifully. Carl was fascinated. The home place was still a plantation. We lived in this big wide open space. You sat on the front porch and looked down the road and there was just nothing but open space, and I think he just enjoyed it. He loved the outdoors. He loved to fish. He didn't hunt, but he loved to fish. My father loved to ride horseback. They had a lot of things to talk about that had nothing to do with life but the fun side of living."

For the senator from Louisiana, 1933 had not gone quite so well. He and the new president, Franklin Delano Roosevelt, had fallen out—Roosevelt had not expressed sufficient gratitude for Long's 1932 support. And in August, Long had suffered an accident that made him a laughingstock. A problem drinker of longstanding, Long had emerged from the men's room of Long Island's upper-crust Sands Point Bath and Country Club with a freshly blackened eye. He claimed that gangsters had mugged him, that he had bravely resisted and escaped. Nobody believed him. The grapevine tittered that Long, in his cups, had been slugged for clumsily wetting another man's trouser leg.

But such antics must have seemed remote to Carl and Yvonne that year. On December 27, 1933, they were married in St. Landry Catholic Church in Opelousas with the full blessings of both families and took a short honeymoon to the San Carlos Hotel, in Pensacola, Flori-

da. When they came home, they brought a Doberman pinscher pup named Peter.

Upon their return to Baton Rouge, Weiss's life became more highly focused and directed even than before. As always, he followed the path of dedicated hard work. Deciding that the community lacked adequate x-ray facilities, Weiss bought an old x-ray machine and rebuilt it, teaching himself how to develop the images in the meantime. He became active in the Kiwanis, the Young Businessmen's Association, and his church, and filled his days and many nights with patients. Yvonne continued to work on her master's degree thesis.

Living simply—no one had much money in those Depression days, and a young doctor just starting out had less than most—they took occasional meals with friends from the LSU faculty and the medical profession. But mainly their life was centered on work, family, faith— the values that Carl Adam had so carefully imparted to his sons. They lived for a time in a furnished apartment in Baton Rouge—a flat with a stairway so steep that it posed a threat once Yvonne got pregnant in late 1934. Carl, meanwhile, had begun to draw up plans for a combination home and office—a Doc in a Box, his brother called it—of the kind he'd seen back east. In the interim,

the couple planned to move into one of several houses that the Weiss family owned on Baton Rouge's Lakeland Street, a small frame bungalow with three bedrooms and a screened porch. Tom Ed and Carl started refurbishing the place.

"Houses in this area and in those days were very poorly built," recalled the younger brother, "and it was usually a frame on which they put weatherboard on the outside and inside there were wide planks. I remember saying the wall bulged when the wind would blow." Working for four or five weeks, he said, often until 10:30 or 11 at night, the two young men cleaned out the house, grained the floors, stripped and repainted the interior, and strengthened the walls. The refurbished place on Lakeland looked pretty good, according to Tom Ed, and was well located, only a block and a half from the brand new state capitol.

On June 7, 1935, Yvonne gave birth to a son, Carl Austin Weiss Jr. The proud father personally carried his baby into the sparsely furnished new home—"You carried him out, I'm going to carry him in," he quipped to his wife—and hired nurses to help take care of the infant. An adoring parent, Carl hovered over his newborn son, giving him his 2 a.m. feeding, changing his diapers,

Their first child due in June 1935, Carl and Yvonne Weiss
moved to this family-owned bungalow at 527 Lakeland
Street, not two blocks from the capitol.

pushing him in the carriage, and taking innumerable snapshots. "He was better at it than the mother," recalled Ida Pavy Boudreaux.

The advent of a child in his life seemed to focus the 29-year-old doctor more than ever on the future. On the evening of Thursday, September 5—the Thursday after Labor Day—Weiss and his wife went shopping for new dining room furniture. It was scheduled for delivery the following week. The next evening Carl's mother came to visit, and Carl told her he was considering installing a costly heating unit under the dining room, to replace the dangerous space heaters then in common use. Mrs. Weiss advised against it, pointing out that Carl and Yvonne would be living in their own home soon. No, Carl replied, "I'll be in this house for 10 years at least." He ordered the unit; it was to be installed on Monday, September 9. On Wednesday, the 11th, the young couple had a date to go swimming with friends.

Despite that summer's powerful omens of life and continuity, the towering capitol began to cast a pervasive shadow over Weiss's life. Huey Long's consolidation of his power had made him a palpable presence in every Louisianan's life, and the Weiss-Pavy clan was no exception. In August Yvonne's uncle, Paul Pavy, was dismissed as principal of Opelousas High School, and her sister Marie had lost her third-grade teaching job in nearby Eunice. Both were victims of Long's control of the school board in St. Landry Parish and of the Kingfish's ability to strike at such enemies as Judge Pavy by destroying his relatives' careers. A good friend of Yvonne's was dismissed by the Baton Rouge school board. One of Weiss's patients, a young teacher supporting a widowed mother, reportedly lost her job to Long's manipulations of the school system.

By the end of August, it had also become clear that Long intended to drive Benjamin Pavy from his position as district judge of Louisiana's 13th district. In the first

Judge Benjamin H. Pavy, Yvonne's father, opposed Huey Long's political machine.

bill up for consideration at the special session called for the weekend of September 7, Pavy's St. Landry Parish—the fourth largest county in the state and one of the last bastions of anti-Long sentiment there—would be gerrymandered out of the 13th district, which it shared with smaller, pro-Long Evangeline Parish, and put in the 15th district with a larger parish controlled by the Kingfish. The redistricting guaranteed that Pavy, who was first elected to his bench in 1910, could never be reelected.

Later, there would be talk of another, more sinister tactic used before by Huey Long—a racial slur against the house of Pavy. In the hard-fought 1910 campaign that had first elevated him to his judgeship, Benjamin Pavy had an opponent who'd alleged that some distant in-law of Pavy's had Negro blood. Some historians have attributed this to an anecdote told of an ancient Pavy who'd turned Republican during the post-Civil War Reconstruction— and was dubbed "Nigger Pavy" for crossing to the Yankee side. Although no one has ever verified it, anecdotal evidence suggests something evil in the summer air in 1935: a hint that Long had either revived or planned to revive the racial slur— and that Carl Weiss may have known it.

In the enlightened South of the 1990s, such an attack might be trivial. But in the strictly segregated South of the 1930s, to be labeled African American was to be disenfranchised totally. Because any black ancestry was enough to alter one's racial identity, the threat went well beyond mere racial purity—particularly if the charge came from someone as all-powerful as Huey Long. "We're not talking about somebody just saying that about you," Louisiana State Police captain Donald Moreau has explained, "we're talking about a man who could change your birth certificate, a man who could make it stick. If Huey had said that, that would have made Carl Weiss's wife black, that would have made Carl Weiss's son black, that would have meant that Carl Weiss's son was not going to get an education. He wasn't going to be a doctor. He was going to be a sharecropper or work on the levees. He was going to view life through the back end of a mule." There was talk of a slur—but never more than talk.

No one knows whether Long intended to revive the damaging rumor or whether Carl Weiss had discerned this real or imaginary threat. Weiss gave little outward sign of any agitation and remained to the end a nonpolitical man, or so it seemed. "All we know," his grieving mother would say, "is that he took living seriously. Right with him was right above everything else." Most people who knew Carl well agreed that he was indeed a serious man, and an ethical one, and a man whose feelings ran very deep.

Carl Weiss's mask, if that is what his secret zone of calm really was, may have slipped on only one occasion, in early September of that year. "A number of us were sitting around one afternoon," an anonymous surgeon told the Baton Rouge *Morning Advocate,* "in the amphitheater of a local hospital. Dr. Weiss was sitting on an operating table, one leg drawn up under him, taking little part in the conversation. The conversation veered around to politics. Several of the doctors present at that informal conference began panning Senator Long, criticizing him for the methods employed in his operation of the state government. The talk became heated. Suddenly I looked across at Dr. Weiss. He had said nothing, but great big tears were rolling down his cheeks. He got up from the table and walked out of the room, still without saying a word."

Nevertheless, if Weiss brooded about Huey Long, he evidently gave no other outward sign of agitation. Sunday, September 8, 1935, was, in a homey sort of way, one of his happiest. That morning the Weisses went to Mass, as was their habit, leaving the baby with Carl's parents. Along with Mass, the family routine called for Carl, Yvonne, and the baby to be at his parents' home by 1 p.m. for Sunday dinner. It was the usual fare that Sunday—fried chicken, rice and gravy, and vegetables. Carl chatted cheerfully during the meal, ate well, and complimented the family cook on the chicken.

Years later, Yvonne would tell reporter David Zinman, author of *The Day Huey Long Was Shot,* that sometime that Sunday, probably in the morning, the subject of Long's move against her father had come up.

"You know Long is out to get your father," she quoted Carl as saying. "Your father is going to be gerrymandered out of office."

Yvonne had not been especially concerned. Her father, she knew, was a tough and savvy political veteran who wasn't taking the gerrymander personally. And her mother, mindful that Pavy would fare better financially as a lawyer in private practice than he ever had as a judge, was delighted: "The ambition of her life was to get him out of that judgeship," Yvonne said. "So there was no great grief. Nobody was complaining." Besides, it was hardly news to the Pavys that Huey Long played hardball. But old Dr. Weiss, who was more political than his son, was livid. According to Yvonne, she and Carl urged calm, pointing out that the judge wouldn't suffer in any case and that Long was simply different from them—a lower form.

In the enveloping midday heat that followed the meal, it was decided that the group would drive the senior Weiss's Buick sedan to the family's little cabin along the Amite River near Baton Rouge. Tom Ed and some friends of his drove south beyond New Orleans, to scout out a college dance band. At the cabin, while the older couple lounged on a porch swing, Carl and Yvonne went swimming.

His mother remarked on how thin her son looked in his bathing suit—his 130 pounds were scantly distributed along his five-foot-ten-inch frame. Eventually the young folks finished their swim in the river, changed into dry clothes, and joined their elders out on the porch. The men talked about medicine and the women cooed over the baby as the idyllic late-summer afternoon drifted quietly on.

Toward evening the family started back to town. Carl dropped his parents off at their house before nightfall, borrowing the Buick for the night's house and hospital calls—young Weiss was not yet able to afford an automobile of his own. It was the last time the old doctor would see his son alive.

At his own home, Carl supped at the kitchen table on sandwiches and milk while his little son slept nearby, then helped his wife dry the supper dishes. He telephoned a colleague who was to assist him in a tonsillectomy the following morning, making sure the other doctor knew of a change in venue for the operation. That done, he showered and dressed in the clothes he'd worn to Mass that morning—a white linen suit, black shoes, and a Panama hat. Yvonne read the Sunday funnies in bed. Her husband kissed her goodbye, saying something about making arrangements for an operation. And even at this point, there appears to have been no signal from her husband; many believe that he himself was not aware what awaited him in the hot Louisiana night. Certainly his actions were not those of man who knew he would never return. Even the self-absorbed Lee Harvey Oswald, after all, would leave mementos and money for his wife and children.

Weiss got into his father's Buick, placing his medical bag on the front seat beside him. A gun—the Browning .32 he'd brought back from France—was in the glove compartment wrapped in a sock that protected it from dust and the compartment from oil stains. Even in rural Louisiana in the 1930s, there were addicts who might try to rob a doctor of his drugs. He backed out of his driveway and drove off to make a house call at the Morgans', who lived about 15 minutes southeast of town. The stop had become a Sunday night ritual. He'd removed the tonsils and adenoids of Elemore Morgan Jr., and for two years he had confined the senior Elemore to bed for an as-yet-undiagnosed throat disorder that the doctor feared might be tubercular. Some time afterward, according to one source, Weiss went by Baton Rouge General Hospital on his way home.

Inexplicably, a block and a half from his own house and family, Carl Weiss pulled up in front of the brightly illuminated state capitol, where another night of Long's special session was about to end. What Weiss thought, what had happened between his visit to the Morgans

This studio portrait of Carl Austin Weiss was taken shortly before his death in September 1935.

and his arrival here, what his intentions were—no one will ever know. By 9:20 that night, however, he was in the rear hallway of the building's first floor.

Huey Long, as he neared his own appointment with catastrophe, was bustling about with his usual energy. Toward the end of August 1935, he and three of his favored bodyguards had left Washington for New York and a couple of days' recreation. August 30th had been the Kingfish's 42nd birthday, and he'd wanted a little time to celebrate before resuming his political agenda. From New York the entourage went to Harrisburg, Pennsylvania, where Huey met with a potential publisher of his new manuscript, *My First Days in the White House*. The book was a fanciful sort of future history about the beginning of his presidency. It was Long's second literary endeavor. The first, *Every Man a King*, published in 1933, dealt with his accomplishments on behalf of the downtrodden. From Harrisburg it was on to Oklahoma City for a Labor Day appearance—a parade, a press conference, a speech flaying both Roosevelt and the Republicans and hinting that he himself might be a good alternative to both. From Oklahoma the Kingfish headed for Baton Rouge to confer with his troops about the upcoming special session.

By Thursday, September 5, plans had been completed to Huey's liking, and bodyguard Murphy Roden picked him up and drove him to New Orleans. As usual when in the Crescent City, the Kingfish headed for his suite at the Roosevelt Hotel, whose proprietor, Seymour Weiss—no relation to the Baton Rouge Weisses—was Huey's most trusted friend. Long did a three-hour radio broadcast from the

About 15 minutes before his fatal wounding, a complacent U.S. senator Huey Long *(second from right)* chats with Louisiana House Speaker Allen Ellender *(right)* on the dais of the state legislature Long still held in the palm of his hand.

hotel that evening. The meat of his address involved a plan set for the following year to give 1,000 Louisiana high-school students virtually free college educations at LSU. After the speech Huey spent the night with Rose and the children at the house on Audubon Boulevard.

The next day, Friday, the Kingfish was back at the Roosevelt, receiving a steady stream of callers who had political business with him. Much of the discussion concerned whom Long would back in the upcoming gubernatorial election; at the time, the incumbent could not succeed himself. Huey dined in the hotel lounge that night with Seymour Weiss, and the two made a date to play golf the next morning at Audubon Park.

Huey enjoyed the game—he played badly but with zest—and he was glad to have a chance for a private chat with Weiss. The hotelier would recall that, among other things, Long chortled about how big the war chest was for his presidential campaign. The money was in the deduct box (pronounced DEE duct, southern style), so called because part of its trove came from the kickbacks Huey deducted from state employees' salaries. The deduct box was kept in Riggs National Bank in Washington, but Huey surprised his friend by revealing he'd moved it. He didn't say where, and Weiss didn't ask.

After lunching with Seymour Weiss on Saturday afternoon, Huey headed back to Baton Rouge and the suite the state maintained for him on the 24th floor of the capitol. The House convened that evening to begin the process of passing Long's bills, including the bill that would gerrymander Judge Pavy out of office in the next election. He stayed on the main floor of the capitol until the House adjourned, rushing between the governor's office and the House chamber, overseeing every last detail of the legislative process. At last he went upstairs to his suite and went to bed.

Sunday he spent the entire day in the capitol. He had the cafeteria send up breakfast. Then he telephoned his male secretary, Earle Christenberry, in New Orleans, reminding him to be in Baton Rouge by that afternoon to discuss Huey's federal income tax return. Long was late filing, and he was about to run out of extensions; he'd also begun to feel pressure from the Bureau of Internal Revenue. In fact, just the day before, T-men meeting in a Dallas hotel had decided to seek an indictment against Long for tax evasion. Christenberry dutifully showed up

for the conference, but it had hardly begun when Huey, never patient with paperwork, threw up his hands. He told Christenberry to go back to New Orleans and fill out the forms. He'd sign them later.

The dregs of the afternoon Long spent in conference with various political vassals, mostly discussing the prospects for a successor to Governor O. K. Allen. Then the senator had supper, catered again by the cafeteria and brought to him by bodyguard Murphy Roden. About 7 p.m. Huey, spiffily dressed in a pale linen suit and black and white shoes, descended to the main floor and went to the governor's office. Sitting in the governor's chair—which O. K. Allen seldom occupied when the Kingfish was in town—Huey summoned his legislative leaders one by one, rehearsing what steps they were to take to finish pushing his bills through.

After drilling his legislative troops, Huey headed for the House floor at a fast trot. The capitol was filling up by now; sightseers always packed the place to see the show when he was in town. At 8:30 p.m. Speaker Allen Ellender gaveled the House to order. The Kingfish ambled up the dais and sat down in a swivel chair to chat with the Speaker and watch his minions go through their paces. Everything was going as planned. About 9:10 p.m. Long noticed one of his public service commissioners, 29-year-old James P. O'Connor, smoking a cigar. Huey had given up both booze and tobacco in 1934 in an effort to improve his image, but the sight of O'Connor's contented puffing was more than he could stand. He called the young man over and directed him to go to the cafeteria in the basement and pick up some smokes for him.

The House had nearly completed the night's business—it never took long to rubber stamp Huey's bills—so the Kingfish headed out of the House chamber, through the lobby, and into the capitol's 10-foot-wide rear corridor on the main floor. Cronies and guards tried to school around him: Murphy Roden led the way, followed by the senator and then by Elliott Coleman, a big man from Louisiana's Bureau of Criminal Identification and Investigation; cossacks Joe Messina and George McQuiston brought up the rear. Long pushed into the governor's office, apparently failed to see whomever he was looking for and darted back into the hallway. Roden said later that he managed to get back ahead of Huey only with difficulty and that the Kingfish had come up abeam of him as they entered the hall. Then the governor's secretary, A. P. White, emerged, and Huey urged him to get some missing legislators into place by the next morning's vote. Long turned to Judge John B. Fournet, a key crony and Louisiana Supreme Court justice, who'd been waiting to speak to him. The other bodyguards eddied nervously as Long talked to Fournet. It was now 9:21.

The only witnesses to what happened next were Long's minions and admirers; their version of events that night has become the official one. According to these accounts Huey finished talking to Fournet and stepped toward the center of the hallway, which widened somewhat near the governor's office to form a rectangle framed by four marble pillars. As he moved forward, a slender man in a white suit stepped out from one of the pillars and approached him. The man was carrying a small, black handgun, partially concealed behind his Panama hat. Neither he nor Huey said a word. Seeing the pistol, Fournet reflexively dealt the man a backhand swipe with his own Panama hat just as the gun fired. Bodyguard Murphy Roden would recall that it was he who hit the assailant's gun hand, deflecting a shot aimed at Huey's heart. Huey gave a single whoop, then whirled around and ran some 20 feet west toward the senate side of the corridor before taking a sharp left into a stairwell that led to the basement.

In that same instant, the compact, powerful Roden was on the man, and the two fell to the slippery marble floor, grappling for the gun. Roden believed that the webbing between his right thumb and forefinger struck the back of the operating slide, preventing the cartridge from ejecting fully and jamming the gun. He would tell a coroner's jury that the assassin fired only once, but 25 years later he would tell an interviewer that the assailant fired twice and that the second shot had grooved Roden's left wrist and torn off his watch, which was said to have been dented by a small-caliber round—a claim that subsequent scientific tests failed to verify.

Roden yanked himself loose from the assailant, stepped back, and drew his own shoulder-holstered gun, a .38 revolver on a .45 frame, loaded with hollow-point bullets. He fired up into the man's throat and saw the flesh explode from his head. By now the other body-

guards, weapons drawn, had leaped forward, and all of them began emptying their powerful .38s, .44s, and .45s into the man who would shortly be identified as Dr. Carl Austin Weiss.

Elliott Coleman, who by the end of his long career was said to have killed a good many men, told a slightly different story. He said that he'd struck Weiss in the face after the young doctor shot Huey and that he'd then been the first bodyguard to shoot the assailant. Another witness thought that Coleman might have punched Huey by mistake, although Coleman vehemently denied it. Joe Messina, a veteran bodyguard, emotionally testified that he'd run up and shot the man who'd shot Senator Long. George McQuiston refused to talk about it.

"The first time he was shot, Weiss shivered," Fournet would tell Zinman. "Then he quit trying to shoot Roden. He shivered again when the second shot hit." As the corridor filled with gun smoke, ricocheting bullets, and the thunder of the bodyguards' fusillade, Weiss's small body collapsed slowly to the floor, his face bending forward, cradled in the crook of his right arm. The

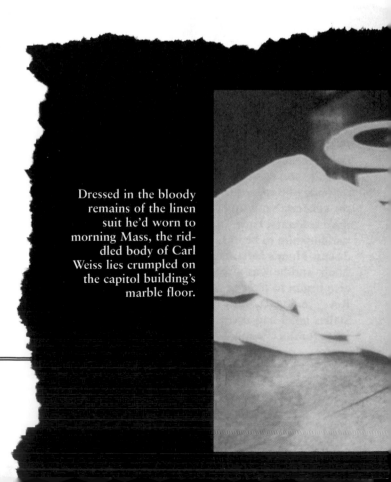

Dressed in the bloody remains of the linen suit he'd worn to morning Mass, the riddled body of Carl Weiss lies crumpled on the capitol building's marble floor.

last sound he made was a single groan. As he lay on the floor the guns still blazed, causing the thin body to twitch each time it was hit. The white of the dead man's suit gave way to red as he bled from scores of wounds. The entire episode had taken about six seconds.

The official version concludes at that point, although the story of the Kingfish's fall was just beginning. For now, as the bodyguards recovered from their frenzied firing in the smoke-filled, bullet-spattered corridor, they came to the frantic realization that their boss was nowhere to be seen.

Fleeing down the basement steps, Long had run into James O'Connor, who was on his way back with the Kingfish's Corona Belvederes. According to legend, the astonished O'Connor asked what was the matter. "Jimmy, my boy, I'm shot," Huey panted.

"The blood came gushing out of his mouth," O'Connor said. "At first I thought he had been shot in the mouth. Later, in the hospital, I saw a membrane had been cut inside his lower lip."

But this is how O'Connor described the incident to Louisiana attorney and legislator Ben Bagert in the early 1970s, when O'Connor was a New Orleans juvenile judge. "He took me back and walked me through his role in the assassination," recounted Bagert in a 1993 interview. "First of all he told me that he really wasn't buying cigars, that he was flirting with the girl at the cash register. Then he told me that he heard what he thought were firecrackers upstairs. I believe he said he had turned to the door to find out what was going on and Huey came down and that he saw right under his pocket a little blotch of red as though an ink pen had been leaking, a little spot of red on his shirt, and that Huey looked at him and said, 'Jimmy, they shot me.' Now when he said that he paused and looked at me ominously to the point where it made me feel uncomfortable. My read on what he was trying to do was he was trying to tell me something. It wasn't just a brief pause. And he went back and repeated it and when he said it, he said it kind of this way: 'Benny, he looked at me and he said, "Jimmy they" '—he paused and stared at me with an ex-

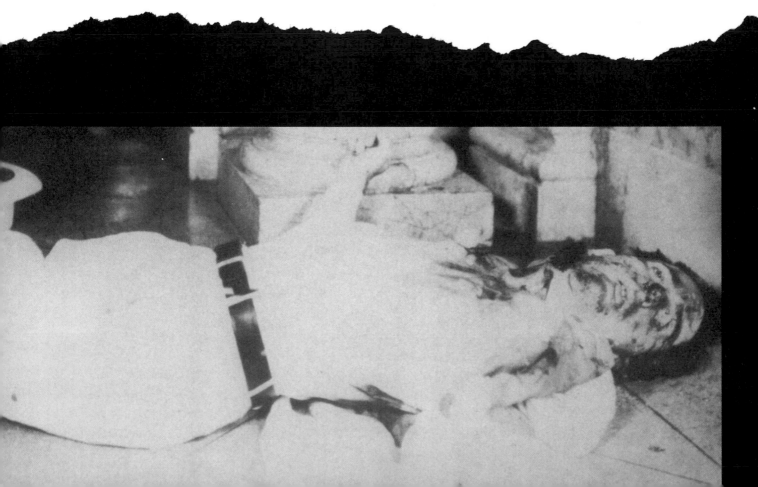

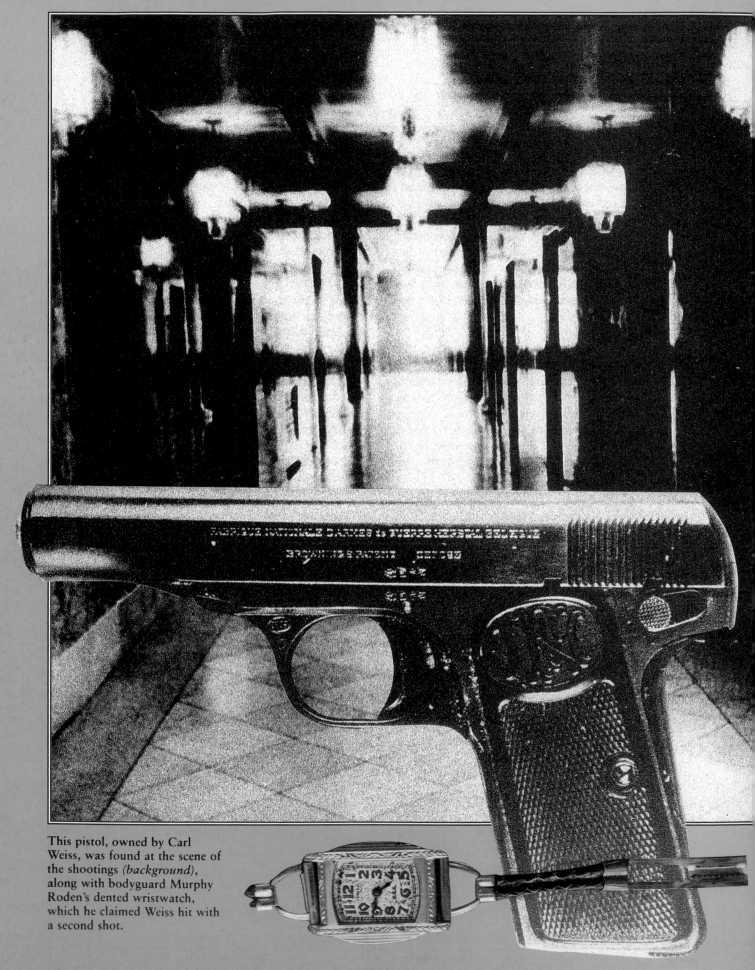

This pistol, owned by Carl Weiss, was found at the scene of the shootings *(background)*, along with bodyguard Murphy Roden's dented wristwatch, which he claimed Weiss hit with a second shot.

pression that really punctuated the word *they*—' "shot me." ' I think what he was trying to tell me was that maybe they did shoot him."

O'Connor grabbed Long and took him outside, where he conscripted a man with a Ford to drive him and the wounded senator the quarter mile to Our Lady of the Lake Sanitarium—the site of so many of Carl Weiss's operations. The young commissioner sat on the sedan's backseat with Long leaning against him. At the hospital O'Connor dragged Huey out of the car, shoved him onto a wheeled stretcher, and pushed him into the lobby. There a nurse helped him get Long into an elevator and up to a third-floor room. It was there that a most peculiar episode in American medicine began to unfold.

Dr. Arthur Vidrine was examining Long—a man to whom the doctor owed much. Vidrine, a graduate of Tulane Medical School, had been a young surgeon in Ville Platte before Huey had plucked him from relative obscurity and made him director of the huge Charity Hospital in New Orleans and of LSU's new medical school. The 39-year-old Vidrine was no political hack, however; he had talent. He'd been a Rhodes scholar, and not even Huey could have arranged that.

Vidrine looked at the wound and ordered blood tests for a transfusion. Even as he went about his work, the room began to fill with the Kingfish's political functionaries, with his bodyguards, and with curious interns and nurses. The doctor left his patient briefly to talk with the aides and to call in more physicians. For a few moments Huey Long found himself alone with the nurse, Sister Michael.

"How bad is it?" he asked.

She replied that gunshot wounds were always serious.

Long, a nonchurchgoing nominal Baptist, asked the nun to pray for him. She said that he'd have to pray too. Thus he followed along as she said aloud the Roman Catholic Act of Contrition. He was sorry for his sins, the Kingfish said. He would atone. He would amend his life.

By now, Tom Ed Weiss had returned from hiring a band in Donaldsonville and was riding around Baton Rouge with some LSU friends, including fraternity brother Guy Riché. "There was nothing much to do here in Baton Rouge on Sunday night but ride around or go to the capitol and watch the legislature," Riché recalled. "So we decided to go to the legislature. We were in my car, and we got near the capitol and there was such a crowd of people, a lot of cars there, big session going on." Finding parking scarce at the capitol, the young men headed for the downtown offices of the *Morning Advocate*. "When anything big happened, like a Dempsey-Tunney boxing match," Riché explained, "everybody went down and stood in front of the newspaper office, and a man sat in a window on the second floor with a megaphone and gave you a blow-by-blow description of whatever was going on." Riché and Weiss made their way through a crowd gathering outside the newspaper. "Tom Ed asked a man, 'Well, who was it that shot Huey Long?' He said, 'Well, it was some young doctor, a Dr. White or something.' And Tom Ed said, 'My God, that's my brother, he's saying *Weiss*.' "

By the time Tom Weiss got home, his father had already heard the bad news. A 9:30 p.m. addendum to Walter Winchell's radio news show had reported that Long had been shot and that Dr. Carl Weiss had been his assailant. But his mother had left the room where the radio murmured its dread tidings after Winchell signed off. Carl Adam tried to call his son's home but, ominously, the line was out. "My father was coming down the steps of our residence," Tom Weiss recalled. "I ran to him and said, 'Dad, what's happened?' He said, 'I don't know. Don't go in the house. Your mother's busy. I'm trying to get in touch with Carl.' " Finding the phone line still dead, Tom Ed hurried to his brother's home. "There were little clusters of people in and out of the shadows," he recalled, "standing around talking." He found his sister-in-law shaken. Her husband was overdue, and the atmosphere had become dense with trouble. "She said, 'What are all these people doing, they're walking all over my porch and my backyard?' and I said, 'Yvonne, I'm afraid something's happened to Carl; he may have been killed,' and she fainted." Some neighbors later said that they'd seen Yvonne Weiss moving restlessly about her cottage earlier in the evening, and she herself told one historian that she'd gone to the drawer where the .32 was usually kept and had been upset to find it missing. "I guess we've all wondered what led her to look for the gun," said Tom Weiss. "But I think by the time that 9:30, 9:45 arrived, a lot of things were going on outside. She possibly was afraid."

Cut off by his dead telephone, old Dr. Weiss, with typical impatience, grew restless. He told his wife that he was going to go over to Carl's and left. While he was gone, a reporter from the *Advocate,* who knew Viola Weiss, slipped through the shadowy figures eddying in the street outside and knocked on the door. When she answered, the reporter said he wanted a picture of Carl. "She wanted to know why," said Tom Weiss, "and he told her that Long had been shot and Carl had been killed. He meant no harm and was most apologetic. But this is how she was informed of Carl's death."

Back at the capitol, the tattered remains of her older son lay horribly sprawled on the gory marble floor of the rear hallway, guarded by a ring of highway patrolmen. In time, East Baton Rouge Parish coroner Thomas R. Bird arrived, made a cursory examination of the body, and identified it as that of Weiss, a man he'd known for several years. Later, Bird would testify that there were 30 wounds in the front of the body, 29 in back, and two in the head. He inventoried the contents of Weiss's pockets—a fountain pen, a pocketknife, some identification, a wallet with six dollars, a tax receipt, an engraved calling card. A .32-caliber Browning pistol was found near the body.

At the hospital, doctors were assembling from various parts of the state. But the surgeon specifically requested by Huey, Urban Maes of New Orleans, was not among them. Maes's car had run into a ditch en route; he was stranded.

Vidrine surmised that Long's wound had been caused by a single bullet passing through his body, leaving a hole whose diameter was no larger than a fingertip. What Vidrine took to be the bullet's entry wound was just below the right lower rib; the presumed exit wound, a second small puncture, was found slightly higher, near the midline of the back.

Jewel O'Neal, a student nurse who was helping Vidrine, heard the doctor ask Huey, "How about this place on your lip?" The nurse looked and saw that the lip was cut. "That's where he hit me," Huey replied. He didn't identify the "he." He seemed intent only on the question that he asked over and over, in various ways: Would he recover? Was he going to live?

Huey received a blood transfusion, and a local physician named Cecil Lorio began checking his pulse and blood pressure every 15 minutes—and finding only bad news. The pulse rate kept climbing and the pressure dropping, likely signs of a heart trying to compensate for internal bleeding.

Vidrine's anxiety at that point can only be imagined. Before him lay one of the most powerful men in the United States. All around hovered his allies and henchmen, watching every move the doctors made. A mistake could cost Vidrine his career, he knew, and it was not inconceivable that it could cost him his life as well. He also knew from training and experience that, because of the potential for hemorrhage and infection, abdominal wounds could be deadly.

Inexplicably, medical records of the historic case are virtually nonexistent—as though no one wanted to be held responsible for the outcome. However, reliable reports indicate that it was probably Huey himself who, understanding the import of the failing vital signs, said, "Come on. Let's go be operated on." It was now after midnight, almost three hours since the shooting. The doctors consulted. Vidrine would do the surgery.

The operation was performed amid a crowd of spectators—politicians and police, as well as medical professionals—all jostling for position to get a look at how things were going. "It was a vaudeville show," Dr. Lorio would recall. The star of the show made one last comment as the anesthetist's mask moved toward his face. "Nobody is to say anything about this," Huey ordered. "I'll do all the talking."

The only known medical account of the operation is a report by New Orleans surgeon Frank L. Loria, published in 1948 in a professional journal. According to Loria, who interviewed Vidrine and others who'd been on the scene, the only damage Vidrine found after opening Huey's peritoneal cavity—the abdominal space that houses the intestines, liver, gallbladder, and stomach—was a little puncture of the large intestine. The penetration left entrance and exit wounds that had allowed a small amount of waste matter to escape into the cavity, and there was a moderate amount of blood. Vidrine examined the area for further damage, cleaned the cavity, sutured the wounds shut, and closed the incision.

What Vidrine, Baton Rouge surgeon Clarence Lorio, and the other doctors had failed to do by that point, for some unknown reason, was to explore directly what

damage the bullet had done beyond the back wall of the abdominal cavity. They felt the kidney, but blindly, and detected no wound. Had they exposed the organ, however, they might have seen that Huey Long was bleeding to death from a hidden injury. By the time this damage was discovered, it was too late to treat; the Kingfish had sunk too low to live through a second operation. "My private opinion," observed New Orleans surgeon Joseph Sabatier Jr., who assisted at Long's operation as a medical student, "is that he died of a committee. I don't think anyone was totally in control."

As much of the nation kept vigil, Huey survived the shooting for 30 hours and 44 minutes. He died before dawn on Tuesday, September 10. Toward the end he drifted in and out of consciousness as family members and political intimates came and went. Seymour Weiss

The wounded Huey Long was hurried to this nearby hospital, Our Lady of the Lake, where Dr. Carl Weiss had performed many operations.

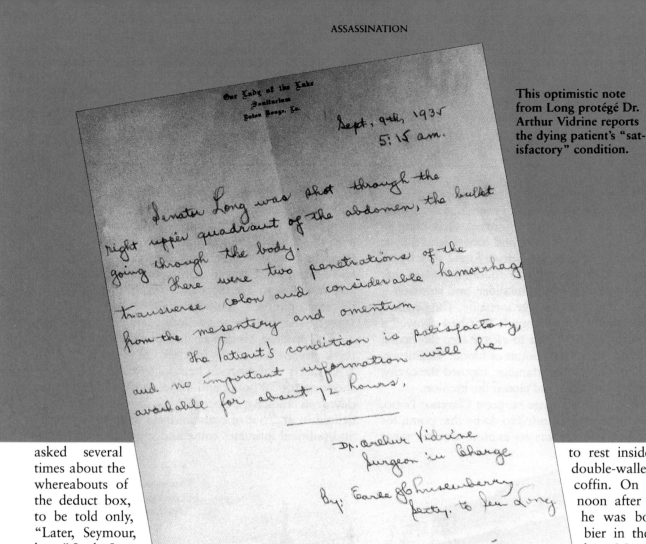

Our Lady of the Lake
Sanitarium
Baton Rouge, La.

Sept., 9th, 1935
5:15 am.

Senator Long was shot through the right upper quadrant of the abdomen, the bullet going through the body.

There were two penetrations of the transverse colon and considerable hemorrhage from the mesentery and omentum

The Patient's condition is satisfactory, and no important information will be available for about 72 hours.

Dr. Arthur Vidrine
Surgeon in Charge

By: Earle J Christenberry
Secty. to Sen Long

This optimistic note from Long protégé Dr. Arthur Vidrine reports the dying patient's "satisfactory" condition.

asked several times about the whereabouts of the deduct box, to be told only, "Later, Seymour, later." In the Long mythos, the fabulous box would take on the role of the Grail, eternally sought but never found. Its fate remains unknown.

Like so much else in his life, Long's last words were a subject of controversy. A sobbing O. K. Allen told the press that Huey had said, "I wonder what will happen to my poor university boys"—meaning, presumably, the ones he planned to educate for free at LSU. A family physician recalled that Long's final words were "Oh, God. Don't let me die. I've a few more things to accomplish." Both quotes did credit to the legend already accreting around the fallen leader. However, a retired nurse said to have been taking Huey's final pulse reported a different, and more plausible, last utterance from the profane Kingfish: "Shit."

The remains of Huey Pierce Long were carried to the Rabenhorst Funeral Home in Baton Rouge to be prepared for a funeral befitting his stature. He was dressed, somewhat incongruously, in a tuxedo and laid to rest inside a huge, double-walled bronze coffin. On the afternoon after his death he was borne to a bier in the capitol's huge Memorial Hall. Seymour Weiss and O. K. Allen had arranged the proceedings, and after they and the Long family had said their final goodbyes, the statehouse doors were opened to the public.

For 25 hours, untold thousands filed by Long's body. There were dignitaries and fashionable city dwellers in attendance, but they were lost in the throngs of Huey's army—the multitudinous poor from the hick towns and backwoods and bayous who came to weep for this man who they believed, whatever his faults, had never broken faith with them. And they were there for the funeral the next day—they and more besides. In the wet, withering late-summer heat, an estimated 100,000 men, women, and children, black and white, surged toward the capitol grounds.

The Kingfish was buried there, in the sunken gardens facing the statehouse. A concrete crypt was sunk seven feet into the ground, and a seamless copper box inside it cradled the bronze casket. The box was sealed after the burial, and later a bronze statue of Huey was erected over the grave.

Newspapers all over the world bristled with editorials

and obituaries about the Kingfish, and important people made the usual appropriate comments. President Roosevelt, for instance, wired Huey's widow to say that he and Mrs. Roosevelt sympathized with her loss.

The Rabenhorst Funeral Home had overseen another funeral the Monday before Huey's. It was nowhere near as grand, but neither was it the obscure, unmourned ceremony that awaits most alleged assassins. Several hundred people stood in a drenching rain to pay final respects to Carl Austin Weiss. Almost every doctor in Baton Rouge crowded into St. Joseph's Catholic Church for Weiss's service. There were also business and social notables, a congressman, and a former governor present. Yvonne Weiss, dressed in white, was accompanied by her brother-in-law, Tom Ed Weiss, and by her mother. Her father, Judge Pavy, stayed in Opelousas. "He could never get over the suffering," said Ida Boudreaux, "the grandchild without a father. That was their first grandchild, you see." As for his physical state, his daughter, about 12 at the time, recalled only that her brother had put him to bed because of chest pains and argued against his going to the funeral.

"I'm not sure there was a eulogy," Tom Weiss recalled. "We were all under a lot of stress. I guess there was greater satisfaction for Mother and Dad and Yvonne that seven or eight priests were on the altar. There was some question the night before whether he could even be buried within the church." Dead at 29, Carl Weiss was buried at Roselawn Cemetery beneath a moss-draped oak. The graveside service was brief, but it entailed the full ritual and panoply of the Catholic Church. Apparently, the church did not accept that Carl Weiss died with the mortal sin of murder on his soul.

Like the Long family, the Weisses received many messages of condolence. A lot of them said that Carl had been a martyr, or a hero. The family would never agree, of course. To them, Carl had never murdered anyone. Perhaps the most telling argument for the young doctor's innocence was expressed by his grieving father the day after the shooting.

"My son was too happy to think of doing what he is accused of trying," Carl Adam Weiss told the press, "too brilliant, too good, too superbly happy with his wife and child, too much in love with them to want to end his life after such a murder. He would have known that it was suicide he was walking into, cold, deliberate self-destruction under the guns of the bodyguards." Weiss survived his son by 12 years, but he never recovered from losing Carl, and he never stopped trying to clear his son's name. He wrote letters of protest to every publication in which he encountered Carl described as Huey's assassin. The many monetary contributions that flowed in from around the country were returned, with thanks, to the senders.

Certainly, in the weeks and days prior to the shooting, Weiss hadn't behaved like a man who planned to kill or to die—nor, say those who think him innocent, did he have any strong motive to kill Long. He wasn't sufficiently interested in politics to despise Huey with the intensity felt by hundreds of other, more violently inclined men in Louisiana. As for the Pavy gerrymander, not even Judge Pavy was especially upset by it; surely his son-in-law could not have taken it so much to heart. The rumored racial slur against the Pavy family has never been confirmed, and it would have been easy for Weiss, a man at home in the eastern United States as well as Europe, to have escaped the South.

The family, and many other students of the Long shooting, believed the incident must have unfolded something like this. On the night of September 8 the doctor had finished his visit to the Morgans and on his way home passed by the capitol grounds, as he often did; but then, perhaps reminded by the glut of cars of the special legislative session and of Huey's presence in the statehouse, he'd hesitated. On the spur of the moment, Weiss decided to try to air his grievance against the senator, man to man, much as he had once spoken up to the rude priest and the senior physician. He'd entered the capitol and waited.

According to one unverified account, he'd seen Huey come and go and had been snubbed twice by the hurried Kingfish. In their final encounter there had been angry words exchanged, and Weiss had slugged Huey, causing the cut on Long's lip that several people would comment upon afterward. Roden had attacked Weiss, then stepped back and drawn his pistol. Carl Weiss, if he had carried the .32 at all, had pulled the gun in self-defense—many maintain, however, that he'd entered the capitol unarmed.

Murphy Roden and the other bodyguards had emp-

Despite a camera ban, this clandestine photograph records the body of Huey Long lying in state at his capitol as thousands of mourners file by.

tied their weapons into the young doctor, who, under their withering fire, had curled up defensively, his arms raised in a futile attempt to shield his head. In the ensuing barrage of high-velocity projectiles, a stray bullet had struck Huey.

Then, in this scenario, Long's followers tried to cover up what really happened in order to protect the bodyguards and because the assassination issue would be useful in the upcoming political campaign—indeed, they would paint the opposition as the Assassination Party. The charges of a cover-up were reinforced by the failure to do an autopsy on Long—his widow reportedly didn't want one—and a 1935 inquest in Baton Rouge into the circumstances surrounding Weiss's death merely reproduced the official line from witnesses who some critics said had been carefully rehearsed.

In 1939 Yvonne Pavy Weiss took her young son and went to live in Paris and then in the French Pyrenees. Her father persuaded her to return to America in 1941 when fascism in its Nazi form started to inch too close to her mountain retreat. Upon her return to America, Yvonne got a Ph.D. in French in 1944 from Columbia University and another in library science at St. John's University in New York. In 1950 she married a textile businessman named Henri Samuel Bourgeoise of New York. She died of cancer in 1963 at the Pavy family home in Opelousas.

Carl Weiss Jr. learned about his father's death accidentally. He'd been told that there had been a shooting accident, and little more. Then, when he was about 10 years old, the son had seen his father's final night emblazoned on the pages of an old *Life* magazine. Bearing a strong resemblance to the parent he never met, the boy set out consciously to emulate him. He'd become a doctor, specializing in orthopedics, and had trained at Bellevue. He traveled to Vienna and Paris, following the footsteps of the dead father, and tried, to the degree he could, to shape himself in the image of Carl Austin Weiss. Having done that, the son noted in a 1993 interview, he had come to the certain knowledge that such a man could not commit such a deed.

Some 50 years after the shooting, this Dr. Weiss met another Senator Long, not in the Louisiana capitol but in a New York hotel. Russell Long, who was 16 when

his father died, and Carl A. Weiss Jr. had breakfast together on June 25, 1985. It was a cordial meeting, Weiss would say later. Of course, they discussed the ways their fathers had died, and neither man changed his mind: Russell Long has always espoused the official version; Carl junior has always insisted that his father was not a killer. In 1993, more than half a century after the event, Russell Long asked to meet with the other Weiss survivor, Tom Ed, in Baton Rouge. Such contacts suggest that, like it or not, the two families are bound by an incident they still find bewildering.

But intimations of conspiracy continue to rise from the shooting of Huey Long like mist rising from the Louisiana bayous (*page 118*). From time to time new bits of information have emerged, however—often fascinating but never definitive—that hint at serious flaws in the official account but fail to displace it.

There was, for instance, the story told in a 1993 interview by Colonel Francis Grevemberg, who, from 1952 to 1955, was superintendent of the Louisiana state police. In 1953, Grevemberg said, veteran trooper Johnny Dearmond told another trooper that he'd seen a bullet fired by bodyguard Joe Messina ricochet and hit Huey. When the shooting stopped, according to Grevemberg, the bodyguards found that Weiss was unarmed. Dearmond said he gave Murphy Roden a .25-caliber handgun that he'd confiscated in a vice raid. But this gun was judged to be too small by General Louis F. Guerre, head of the Bureau of Criminal Identification and Investigation, a precursor to the state police; besides, it had a broken firing pin. Guerre allegedly substituted a .32-caliber pistol. A police captain would later repeat to Grevemberg a story that troopers had taken Weiss's keys off his body, located the Buick, and discovered the .32 in the glove compartment.

Tom Weiss, who examined the Buick parked in front of the capitol, reported that his brother's medical instrument case looked as if it had been rifled and there was an oily sock on the floor. Someone moved the Buick to a different parking spot before Tom Ed could return with another set of keys to take it home.

Finally, the story goes, Guerre ordered the men at the scene to stay silent about what happened, his motive being to protect Messina and the other bodyguards. The account is, of course, hearsay—Grevemberg said he

Who Killed the Kingfish?

No theory quite accounts for the many ambiguities in the case of Huey Long. The apparent absence of a truly compelling motive, taken with Carl Weiss's record as a man, husband, doctor, and father, has rendered Weiss a poor candidate as Long's assassin. And yet, unarguably, he was in the Louisiana capitol that night and may have gone armed. But there are other disturbing mysteries too. Medical and police files inexplicably vanished—along with the alleged murder weapon, Huey's clothes, and other evidence—days after Long's death. Neither Long nor Weiss was autopsied. The district attorney tried four times to call an inquest, and only on the fifth round managed to bring out all the witnesses—all from the Long camp—to testify. Such irregularities have spawned many alternative scenarios for the death of Huey Long, among them:

The Bodyguards Did It—Accidentally. K. B. Ponder, an investigator for the Mutual Life Insurance Company of New York, the holder of Long's $20,000 double-indemnity policy, had this to say in his November 1936 report: "Weiss, when he approached Long in the capitol Building, spoke to him and when Long replied, Weiss struck him in the mouth with his fist. It is an established fact that when he got to the hospital Long's mouth was bruised and there was some bleeding. There is nothing to show that it is possible for him to have received this bruise any other way. Long's bodyguard rushed Weiss and he attempted to draw a pistol. The bodyguard started firing their pistols and Long was killed by a bullet fired by one of his own bodyguard. One of the bodyguard, Joe Messina, was later sent out of the State for a time, following a drunken remark to the effect that 'I killed my only friend.' There was some rumor at the time that he was being confined to the State Insane Asylum but this cannot be verified. This version of the affair is believed to be true by most unbiased informants."

Weiss Did It with Others. Long's followers tried very hard to establish after the shooting that Carl Weiss had not merely been in the wrong place at the wrong time but had stalked Long, intending to kill him.

They claimed Weiss had participated in a meeting of Long enemies where an assassination was proposed and straws drawn—Weiss, they said, had drawn the short straw and would be the assassin. The meeting had taken place on July 21 and 22 at the DeSoto Hotel in New Orleans. But Weiss, it turned out, was in Opelousas treating patients at the time, and men who'd attended the meeting, which they claimed was merely a caucus of the opposition, didn't know Weiss. Given Weiss's personality and background, this scenario has few adherents.

Elliott Coleman Did It. The man who became the sheriff of Tensas Parish in northern Louisiana was one of the bodyguards in the corridor that night. Many years later, a Baptist minister told relatives that Elliott Coleman had come to him, knelt, and confessed to the deliberate murder of Huey Long; he'd had to kill Long when it appeared Weiss had failed. A similar anecdote from a former deputy reported Coleman's flourishing a .45 and claiming it was the gun that killed Huey. But other friends and relatives note that Coleman had no time for clergy and that he'd remained a dedicated Long man to the end.

The Mafia Did It. Long allegedly formed an uneasy alliance with Chicago's notorious Al Capone for bootlegging operations on the Mississippi. When the Kingfish reneged, Capone retaliated with murder. In this scenario, Weiss would have been lured to the capitol, or taken there at gunpoint, and set up to take the lethal barrage from the bodyguards. But Long's real killer would have been someone else, possibly a bodyguard sent down from Chicago.

Roosevelt Did It. Fed by Long's rising paranoia, the idea of a federal conspiracy to kill him has taken root among some surviving admirers of the Kingfish. This scenario holds that Franklin Roosevelt, or his minions, fearing Long might capture or spoil the 1936 election with a third-party bid, decided to remove him. The theory is fueled partly by FBI director J. Edgar Hoover's refusal to investigate Long's murder.

could never get anyone to go on the record—and to it the colonel added another bit of unsubstantiated lore. His father, he said, had been a friend of Dr. Arthur Vidrine's, Long's surgeon at the end. Vidrine had confided to him that the official account of the operation was a lie: Vidrine had found two .38-caliber bullets in Huey's body. He'd been afraid, he claimed, to tell the truth at the time.

Another bullet was injected into the discussion by Baton Rouge publicist Ed Reed, author of *Requiem for a Kingfish,* who recounted a story told by Merle Welsh, who was manager of the Rabenhorst Funeral Home at the time of Huey's death. Welsh told Reed that, while preparing Long's body, he'd assessed the two holes in it not as an entrance wound and an exit wound but as two separate entrance wounds. He believed that Huey had

actually been shot twice and that the bullets might still be in his body.

Welsh also reportedly told Reed that, on the morning Long's remains arrived at the funeral home, Dr. Clarence Lorio had come to Rabenhorst and asked to see the body. Lorio, Welsh claimed, had opened the sutures from the surgery, felt around inside the body, and pulled out one bullet—a large one, although the undertaker could not say what caliber. The bullet supposedly ended up as a pendant belonging to one of Welsh's assistants, who was fond of displaying it as the missile that had killed Huey Long.

During the 1990s two serious efforts were made to resolve the many ambiguities of the case through physical evidence. The first was a forensic examination of Carl Weiss's exhumed remains. The exhumation, approved

On their way to a life in France, Yvonne Pavy Weiss and son Carl junior share this 1939 passport photograph.

by Weiss's son, was done in October of 1991 at the behest of James E. Starrs, a professor of forensic sciences at George Washington University in Washington, D.C. Little was left but the skeleton, but the examination was nevertheless able to show the directions from which the bodyguards' bullets struck Weiss's body. Contrary to their testimony, the bodyguards had shot Weiss in the back with more than half of the 22 bullets that had left their imprint on his bones.

Of special interest to the forensic scientists, however, was a hollow-point .38-caliber bullet lodged in Weiss's cranium. This high-powered round should have exited the skull; that it did not suggested to the investigators that the bullet had been slowed before it struck the head. A closer look revealed that the bullet bore white linen fibers matching the suit Weiss had been wearing when he died. From the fibers and the projectile's angle of entry into the head, investigators came to the conclusion that the bullet probably passed through Weiss's left wrist before lodging in his skull. This, in turn, indicated he might have had his arms thrown up in a defensive posture—and was not on the offense—when the bodyguards started shooting.

Even more intriguing was an offshoot of Starrs's probe. He discovered Carl Weiss's .32, a piece of evidence missing since 1935. General Louis Guerre, who had protested for years that he didn't know where the gun was, died in 1966, leaving a will through which the weapon passed to his daughter, Mabel Guerre Binnings of New Orleans. Another bit of Guerre's legacy was a spent .32 bullet, evidently the one he believed had fatally wounded the Kingfish.

Analysis of these finds showed that the bullet was flattened at two places near its nose and bore a residue of calcium carbonate, a common constituent of marble—facts consistent with it having passed through Huey and ricocheting off a marble wall in the capitol corridor. But Starrs reported that ballistics experts with the Louisiana State Police test-fired Weiss's pistol using a 1935 .32 cartridge—the same type of bullet as the one in Guerre's estate—and then compared the two spent rounds. From marks left by the rifling inside the gun barrel, the experts concluded that the bullet from Guerre's estate—what some believed was the fatal bullet—could *not* have come from Weiss's .32.

Sparked by Starrs's discovery, the Louisiana State Police reopened their own investigation of the Huey Long shooting, under the direction of then-lieutenant Don Moreau. Their report, released on June 5, 1992, supported the official version of the assassination. One of its objections was that no chain of evidence existed to link the Weiss gun and bullet from the Guerre estate with the decades-old crime.

Starrs turned up more than the Weiss weapon, however. He uncovered in General Guerre's estate the Louisiana State Police investigative records of the Long shooting, which also had been missing since 1935. Among these documents were photographs that appeared to show clothing Long was wearing on the night he was shot—an undershirt, a long-sleeved shirt, and a suit coat, all bearing either store labels or hand-written annotations linking them to Long. The garments had been slit open and tacked to a display board. All showed apparent bullet entry and exit holes.

What caught the eye of the Louisiana investigators was what their report called "obvious tearing and sooty residue on the front of the suit coat." To them, the residue—powder burns—bespoke an assassin who fired at Huey almost point-blank—as Weiss allegedly did. Of course, there was no way to guarantee that the residue had been left the night of the killing—or in some subsequent attempt to alter evidence by shooting through the clothes. Nor was there any attempt to explain why no mention had ever been made of powder burns on Huey's body; there should have been some if the police scenario were correct.

In the end the only certainty about events at the Louisiana statehouse on the night of September 8, 1935, was that two remarkable men died there. Few think today that Carl Weiss entered the capitol intending to shoot Huey Long, although some cannot imagine that he did not. Some believe a bullet from his pistol killed the Kingfish, but one hears again and again that it could only have been the bodyguards, accidentally drilling their boss. No one knows; the simple truth, if there is one, may be lost forever. The young doctor, the bodyguards, the cronies, the only witnesses to the night's events, are gone now. If they had secret knowledge of how and why and by whom Huey Long was slain, they took it with them to the grave.◆

The Death Card

Among the cards used in the high-stakes games of practical politics, assassination may seem a powerful trump. When negotiation, threat, sanctions, and sabotage fail, nations may try murder. Sometimes it is a solution; more often it is not. The sudden, violent death of a leader can reduce a party, a nation—indeed, a planet—to rubble. From every "strategic" killing, waves of death go rippling out—World War I ignited around an assassin's bullet in Sarajevo; thousands died in the deaths of three Indian leaders named Gandhi. Political murder unleashes forces that are often impossible to control.

Yet people still play the death card. In these stories, the scent of superpower money mixes with that of ideology in a Turk's attempt to kill Pope John Paul II and in Stalin's execution-at-a-distance of exiled Soviet leader Leon Trotsky. But the assassins might call these tales the patriot's revenge—for annexing a homeland, appeasing a minority faction, violating a shrine, meddling in another nation's revolution. There is always a compelling reason to kill, and someone eager to do it.

A Shot in Sarajevo

Gavrilo Princip was just 14 years old when the Austro-Hungarian empire of the Hapsburgs annexed his homeland of Bosnia and its neighbor Herzegovina in 1908. The son of a poor farmer and mail carrier, Princip had recently moved from his remote Bosnian village to Sarajevo to attend school. There he joined a group of students critical of the Hapsburg rule who met secretly to share propaganda calling for Serb and Croat residents of the occupied territories to band together to create an independent Serbian nation.

A crisis in Europe seemed inevitable. The continent was torn between the aggressive expansions of the stronger powers and a growing pressure from within to throw off the creaky apparatus of the ruling dynasties. To many, the militaristic style of the Hapsburgs appeared wildly out of step with the times, but the aging emperor Franz Joseph turned a deaf ear to any protests.

Archduke Franz Ferdinand, heir apparent to the Hapsburg throne, saw merit in some of the demands of the occupied nations and may have been an agent of change, if he had lived. But those changes would not come soon enough for Gavrilo Princip. The young man became an outspoken antigovernment protester. When his activism got him tossed out of school in Sarajevo in 1912, he left on foot for the Serbian city of Belgrade, more than 100 miles away. There he fell in with a group of like-minded radicals and passed a great deal of time in a local café railing against the Hapsburgs. He volunteered for the Serbian army, but the slight young man was deemed unfit for military service.

Stung by the rejection, Princip resolved that he would fight for Bosnian independence by whatever means came to hand. Together with a pair of student friends, Nedeljko Cabrinovic and Trifko Grabez, he formed a secret society pledged to the cause of Serbian nationalism. For all the trio's fiery dedication, it is unlikely that they would have achieved anything had Princip not made contact with a secret Bosnian revolutionary group known as the Black Hand. Led by Colonel Dragutin Dimitrijevic, an officer of the Serbian army, the Black Hand was said to reach to the very highest levels of government.

The colonel himself, known as Apis, after the sacred bull of ancient Egypt, had become a figure of legend to Princip. Eleven years earlier, the colonel and a small band of officers had dynamited the doors of Belgrade's Royal Palace in a murderous attack on King Alexander and Queen Draga. Cornering the royal couple in their bedroom, Apis and his men riddled them with bullets, then hacked the bodies to pieces with their sabers and hurled the remains out a palace window.

Under the influence of the Black Hand, Gavrilo Princip's student idealism hardened into deadly resolve. When Archduke Franz Ferdinand announced plans to visit Sarajevo in June 1914, Princip saw his chance for glory.

The plot to assassinate the archduke may well have been Princip's, but the seed was likely planted by the Black Hand. In either case, the plan soon had the backing of Colonel Apis himself. Princip, Cabrinovic, and Grabez received weapons and were trained in how to use them.

In Belgrade on the night of May 27, the three conspirators were herded into a basement room illuminated by a single candle. Behind a table sat three men clad in black robes and hoods. Spread out before them were the symbols of the Black Hand—a crucifix, a skull, a dagger, a revolver, and a bottle with a skull-and-crossbones label. After swearing an oath of loyalty, each of the young men was handed a small cardboard box. Inside was a capsule of cyanide.

The next morning Princip, Cabrinovic, and Grabez each donned a loose overcoat that concealed a private arsenal—two powerful explosive charges, a loaded Browning revolver, and extra ammunition. The three men then set out for Sarajevo, traveling first by steamer, then by train. Along the way they received shelter and assistance from a number of Serbo-Croatians sympathetic to their cause, some of whom would later pay dearly for their role in the plot. It remains unclear why such stealth was necessary. As Bosnians living under Hapsburg rule, the three travelers required no papers or passports to cross into Austrian territory. Princip may have believed he was under surveillance, or perhaps he was simply caught up in the drama of his mission.

Arriving in Sarajevo a week later, the conspirators finalized their plans. Then, on the night of June 27, they slipped into the Kosovo cemetery to swear a silent oath at the grave of a Black Hand martyr. Princip brought a handful of soil from "free Serbia" to place on the grave.

The next morning, June 28, Archduke Franz Ferdinand and his wife, the duchess Sophie, began their official visit to Sarajevo. The couple's itinerary, which had been published in a newspaper, included a tour of the city in an open-topped car, a ceremony at the town hall, the opening of a new museum, and lunch. For most of the Bosnians lining the parade route, it would be their first glimpse of the archduke.

Cannons sounded a 24-gun salute as the seven-car procession made its way slowly toward Cemaszula Street, re-named Franz Ferdinand Boulevard in honor of the occasion. Hundreds of portraits of the archduke were on display, and well-wishers along the parade route held up banners and medallions.

In the crowd, spaced at regular intervals, Princip, Cabrinovic, and Grabez waited for the opportunity to strike. As the line of cars approached his position at about 10:10 a.m., Cabrinovic asked a policeman which of the seven vehicles held the archduke. Receiving an answer, Cabrinovic retreated into the crowd and reached beneath his coat for one of his explosive charges. Stepping forward, he struck the detonator cap and hurled the device toward the archduke's car.

The archduke's driver heard the sound of the detonator and mistook it for a pistol shot. He stamped down on the accelerator, but Cabrinovic's bomb had already landed in the folds of the car's top. The archduke, according to witnesses, reached back and pushed it into the street. The device rolled beneath the car following and exploded, sending up a cloud of oily smoke.

At the sound of the blast, the arch-duke ordered the procession to a halt. Though he surely realized the assassin must be close at hand, he demanded to know of any injuries to his party. A Bosnian nobleman by the name of Count Harrach ran back to report on the damage: Colonel Merizzi, one of the archduke's aides-de-camp, had been slightly wounded, as were several spectators standing close by.

Cabrinovic, seeing that his attempt had failed, fought his way through the crowd, leaped over a parapet, and jumped into the Miljacka River, where he was soon seized by police.

Franz Ferdinand, meanwhile, had ordered his driver to continue on. Princip

Sarajevo police seize Gavrilo Princip (*second from right and inset*) after he fatally wounded Austria's archduke Franz Ferdinand and his wife Sophie.

and Grabez, still waiting along the route, were unable to get a clear shot as the archduke rode by.

At the Sarajevo town hall, an array of city dignitaries waited on the front steps for Franz Ferdinand's arrival, unaware of the attempt on his life. The mayor of Sarajevo launched into an elaborate speech to welcome him, but the archduke cut him short. "To hell with your speech!" he shouted angrily. "I have come to visit Sarajevo and am greeted by bombs! It is outrageous!"

The mayor, taken aback, appeared at a loss. Then a calming word from the duchess seemed to quiet Franz Ferdinand's rage, and the mayor was permitted to continue. In the confusion of the blast, the archduke had left the text of his own speech behind, and an aide was dispatched to retrieve it from the damaged car. Only then did the gravity of the assassination attempt become apparent to all: The pages of the speech were stained with Colonel Merizzi's blood. The archduke stoically wiped the blood away with a handkerchief and read his address.

When he finished, Franz Ferdinand announced his intention to carry out the rest of his itinerary—after paying a call on Colonel Merizzi in the hospital. His hosts objected strenuously, arguing that they could not guarantee his safety, but the archduke stood firm. It proved to be a costly act of charity. As the procession set out for the hospital, the driver of the lead car made a wrong turn onto Franz Joseph Strasse, the route he would have taken to reach the museum. When the error was realized, the procession came to a halt. Standing on the pavement less than five feet away was Gavrilo Princip.

Princip reached first for a bomb, then thought better of it. He drew his revolver. Stepping forward, he aimed the Browning at the archduke and fired twice. The first shot pierced the car door and struck the duchess in the side. The second caught the archduke in the neck, lodging in his spine.

The car sped off toward the Konak, the governor's residence. Count Harrach, the Bosnian nobleman, was clinging to the running board of the car. He had hoped to shield Franz Ferdinand from any further assaults, but he was on the opposite side of the car from Princip. Harrach was the first to realize what had happened. "As the car quickly reversed a thin stream of blood spurted out of His Imperial Highness's mouth on to my right cheek. With one hand I got out my handkerchief to wipe the blood from the Archduke's face, and as I did so Her Highness called out, 'In God's name what has happened to you?' Then she collapsed, her face between the Archduke's knees." According to Harrach, Franz Ferdinand then implored his wife, "Don't die! Live for my children." Harrach asked the archduke if he was in great pain. "He answered distinctly, 'It is nothing.' Then he turned his face a little to one side and said six or seven times, more faintly as he began to lose consciousness, 'It is nothing.' " By the time the car arrived at the Konak, Sophie was dead; Franz Ferdinand died a few minutes later.

Back on Franz Joseph Strasse, Gavrilo Princip had one more grim task ahead of him. As the imperial car sped away, the young assassin placed the Browning to his own head. A bystander tore it from his grip. Undeterred, he bit into his cyanide capsule, but just then a policeman's club cracked down on his head, knocking the poison from his mouth.

Within the hour, Princip and Cabrinovic were in police custody; two days later Grabez was apprehended. In the coming days, police would interrogate hundreds of suspects—so many, in fact, that Princip soon made a limited confession from his prison cell, hoping to head off further arrests.

Though he freely admitted his guilt, Princip showed no remorse. "I am not a criminal," he declared, as the trial of the assassins got under way. "I have killed a man who has done wrong; I think I have done right." If Princip had any regret at all, it was over the killing of the duchess, which he had not intended.

On October 28, 1914, Princip was sentenced to 20 years of hard labor—with the provision that he fast one day of each month and spend the anniversary of the assassination in solitary confinement. Only his youth saved him from the hangman's noose.

Cabrinovic and Grabez received the same sentence as Princip, while others, perhaps less guilty, received life imprisonment on charges of conspiracy. Three men, some of whom had assisted only in helping the conspirators reach Sarajevo, were given the death penalty. Strangely enough, the Black Hand was never linked to the plot.

Even before the verdicts were rendered, the concussive effect of the fatal shots was felt across Europe. "It is feared," said one newspaper article, "that the Sarajevo tragedy will still further embitter the none too friendly relations existing between Austria and Serbia." This proved to be an understatement. Immediately following the assassination, the Austrian government issued an ultimatum accusing Serbian officials of complicity in the murder. Germany threw its support behind the Austrians, while Russia backed Serbia. Within weeks, the world was at war.

Out of the chaos and bloodshed the conspirators' actions precipitated, an independent Yugoslavian nation arose. But none of the trio, who all suffered with tuberculosis, lived to see it. Nedeljko Cabrinovic died in prison in 1916, before reaching the age of 22. Trifko Grabez died nine months later. Gavrilo Princip survived his two comrades by only two years. He succumbed in April 1918, at the age of 23.◆

Courtly Assassin

To Sylvia Ageloff, an American working in Paris in 1938, Jacques Mornard seemed the ideal suitor. The elegant, 25-year-old Belgian spoke several languages, had plenty of money, and was a perfect gentleman. In her private moments, Ageloff may have wondered what this suave diplomat's son saw in her—a social worker and part-time translator from New York. In her wildest imaginings, though, Ageloff could hardly have guessed the truth: Virtually everything Mornard told her was a lie—his nationality, his background, even his name. In fact, he was a Spanish Communist named Ramon Mercader, and he was an assassin.

As Mercader squired Sylvia Ageloff around Paris, he was laying the ground-work for one of the grisliest political assassinations of the 20th century. Ageloff had something he needed, and it was this one thing that bound him to her: She was in Paris to serve as a translator at the founding congress of the Fourth International, a revolutionary movement led by Russian dissident Leon Trotsky. Trotsky had been second only to Lenin as a leader of Russia's 1917 Communist revolution and was a political rival of Joseph Stalin, iron-handed dictator of the Soviet Union. Trotsky was the man Ramon Mercader was plotting to kill.

In a sense, Mercader had been born to the role of assassin. His mother was a fanatical adherent of Stalinist policy and eventually became the mistress of a senior official of the Soviet secret police. Her devotion was passed on to her son, who trained as a Soviet agent in both Spain and Moscow.

In October 1939 Mercader moved to Mexico City, telling Ageloff he was to work for an import firm. But it was not business that drew him to Mexico City. It was Trotsky. The city was home to the exiled revolutionary and provided a safe haven from which he could renew his attacks on the Stalin regime.

Trotsky had become locked in a power struggle with Stalin, then the general secretary of the Communist party, following Lenin's death in 1924. By 1928 Trotsky was forced out of office and exiled to Siberia, while Stalin moved to suppress his rival's supporters. A year later, Trotsky was banished from the Soviet Union.

For nearly 10 years, Trotsky lived under constant threat from the Soviet secret police, and tragedy dogged his steps. Within the span of five years, three of his children died under questionable circumstances. And in 1938, in Paris, the dismembered body of Rudolf Klement, once a secretary of Trotsky's, was found floating in the Seine.

By 1937 Trotsky, his wife, Natalia, and their young grandson Seva had settled in Mexico City. Mercader arrived in the fall of 1939, and Sylvia Ageloff joined him a few months later. Her command of the Russian language made her useful to Trotsky, and soon she was working for him. Mercader, however, did not press the advantage. He drove her to the Trotsky house every day but did not insist on going inside. Occasionally he brought small gifts for Natalia and Seva. Armed guards were posted

Exiled Russian revolutionary leader Leon Trotsky *(above)* lies dying in a Mexico City hospital, mortally injured by assassin Ramon Mercader *(inset)* on the orders of Soviet dictator Joseph Stalin.

outside the house, but Mercader soon developed an easy familiarity with them.

His generosity apparently knew no bounds. Once, while visiting New York on what he claimed was a business trip, he left his car at the Trotskys' disposal. But Mercader returned from this trip a changed man. His once fastidious appearance gave way to a shabby disregard. He developed a facial twitch and trembling hands. With Sylvia Ageloff, he alternated between moody silence and boastful talkativeness.

It is possible that Mercader received his final orders to kill Trotsky while in New York, which may account for his increasingly strange behavior. But whatever fears or doubts he may have felt, he did not wait long to act.

Early in the morning of May 24, 1940, Trotsky and his wife were jolted awake by the sound of gunfire. Groggy from a sleeping pill, Trotsky dismissed the noise as fireworks. Natalia, instantly recognizing the danger, pushed him off the bed and covered his body with her own—just as a stream of bullets tore through the room. From a nearby room, the Trotskys heard the screams of their grandson Seva. The couple was pinned to the floor and couldn't help the boy, but when the gunfire subsided, Natalia hurried to find him. The child, who had run out into the garden, had received only a slight wound in the foot. But in the garden Natalia Trotsky also discovered a bundle of dynamite that had failed to explode.

The guard on duty that night was missing. A month later, the Mexican police found his body several miles from the house with a bullet through the head. In time, the police concluded that the attack had been led by a man named David Siqueiros, who was arrested some months later. Many more months would pass, however, before they connected the office address used by Ramon Mercader with a building occupied by David Siqueiros. By then it would be too late.

Four days after the attack on the Trotsky home, Mercader and Trotsky met for the first time. Trotsky was impressed by the polite young man, and Mercader became an even more regular presence in the household.

By August Mercader had cultivated such an intimacy with Trotsky that he asked the older man to give an opinion of an article he had written. Trotsky agreed, but found the meeting to be a strange one. Mercader sat in a corner without removing his hat and kept his coat tightly clutched around him. Later, it would emerge that Mercader had come armed with a gun, a dagger, and a steel-bladed pickax. At the last moment, however, he lost his resolve.

Three days later, on August 20, Mercader returned once more seeking help on his article. He again sat in a corner while Trotsky looked it over. Then, finding his courage, the assassin reached inside his coat and withdrew his pickax. He stood and raised the ax high above his head. Trotsky looked up just as Mercader brought the sharpened point crashing down.

Though badly wounded, Trotsky put up a furious struggle, pelting Mercader with heavy books, an inkwell, and even his dictaphone. Trotsky then managed to grab hold of Mercader's hand and bit it savagely. Pulling free, Mercader backed away, knocking over chairs and a bookcase. Natalia heard the noise and hurried to the office, where she found her husband sagging against the door frame, his face a mass of blood and gore. Calmly and without bitterness, Trotsky spoke the name of his attacker.

By now, security guards had pounced on Mercader and were pummeling him with their fists and revolver butts. "They made me!" screamed Mercader. "They've got my mother!" Trotsky, hearing the noise from another room, struggled to speak clearly. "He must not be killed," he declared. "He must talk."

Trotsky lost consciousness on the way to the hospital, where a team of five doctors performed emergency surgery. The ax had splintered a bone, driving shards deep into the brain. He lingered on for nearly 26 hours, then died.

Even as the murder trial got under way, the mystery of Ramon Mercader—who was still using the alias Jacques Mornard—remained impenetrable. It was generally accepted that he was a pawn of the Soviet secret police, but the connection was never proven. Nor was any source of Mercader's considerable income ever uncovered. In his pocket he carried a lengthy typewritten document purporting to be a justification of the murder. It claimed, in part, that he had grown to hate Trotsky for coming between him and Sylvia Ageloff; soon Ageloff was arrested as an accomplice. When police officials brought her face to face with Mercader, however, she flew into a wild rage and attempted to spit in his face. "Kill him!" she shouted. "He has murdered Trotsky! Kill him! Kill him!" Ultimately the charge of complicity in the murder was dropped.

Mercader received a total of 20 years' imprisonment for the crime. But it was not until 1950, when a police psychologist matched his fingerprints with a set on file with the Spanish police, that the true identity of Ramon Mercader was finally established. Any doubts about his link to the Stalin regime were dispelled when it was learned that his mother had accepted the Order of Hero of the Soviet Union on behalf of her son.

In 1960, within an hour of Mercader's release from a Mexican penitentiary, he was met by two guards from the Czechoslovakian embassy. They handed him a diplomatic passport in the name of Jacques Vandendreschd. Leaving all traces of Ramon Mercader behind, he boarded a Cuban airliner and disappeared behind the Iron Curtain.◆

Young Turk

More than 10,000 of the faithful packed St. Peter's Square in Rome on the afternoon of May 13, 1981. They strained for positions at the wooden barricades that bordered a narrow path around the perimeter of the square. Standing in the back of a white Jeep-like vehicle slowly driving the path, Pope John Paul II bent to bless those nearest to him. Again and again, the Jeep stopped so that this thin, wry man from Poland, the spiritual leader of nearly 600 million Roman Catholics, could touch the outstretched fingers. At about 5:15 p.m., as the vehicle paused near the Vatican's Great Bronze Door, the pope reached down once more to the sea of waving hands, unaware that one held a semiautomatic pistol. Two rapid shots cracked the air. One grazed the pope's right arm and left hand; the other struck him in the abdomen. People watched in horror as the Holy Father raised one shaking hand to his face, then collapsed, his white garments smeared with blood.

The young gunman, holding tight to the 9-mm. Browning, turned to flee. But Suor Letizia, a robust young nun standing several yards behind him, was already in pursuit. When he tripped on the cobblestones, dropping his weapon, she grabbed him. "Why did you do it?" she shouted into the assailant's thin, dark face. "Not me, not me!" he cried. But she and others held him until police arrived. As the pope underwent the emergency surgery that would save his life, investigators began their long, frustrating search for the answer to Suor Letizia's question.

The would-be assassin, they found, was a 23-year-old Turk named Mehmet Ali Agca from the shantytown of Yesiltepe, a suburb of Malatya. His alcoholic father had died in 1966, when Mehmet Ali was seven, leaving a wife and three children in poverty. As the eldest child, Mehmet Ali sold spring water at the local railway terminal to earn money.

The Turkey of Agca's youth was a violent place, with the extreme right and

Moments before shooting, hitman Mehmet Ali Agca (*inset*) aims a 9-mm. automatic (*circled*) at Pope John Paul II in Rome's St. Peter's Square.

extreme left battling savagely for political dominance. In 1975 a right-wing, anti-West group, the National Action Party, took over the Malatya's Teachers Training High School, where the 17-year-old Agca was studying. Soon he was seen in the company of militant young people belonging to the Grey Wolves, a branch of an organization called Turkish Idealists, which was in turn an affiliate of the National Action Party. Agca's new companions were often arrested, but his own record remained spotless—until June 25, 1979, when Agca, by then a student at Istanbul University, was arrested for murder.

The victim was Abdi Ipekci, the outspoken editor of the leftist newspaper *Milliyet*, shot to death in Istanbul on the night of February 1, 1979. Almost five months later, an anonymous caller told Istanbul police they could find "Ali," Ipekci's murderer, at the Marmara, a right-wing student coffeehouse. Mehmet Ali Agca confessed to the murder, but insisted he'd acted alone, despite eyewitness testimony to the contrary. He was incarcerated at the Kartal Maltepe maximum security prison.

A month into his sentence, on November 23, Agca dressed in an army uniform that had been smuggled in to him, coolly walked past the prison's guards, and disappeared into the night. He left behind a letter for *Milliyet*, in which he called Pope John Paul II "the Crusader Commander" and claimed that the pope's impending visit to Turkey was a Western imperialist plan to erode the unity of "the brotherly Islamic countries." Agca swore he would kill John Paul if he came to Turkey. But the papal visit proceeded as planned, and Agca never appeared. He may have left his mark elsewhere, however. A month after Agca's escape, the Grey Wolf informant believed to have fingered Agca for Ipekci's murder was tortured and killed in Istanbul.

During 1980 the fugitive seemed to wander aimlessly: from Turkey to Iran, back through Turkey, on to Bulgaria for a few months, then to Yugoslavia. By autumn he was in West Germany, where police suspected him of murdering a former Turkish Idealist in Kempten on November 25. A month later Agca turned up in Italy, evidently preparing for his spring day in St. Peter's Square.

Although authorities soon knew the identity and background of the pope's attacker, Agca remained something of an enigma. Some observers felt that the *Milliyet* letter he'd left in prison marked him as a lone religious fanatic. Others found the cool young Turk more political. "He is a terrorist with a capital 'T,' " said an official who questioned him, "cold, lucid and certainly well trained to shoot." Agca himself kept mostly silent, insisting only that he'd acted alone. Asked about reports of another man fleeing St. Peter's Square on the day of the shooting, Agca said nothing, and he refused to reveal how he'd financed his travels around Europe. Police suspected the involvement of Turkey's National Action Party, but couldn't link it to the shooting. In July 1981 Agca was sentenced to life in prison for the attempted murder of the pope.

After 10 months in an Italian jail, Agca told his captors that Bulgarian officials had offered him $1.25 million to kill the pope. Naturally, he'd accepted. The Bulgarian connection had a certain ring of truth. That country's secret police—the DS, or Darzhavna Sigurnost—had been implicated in terrorist attacks and at least one murder and were seen as partners in illegal arms and drug trafficking. Moreover, Agca's account was full of convincing details.

Despite some wariness at taking Agca's word for anything, the Italian government decided to move. In November 1982 they arrested Bulgarian airline official Sergei Ivanov Antonov.

They also issued warrants for embassy cashier Teodorov Ayvazov and Guelio Vassiliev Kolev, secretary of the embassy's military attaché, but both had already fled the country. Eventually four Turks were also arrested.

Agca hadn't finished spinning his tale of conspiracy, however. On July 8, 1983, as he was being moved from police headquarters, he threw questioning reporters an irresistible morsel. "In the attack against the pope," he said offhandedly, "even the KGB took part." Again, the accusation made sense to those who believed that the Soviets wished to silence the pope's vocal support of the Solidarity labor movement in communist Poland. But no Russians were apprehended.

The Italian government eventually tried the three Bulgarians and four Turks for conspiracy to assassinate the pope. The trial, which began in June 1985, depended almost entirely on the reliability of Agca's testimony. "When he starts speaking of facts," the prosecutor said confidently, "he is very believable." Agca swiftly made a liar out of him. On the first day of the trial, the assassin announced, "I am Jesus Christ!" He further devalued his testimony by revealing more conspirators: To the Soviet Union and Bulgaria, he added a secret Italian Masonic lodge and the Italian secret service. After more than nine months of this, all of the defendants were acquitted on the conspiracy charge for lack of evidence.

As of 1994 the man who would have killed John Paul still languished in a high security prison in Ancona, Italy, his contact with other inmates limited. But from time to time journalists can question him. When one reporter asked who ordered the pope's assassination, Agca said, "Some blame the KGB, others the CIA, by now there is not any possibility of knowing." Exhausted Italian investigators would be the first to agree.◆

Gandhi Must Die

To Nathuram Godse, the 1947 partition of India that created Pakistan was more than another humiliating capitulation to his country's Muslim minority. It was a turning point for the 37-year-old Hindu, whose diffuse anger and frustration at what he called the castration and vivisection of India now began to sharpen.

Godse was the editor of the radical newspaper *Hindu Rashtra*—"Hindu Nation"—in Poona, a city 119 miles inland from Bombay in southwest India and a hotbed of Hindu nationalism. Brought up in a strict Brahman Hindu household, Godse developed a passion for politics as a young man. By the age of 27 he had become a follower of Vinayak Damodar Savarkar, a fervent believer in Hindu racial supremacy who advocated violent revolution to advance his cause. Savarkar was also a political assassin. To Godse, he was a master, a mystic, a god.

The young Brahman shadowed Savarkar as he spread his virulent message across India. For years Godse absorbed his master's teachings and attended his every need. In 1944, at Savarkar's behest, Godse and another Hindu extremist, Narayan Apte, began publishing the *Hindu Rashtra*.

By the time of India's partition three years later, Godse's considerable hatred had focused on a man who epitomized nonviolence: Mohandas Karamchand Gandhi. Known as the Mahatma, or Great Soul, by his followers, the elderly Hindu taught that the way to freedom was through passive civil disobedience, not bloody revolution. As a result, Britain had relaxed its hold on the colony, and violence had begun to fade from the quest for liberty.

Gandhi provided a catalyst for Godse's violent impulses in mid-January of 1948. At the time of partition, India had agreed to pay the newly created country of Pakistan its share of existing monetary reserves—550 million rupees (about $166 million). But India's new government, elected in 1947 and led by Prime Minister Jawaharlal Nehru, balked at making good on the agreement. Gandhi countered with a trump card he'd used before: He would fast until India paid Pakistan what it owed—to the death, if necessary.

As Gandhi's fast began in New Delhi and bulletins on the Mahatma's condition went out on the nation's wires, the editor of *Hindu Rashtra*, some 700 miles away, felt his hatred narrow like a beam of light. His itch for action coalesced into an assassin's plot. For selling India out to the Muslims, Gandhi must die.

The idea became a magnet for conspiracy. Godse and his colleague Narayan Apte were joined in the plot by Digambar Badge, who was a purveyor of illegal weaponry in Poona's back streets. Savarkar took a shadowy interest. Innkeeper Vishnu Karkare threw in with the conspiracy and brought along Madanlal Pahwa, a Punjabi Hindu

Radical editor Nathuram Godse, shown above at his May 27, 1948, arraignment on murder charges, conspired with six other Hindu nationalists to kill India's Mahatma Gandhi *(right)* in New Delhi.

whose father had been abused by Muslims. Gopal Godse, Nathuram's younger brother by 10 years, joined in the scheme. By January 18, seven conspirators were converging on New Delhi with grenades and a pair of handguns.

In his sparsely furnished wing of Birla House, the New Delhi home of industrialist G. D. Birla, Gandhi was already close to death. Still, the fast had produced the desired result. Hindus and Muslims had put up their weapons for a time, and Nehru's government agreed to pay the 550 million rupees. Gandhi's spirits soared. Soon he would be strong enough to walk to his evening prayers on the broad lawn of Birla House.

On the afternoon of Tuesday, January 20, however, Gandhi still had to be carried in a litter and set down before the faithful crowd in the garden. The assassins waiting for him there had set up what seemed to them a clever cascade of events: A bomb planted by Madanlal Pahwa would panic the crowd and the assassins would move in and murder Gandhi during the confusion.

But when the bomb exploded, the congregation wavered but didn't run. The screams of a woman who'd seen Pahwa light his bomb brought the police to him. When the other assassins saw their companion dragged into custody, they swiftly melted away.

The bungled attempt depressed and frightened the self-styled heroes of Hindu nationalism—all, that is, but Nathuram Godse. Their scheme had failed, he told Apte, because there had been too many players. Next time, he said, he, and he alone, would assassinate Mohandas Gandhi. Apte and Karkare would accompany him and there would be no bombs, only one dependable pistol. Worried that Pahwa might be naming them as coconspirators, Godse reportedly told the two men, "We must get Gandhi before the police get us."

He needn't have worried. The Indian police acted with puzzling slowness on the information they squeezed from their prisoner. Arrests that should have taken a few hours dragged on for precious days, delayed, according to some historians, by the mistaken belief that the bunglers would not try again.

Thus, when Nathuram Godse arrived at Birla House on the afternoon of Friday, January 30, he entered unimpeded, as did Narayan Apte and Vishnu Karkare minutes later. Gandhi had insisted that none of his audience be searched for weapons, allowing Godse to smuggle in a 9-mm. Beretta automatic purchased just two nights before. Nathuram's plan was to position himself fairly close to the platform where Gandhi sat during his prayer meetings—a moderately difficult pistol shot of perhaps 35 feet. Then fate took a hand.

Gandhi started for that day's prayers a few minutes late, walking with the aid of his grandnieces Manu and Abha. Obsessed with punctuality, he cut across the lawn to his platform. The crowd parted before him, calling, "*Bapuji, Bapuji,*" to the man they affectionately called *Bapu*—"Father."

Nathuram Godse found himself standing only a few paces from the small figure he had come to murder. He eased the Beretta from his pocket and held it between his palms, which were pressed together in a gesture of homage. He stepped into the space just ahead of Gandhi, bowed, and offered a respectful greeting: "*Namaste, Gandhiji.*"

"Brother," protested Manu gently, "Bapu is already 10 minutes late."

But Godse shoved her aside with his left arm. He brought up the black Beretta and fired three shots into Gandhi's chest. "*He Ram!*" cried the Mahatma. "Oh God!" Then he was dead.

Nathuram Godse was arrested on the spot. The police, goaded into action, quickly rounded up the other conspirators. Digamber Badge turned state's evidence and went free. Vinayak Damodar Savarkar was acquitted. Vishnu Karkare, Madanlal Pahwa, and Gopal Godse served long prison sentences, emerging only in the late 1960s.

Nathuram Godse, who claimed to have acted alone, received a death sentence, as did Narayan Apte—he'd sealed his fate by going with Godse to buy the Beretta. At dawn on November 15, 1949, at Ambala Prison, the two assassins were taken to the gallows. Godse is said to have walked unflinchingly to his execution, but Apte, who'd seen a reprieve in the lines of his palm, had to be carried to the noose.

One of Mahatma Gandhi's last visitors, on the day before his assassination, was a 30-year-old woman named Indira Priyadarshini Gandhi. She was not related to the Mahatma—Gandhi was the surname of her estranged husband—but she was part of the movement the martyred leader had begun. Her father, Jawaharlal Nehru, was a close associate of the Mahatma's and was independent India's first prime minister. He was also utterly dependent upon the affectionate aid of his only child, who by 1947 had moved back into his house with her two sons, Rajiv and Sanjay. Her father's hostess until his death in 1964, Indira Gandhi became prime minister herself in 1966; in 1977, after a period of authoritarian rule, the voters rejected her. But she swept back into office in 1980, the same year that her politically promising younger son, Sanjay, was killed in a plane crash.

Like her father, Indira Gandhi believed that India could function as a secular, or nonreligious, democracy—a belief that may have seemed merely silly to the Sikhs of India's Punjab state, whose lives and faith are tightly bound. Distinctive in their turbans and beards, Sikhs follow a religion that is a kind of hybrid of Hinduism and Islam. They had suffered mightily in the 1947 partition, when West Pakistan was ripped out of their homeland. Sikhs were famous for their incorruptibility and ferocious courage, however, and they acquired enormous influence in India. Though composing only about two percent of the population, they made up about 15 percent of the Indian army and were similarly well represented in the government ranks. Thus, when Indira Gandhi returned to power in 1980, her party's president was Zail Singh (Singh, which all Sikh men add to their name, means "lion"). And a police officer named Beant Singh came to be in the inner circle of her residential guard.

Beant Singh was born in 1950 in the Punjab village of Maloya, near Chandigarh. He was just 16 when Indira Gandhi first came to power. Leaving his wife in Maloya, Beant Singh had joined the police in 1975 and was posted to New Delhi's armed police in 1980. In 1982 he'd been tapped for the Special Security District, the prime minister's trusted guards. Big and gregarious, Beant Singh sometimes traveled with her when she went abroad. And he was more than just a bodyguard. He had the same rare blood type as Indira Gandhi—type O negative. His blood could save her life.

Gandhi had allied herself a few years earlier with another Sikh, a humble cleric named Jarnail Singh

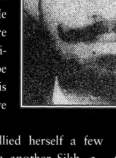

Indira Gandhi *(right)* appears on U.S. television in 1982, two years before Sikh bodyguard Beant Singh *(inset)* and an accomplice murdered her.

Bhindranwale, then preaching in the Punjab. Encouraged by her support, Bhindranwale had evolved radically, urging the creation of a Sikh nation that separatists called Khalistan. Then, gathering the zealous around him in 1982, he undertook a campaign of terror that left hundreds dead in Punjab. For his stronghold, he chose the Sikh's holiest of holies—the Golden Temple at Amritsar—and fortified the shrine against the siege that would inevitably come.

It came in June 1984 while subinspector Beant Singh was on a month's leave in Maloya. Called Operation Bluestar, the Indian army's assault on the Golden Temple quickly went wrong. Instead of poorly armed civilians cowering behind the temple's ornate walls, the army found a force of some 500 highly trained, well-equipped Sikh warriors holding the battle's key vantage points and fields of fire—and ready to die in a good cause.

The militants, Bhindranwale among them, were destroyed in three days' heavy fighting.

A wave of angry revulsion swept through India's Sikhs. Soldiers mutinied, Sikhs demonstrated in the streets. On a tour of the ravaged Golden Temple, President Zail Singh prayed for forgiveness. "Mrs. Gandhi made a fatal mistake," said one Sikh leader living abroad. "Every man who thinks himself as a Sikh can never forget that she has signed her own death warrant."

Sikh bodyguards assigned to protect the prime minister, including Beant Singh, were quickly reassigned to an outer cordon around the New Delhi compound where she had both her office and residence. But Gandhi insisted that the Sikhs be restored to positions of trust. One could not be secular, she insisted, and single out one group.

Among the Sikh detachment, however, an assassination conspiracy had already ignited. At their secret rendezvous—the New Delhi home of Beant Singh's uncle, Kehar Singh—the young guard agreed to do what must be done. Then he brought in constable Satwant Singh, a brawny 21-year-old who'd joined the Delhi Armed Police in 1982. On October 30, Beant Singh asked to change places with a colleague on the next day's duty roster—a routine substitution. He would take his position at the gate on the path that linked the prime minister's home and office building. Satwant Singh, assigned to an outer perimeter guard position, asked to be stationed near the same gate—he had a bad stomach, he said, and needed to be near a lavatory.

At 9:10 a.m. on October 31, the two guards were at their stations. Beant Singh held a .38-caliber service revolver; Satwant Singh carried a Sten, a light submachine gun. Indira Gandhi, leading a procession of aides and bodyguards, approached them from her residence. She was on her way to a television interview on the far side of her office building. Recognizing Beant Singh as one who had spent years at her side, she smiled and greeted the subinspector. He shot her three times in the abdomen. As Gandhi buckled, Satwant Singh emptied his 30-round Sten-gun magazine at her. Her bodyguards scattered for cover.

"We have done what we wanted to," said Beant Singh, dropping his pistol and raising his arms. "Now you can do what you want to."

The two men were quickly hustled away by a special commando unit assigned to guard the compound. Minutes later, in what the commandos described as an escape attempt inside the guardhouse, Beant Singh was shot to death and Satwant Singh was wounded eight times. He recovered sufficiently to be interrogated and, with two of his coconspirators, went to trial.

As word of Indira Gandhi's murder at Sikh hands spread across the subcontinent, fights and riots flared. In three days, some 3,000 Sikhs were killed by mobs in 80 cities, more than 2,000 of them in Delhi.

The surviving assassin lived until 1989. Then, having exhausted all appeals, Satwant Singh was hanged, along with Beant's uncle, Kehar Singh. Their act of vengeance evidently left no shadow on their families in Punjab, however: Beant Singh's wife, Bimal Khalsa, was later elected to parliament, as was his father, Succha Singh.

Even as the Singhs of Punjab were plotting against Indira Gandhi, another threat was looming large. She had also given her government's tacit support to the Liberation Tigers, a budding revolutionary army drawn from the Hindu Tamil population of northwestern Sri Lanka, the tear-shaped island nation at the tip of the subcontinent. This group would prove to be the bane of Indira's successor as prime minister, her eldest son, Rajiv Gandhi.

In the 19th century the British had brought thousands of Tamils across the 26-mile-wide Palk Strait to what was then the English colony of Ceylon to work the island's tea estates. But as the 1947 independence ignited the separatist aspirations of Indian Hindus, Sikhs, and Muslims, it also gave hope to the Hindu Tamils of Sri Lanka, where almost 80 percent of the population is Buddhist Sinhalese. Increasingly a powerless minority, the Tamils campaigned for Eelam—the Tamil homeland—on the northern section of the island.

Indira Gandhi's government did not look too closely at the training camps that sprang up in the Tamil Nadu district of southern India or the traffic that moved furtively across the Palk Strait. By the early 1980s the separatist movement had spawned the Liberation Tigers of Tamil Eelam, or LTTE, which was raiding Sri Lanka's northwestern settlements even before Indira Gandhi was cut down by her guards.

Rajiv Gandhi was less friendly to the Tigers than his mother had been. "I will not allow Eelam," said the new prime minister in a 1985 speech in Madras, the provincial capital of India's Tamil Nadu district. As Sri Lanka sank toward civil war, Rajiv Gandhi moved to intercede. In July 1987 he helped arrange a ceasefire between the Sri Lankan army and the Tamil Tigers—an agreement that Tiger supremo Villupillai Prabhakaran detested, for it was really a call for his troops to lay down their arms.

When the truce collapsed, Gandhi sent a force of 60,000 troops into Sri Lanka. Called the Indian Peace Keeping Force, or IPKF, the army was intended to restore order and protect civilian interests in the north. Although the guerrillas' numbers dropped from some 5,000 in 1987 to fewer than 1,500 in 1988, the stubbornly aggressive Tigers had managed to kill more than 3,000 Indian soldiers by 1990.

Sending in the army, in the view of Prabhakaran and his followers, was an unforgivable affront. But Rajiv was protected by an impregnable Indian security force determined to redeem itself. When Gandhi lost the 1989 election, however, this shield dropped.

In late November 1990 Prabhakaran summoned four of his lieutenants. Rajiv Gandhi's anti-Eelam sentiments were well known, he told them; the Tigers could not risk having the man who'd sent troops against them back in power. They must strike quickly, while Rajiv campaigned for the May 1991 election without the protection of a prime minister's heavy security. And they must strike on Tamil ground: Madras.

The mission was parceled out. Shivarasan, at 33 a senior LTTE agent and the field commander of the scheme, would lead the killers to their prey. Others were charged with finding a safe house and acquiring a proper bomb.

In Madras the conspirators recruited a radical student, whose parents' home became the LTTE hideout. Two freelance photographers, Ravi Shankaran and a man called Haribabu, were inducted to photograph the actual assassination, an LTTE trademark. An electronics expert was asked to design and build the bomb.

Shivarasan reached Madras during the first week of March. He liked the bomb design: Six grenades linked by silver wires and fastened to a denim girdle. Each grenade contained 80 grams of C4-RDX high explosives and 2,800 two-mm. steel shards. The grenades were further encased in TNT. Powered by a single nine-volt battery, two toggle switches controlled the bomb—one armed the circuit, the other detonated the grenades. The bomb's human delivery system would be Shivarasan's young female cousin, Dhanu; another cousin, Subha, would be her backup.

On May 19 the Congress Party announced that candidate Rajiv Gandhi would speak at a rally near Madras two days hence. On the afternoon of May 21, Dhanu slipped into the grenade-packed denim girdle, then dressed in an orange salwar-kameez, the long shirt favored by men and women in urban India; the shapeless garment gave no hint that she was weighted with explosives.

Arriving by bus at the site of the rally, the conspirators took up their positions. Shivarasan stood near the dais. Haribabu, with a borrowed Pentax camera, and Dhanu, carrying a sandalwood garland she would offer Rajiv, waited near the red carpet that Gandhi would follow to the platform. The candidate's motorcade arrived at about 10 p.m., and his progress through the throng toward his murderers was tortuously slow.

Dhanu waited tranquilly among the others flanking the red carpet. Shi-varasan stood less than 10 feet behind her. Haribabu watched her through the Pentax viewfinder, clicking the frames that would preserve this moment in Tiger history. Dhanu flipped the first toggle switch, tripping the circuit, then stepped forward, raising the garland toward Rajiv. An alert female constable held up an arm to stop her, but Gandhi intervened. "Let everyone have a turn," he told her, smiling. "Don't worry. Relax." He turned back to the girl with the garland. Dhanu placed it around his neck, then knelt as if to touch his feet. Gandhi bowed slightly to lift her. The girl smiled briefly at the constable—and flipped the second switch.

Only four of the six grenades detonated, but they were more than enough. The blast ripped Dhanu apart and sent her severed head tumbling through the air. Rajiv Gandhi absorbed much of the explosion. It tore away the left side of his face, crushed his skull, and excavated his abdomen and chest. The photographer Haribabu, who had positioned himself too close to Dhanu, was killed, as were 15 others. Shivarasan, unscathed, was on his way back to Madras minutes after the assassination.

But the film in the unfortunate Hari-

babu's borrowed Pentax survived the blast. Using the damning images from the developed 35-mm. roll, Indian officials quickly rounded up dozens of conspirators and sympathizers in Tamil Nadu. Many others committed suicide to avoid arrest.

For Shivarasan, Subha, and five others, the end came three months later in a shootout near the southern Indian city of Bangalore. Surrounded by commandos and police, the Tiger death squad turned to cyanide. They died on the morning of August 20, 1991—Rajiv Gandhi's 47th birthday.◆

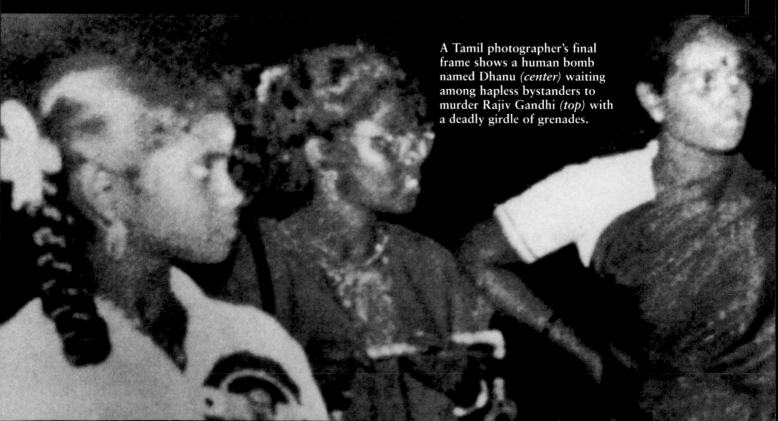

A Tamil photographer's final frame shows a human bomb named Dhanu (center) waiting among hapless bystanders to murder Rajiv Gandhi (top) with a deadly girdle of grenades.

I *don't think there's anything sinister about someone being a loner.*

JAMES EARL RAY

4

Death in Memphis

Perched on a bluff between the Missouri River and the southeast corner of Jefferson City's central business district, the maximum-security state prison was 47 acres of regimented misery. Its 2,000 inmates were held in grim limestone buildings meant to house half that number. Sixteen guard towers studded its 23-foot-high stone walls, which dominated the city's skyline, dwarfing even the state capitol seven blocks away. Jeff City, as the prison was called, was hard time epitomized. Although seven prisoners died rioting for better conditions in 1954, the Missouri prison remained one of the worst in the country. Men were crammed seven to a 9-by-12-foot cell and bitterly segregated—the whites from the blacks, the homosexuals from the rest. Many convicts belonged to racially exclusive gangs within the prison population and armed themselves with shanks, razor-sharp knives fashioned from scraps of metal. Violence, gambling, and illicit drugs were all easy to find within those walls, but so was a kind of security. Only about seven men a year tried to run. Most just wanted to serve out their time and be done with it.

But not inmate number 00416J. He wanted out. "For a lot of prisoners," he would write later, "the idea of trying to escape is frightening, and they want nothing to do with it. For others, the outside wall is a challenge they can't resist. It isn't a matter of heroism or bravery—they don't have a choice. They have to try."

Number 00416J had tried three times. One attempt had landed him in solitary confinement—what prisoners called segregation, or the hole. The last had put him in a psychiatric ward. Rejoining the general prison population, he'd gone to work on another kind of escape and had managed to secure a hearing, now just four days away, asking for a new trial on the robbery charge that had won him 20 years in Jeff City. Despite that prospect, however, the challenge of the outside wall still drew him. On this quiet Sunday morning, April 23, 1967, James Earl Ray was making his fourth attempt to leave.

Ray worked in the Jeff City bakery, which supplied bread for the main prison and for the prison honor farm on the far side of the Missouri River. Every morning, the farm's truck called at the prison bakery for its daily order. But on this morning the truck took away more than loaves: Ray lay concealed in one of the bread boxes, a wooden container four feet long, three feet wide, and three feet deep. The prisoner was fit and slender, and easily folded his five feet ten inches into one of the boxes, which he'd perforated with air holes. He pulled a false floor of heavy cardboard into place over himself, then a friend in the bakery arranged about 60 loaves over the cardboard and put on the box lid.

To leave the prison grounds, the truck had to pass through a tunnel exit, where gates in front of the vehicle and behind it were sealed until the cargo was inspected for contraband and stowaways. The guard glanced at the bakery boxes but saw nothing amiss and signaled the driver to move on. As the truck rumbled out onto westbound Capitol Avenue, past the railroad depot, the governor's mansion, and the capitol, Ray strained upward, trying to raise the box lid; at last it gave way and breadcrumbs showered over him as he pushed through the cardboard and crushed loaves.

The prisoner had stashed 20 candy bars, a razor, a comb, and soap in his pockets, along with a small transistor radio that had his Jeff City number etched on it. He had about $300 hidden in his shoes and, stuffed in his shirt, a pair of black pants purchased from a member of the prison band. His other major asset was a Social Security number that had once belonged to someone else. To add some slack to his escape, he'd arranged with his bakery accomplice to create a false trail. The man would let slip to a known informant that Ray was hiding somewhere inside the prison. It would be hours before the guards realized that he must be outside.

Ray pulled on the black civilian pants, but he was too late to bail out at a traffic light downtown. The truck was already crossing the Missouri River Bridge. When it paused before turning off on a gravel road that led to the prison farm, the convict jumped out, crossed the highway, and hurried into the mosaic of open farmlands and forests of the midwestern countryside.

This was more than freedom. This was a new life. A third of his 39 years had been spent behind bars in four different prisons. His criminal career so far had been a string of petty, bungled thefts, most of them followed by futile attempts to allude capture—memorably inept chases ending in his arrest. He would later say that the biggest goal in his life on this day of freedom was to break out of the country of his birth, where the best he could expect was a chance to finish the 13 years remaining in Jefferson City State Penitentiary, plus a few years' penalty for escaping. He dreamed, he would write, of a life of ease and anonymity in a country that would not extradite him and would let him work.

But the world Ray reentered in 1967 was quite different from the one he'd left when he walked into Jeff City in May 1960. He found himself in the midst of a turbulent decade of Vietnam War protest, a sexual revolution, and rising demands by women and minorities for equal rights. The country was gripped by increasing racial violence and polarization. Some black leaders, including one who called himself Malcolm X *(page 148)*, espoused violent revolt as a solution to the problem of inequality. And from 1965 to 1967, more than 100 American cities erupted in racial disturbances, starting with Watts, a poor black neighborhood of Los Angeles, where six days of rioting took 35 lives.

Another black leader, Martin Luther King Jr., a Baptist minister from Atlanta, had galvanized the nation with his campaign of nonviolent civil disobedience, boycotts, voter-registration drives, and heady oratory. He'd received the 1964 Nobel Peace Prize for his extraordinary efforts. But since that watershed, King had begun to lose momentum to those urging black militancy and separatism. He broadened his appeal by embracing the poor of every race and by turning his attention to protesting the Vietnam War.

On April 4, 1967, not three weeks before James Earl Ray's escape from prison, King had eloquently expressed his antiwar views to the congregation of New York's Riverside Church. He called for an immediate end to hostilities and decried the squandering of billions of dollars that could be used at home to help the poor—whose ranks had contributed more than its fair share to the fighting. Ten days later, King helped lead a massive antiwar demonstration at the United Nations headquarters. To his many followers, the minister's voice had the ring of a messiah's; to others, he was a black agitator, a Communist, an enemy of the people—in FBI director J. Edgar Hoover's words, "the most dangerous man in the United States."

What James Earl Ray thought about all this is unknowable. Some observers have made a case for his acute awareness of current events and for a profound racism drawn from his own roots. But one can argue with equal strength that such things lay outside Ray's experience—out of earshot, so to speak. He'd largely missed the 1960s.

Yet in breaking out of prison on that April Sunday in 1967, Ray embarked on a strange, year-long odyssey that would bring him to a seedy rooming house in Memphis, Tennessee, and to the moment and place where an assassin's bullet would silence Martin Luther King. Some believe Ray always knew where he was going; he insists that he did not.

James Earl Ray's history suggests that he had rarely known where the currents of life would next deposit him—he spent much of his time drifting from place to place, foraging for food and money and paying for it with time in jail. Born on March 10, 1928, in Alton, Illinois, a little steel-mill town 20 miles north of St. Louis, James was the first of Lucille and George Ray's nine children. The family was desperately poor, and the father, who also occasionally used the surnames Rayns, Raines, or Ryan, was arrested for forgery when little Jimmy was six. Although the charges were later dropped, George Ray thought it best to leave town. He moved the family to Ewing, Missouri, to a rundown 63-acre farm owned by his mother-in-law and to a life of grinding poverty.

In 1934 Ewing was a hamlet bounded by ruined farms. Only two of its houses were lighted by electricity and had flush toilets; there was no nice part of town. In Ewing, everyone was poor. But the Rays—Rayns, as they called themselves there—were the poorest of all, pitied and shunned as "white trash" by their neighbors.

Born into poverty on March 10, 1928, in the cellar of this Alton, Illinois home *(inset)*, Ray moved with his family in 1934 to Ewing, Missouri, epitomized by this lonely railroad whistle-stop *(above)*.

There is nothing to indicate that the Rays hated blacks any more or less than did any other poor whites in rural Missouri. During the Depression, everyone's efforts were dedicated to getting by. George Ray eked out a living by hauling farm goods and livestock in an ancient truck and puttering around his farm, which he lacked the energy to cultivate seriously. His wife, called Ceal, tended a garden and chickens and bore child after child.

The Rays waged a desultory, losing battle against their poverty. Then, in 1938, when Jimmy was 10, tragedy struck. His little sister Marjorie, playing with matches, set fire to her clothes and hair, and later died from her burns. After that the mother turned more and more to alcohol for solace; despair hardened around the parents. By 1940 they were pulling up the floorboards of their ramshackle farmhouse for firewood.

Jimmy Ray dutifully pursued his schooling for a time. A ragged, unwashed little boy who sometimes smelled of urine, he was well-intended but very quiet and alone. One heartless teacher, filling in his report card, recorded his appearance as "repulsive." He failed the first grade for missing school a fourth of the time, and as the years went on, his attendance didn't improve much. It wasn't that he was unintelligent; his IQ tested at 108, a solid, average score. In one teacher's estimate, "he had the power between his ears to make it to college." But his family's threadbare existence made him a virtual outcast. Now and then he would rally and his grades would rise. He liked history and his only recorded offense against the rules came in the sixth grade, when he stole the class lunch money. His teacher chased him for blocks on foot, and his mother later returned most of the money—$1.50—still in the box in which the teacher had collected it. It was not, by any means, the teacher recalled, the worst offense of the boys under her charge.

Although fond of his idle and sometimes cowardly father, Jimmy looked for excitement to his Uncle Earl, who seemed game for anything, fearless, and as tough as the part of Quincy, Illinois, he lived in. Earl Ray was in and out of jail for various offenses, including rape and receiving stolen goods; later he would do time for slinging carbolic acid into his estranged wife's face. Hitchhiking the 20 miles to Quincy, Jimmy often visited his uncle when Earl was on the outside, and the young teenager learned to feel at home in dives, flophouses, and brothels in the rough parts of town near the docks. All his life, Ray would gravitate to squalor, whether in Los Angeles, Montreal, St. Louis, or Memphis; he seems to have been comfortable nowhere else.

The decade the Ray family spent in Ewing degraded and depressed them, but it also bound the children and their mother solidly together—to the exclusion of outsiders. The Rays did not have many friends, brother John Larry observed later, "but we don't want none. Having friends is the quickest way of winding up on the end of a rope." James Earl, the brightest, quickest, and most adaptable of the children, was invested with all the family's hopes for something better.

By the early 1940s the grip of the Depression had been broken by a wartime boom, and George Ray bestirred himself to take advantage of it. In the spring of 1944, he found a job as a switcher on the railroad in Galesburg, Illinois, and moved his family across the Mississippi to Quincy—all, that is, but Jimmy.

Young James went instead to live with Mom Maher, his maternal grandmother, who ran a cheap boardinghouse back in Alton. He'd turned 16 that spring and had dropped out of the eighth grade. He found a job in the leather-dyeing room at the International Shoe Company tannery just south of Alton in East Hartford, Illinois. As he would everywhere he ever worked, Ray showed himself to be neat, quiet, and punctual. His grandmother recalled that he "never went out, never runned around." He was, she said, "bashful with girls. No pals of men, either. Just stayed home. Always comes in with a smile on his face. He's quiet and easy." He lived frugally, saving some $1,000 in a year and a half. On visits home, he warned his brothers John and Jerry not to steal: "Stay out of trouble. It's easier working." But he'd already become a small-time thief himself—newspapers in Ewing, minor pilferings with a pal in Alton. And with the war ending, it became harder to stay employed. International Shoe's government contracts dried up, and Ray was laid off in December 1945.

Two months later, in February 1946, Ray joined the Army for a three-year hitch. After basic infantry training at Camp Crowder, Missouri, he was sent to Bamberg, West Germany, and then to a motor pool near Nuremberg, where he learned to drive. Assigned as a Jeep driv-

Characteristically obscure, little James Ray *(circled)* hides behind a classmate in his third-grade picture in Ewing.
Although of average intelligence, Ray performed poorly at school, where the impoverished boy's soiled,
raggedy appearance drew pitying scorn from teachers.

er ferrying guards to and from their posts, he stayed out of trouble and sent money home. That December, Ray was transferred to guard duty with the 382nd Military Police Battalion in Bremen, a northern city that Allied bombs had transformed into a wasteland. This ruined underworld of vice and black marketeering may have whetted his evolving appetite for petty crime, and he is rumored to have dabbled in the black market there.

As East-West tensions intensified during 1947, Private First Class Ray was moved into the newly created 18th Infantry Regiment, First Infantry Division, headquartered near Frankfurt. The summer of 1948, Ray recalled, was spent maneuvering near Grafenau, near the Czech border. By autumn, the 18th was back in garrison near Nuremberg, and its soldiers were pulling guard details. "One day when I was supposed to be on guard duty," he wrote in his autobiography, *Who Killed Martin Luther King?*, "I got sick and missed my shift. This got me confined to quarters pending an investigation. Instead of lying low, I hitchhiked into Nuremberg. While there, a sweep by the MPs caught me and several other soldiers who were where they weren't supposed to be."

Ray was fined $45 and sentenced to three months' hard labor. His enlistment was nearly up, however, and instead of serving out his sentence, Ray was discharged under honorable conditions, though his service record pointed to his poor adaptation to Army life.

After mustering out at Camp Kilmer, New Jersey, Ray returned to the squalid riverside district of Quincy, Illinois, where his family

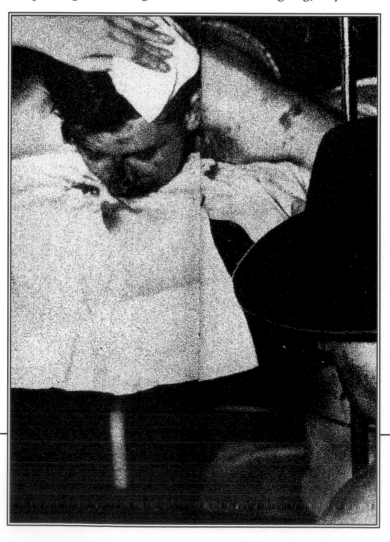

Run to earth by Chicago police after an inept cab robbery in 1952, Ray is treated for cuts and bruises from the chase.

was in a bad way, with Lucille drinking and George out of work. The Rays found their easygoing Jimmy a changed and bitter man—he would always resent the Army's treatment of him. With his mustering out pay, he took a TV-repair course and bought a car—a late-model Mercury—which brought him his first recorded brush with the law, a ticket for reckless driving.

Apparently determined to live clean, Ray headed north for Chicago and found a job at a rubber factory. When, after four months, he was laid off and his car repossessed, his commitment to being a solid citizen began to slide. "When I got out of the Army," he told an interviewer in 1993, "I didn't have too much self-discipline. See, I used to have a lot of discipline when I was young, because I used to work and all that stuff. But in the Army, you know, you come out and you don't have as much responsibility, or something." In a restless search for a warmer climate and perhaps a better fix on where his life was going, Ray took off for Los Angeles in late September 1949, riding the rails hobo-style to get there. Within weeks he was caught trying to steal from a cafeteria in a poor part of town.

That first bungled break-in was to set the pattern for most of Ray's criminal career. He was surprised in the cafeteria's office, hiding behind the safe; he'd already set the office typewriter out on the fire escape. The assistant manager grabbed him, and Ray pulled free and fled, but in the struggle he dropped his Army discharge papers and a savings-account passbook from a bank back home. Four days later, in a freak coincidence, the same assistant manager spotted Ray coming out of a local bank and called the police. Ray claimed he'd just wandered into the cafeteria office by accident, offering the feeble explanation, "I guess I had some beers, or something."

Ray gave officials as little information as he could about himself and his family, saying his father had died in 1946 and that his only living relatives were his mother and an uncle working in construction on the Pacific island of Guam; as a matter of fact, he improvised, the uncle was meeting him in Los Angeles to arrange a job on Guam for him, too. Convicted of second-degree burglary, Ray was sentenced to 90 days in the county jail. He was released two weeks early for good behavior, on condition that he get a job or get out of town.

On the move again in March 1950, Ray bounced from train to train, inching his way back toward the Mississippi by way of Nevada, Arizona, and Cedar Rapids, Iowa, where he was locked up for vagrancy. By May he'd reached Chicago, found a $1.10-an-hour factory job with the Neo Products Company, and bought a 1949 Buick. Two months later, he changed jobs, moving to the Arvey Corporation, an envelope manufacturer. Hoping finally to realize the promise his family had always thought he showed, Ray enrolled in night classes and worked toward his high-school diploma. He also had a girlfriend, someone he'd met at school. "I generally stayed inside the law in Chicago," Ray later wrote.

Just over a year after his arrival in the city, in June 1951, Ray abruptly resigned from Arvey and was soon back in his old haunts along the Mississippi, in Quincy and Alton. The Alton police appear to have marked Ray as a troublemaker, for they began to lean on him for minor infractions—vagrancy, license-plate violations, anything they could think of.

As for the Ray family, life had never been worse. The parents worked only intermittently in the kitchen at Quincy's Lincoln-Douglas Hotel, and the two oldest brothers, John Larry and Jerry, had been convicted on burglary charges and packed off to reformatories. The house, according to probation officers' reports, was "a terrible mess. The mother, Lucille, was drunk all the time. The house was littered with garbage. There was nothing to eat. The closets were full of empty wine bottles." As for the three children living at home, they "were infested with lice. They ran wild in the streets.

They urinated out the windows and shouted obscenities at people who were passing by." In August Ceal bore her ninth and final child.

By then, James, evidently repelled by the mess at home, had returned to Chicago and had found a laborer's job. But when a friend suggested that they rob a clandestine bookmaker, Ray readily joined in—it seemed hardly a crime, to rob people who were engaged in illegal activities.

According to Ray's account, the robbery went off with the backfiring ineptitude of a Keystone Kops chase. He would drive a getaway car while his partner did the actual robbing. To confound pursuers, Ray parked his Buick some blocks away from the target, then tried to commandeer a cab. But when he pointed his .38 revolver at the driver's head and ordered him to hand over the keys, the man flipped them out the car door; when Ray didn't pull the trigger, the man got out and ran. So did Ray, pursued by a fleet-footed bystander. "When I passed my Buick," he commented wryly, "my partner took off in the opposite direction." As police joined the chase, Ray was herded into a blind alley and grazed by a bullet after he jumped through a basement window. He drew one to two years and was sent first to the Illinois State Prison at Joliet, then on to the medium-security honor farm at Pontiac, where he served 22 months.

Free again in March of 1954, Ray returned to Alton, where his family had all but disintegrated. His father had abandoned his mother and Ceal had become a hopeless, derelict alcoholic. Ray moved back in with his grandmother Maher, got a job pumping gas, and drifted back to petty crime, with his usual comic ineptitude.

On a rainy night in August, an East Alton police officer on routine patrol and a private security guard noticed a broken windowpane at a dry-cleaning store. They disabled what looked like a getaway car in the alley and called the shop's owner to let them into the establishment. As one recalled it, "We went inside, then over to the pressing room, where the window was open. I couldn't believe my eyes. I saw this guy at the window. He was outside and coming back in!" The officer shouted, and the intruder dropped back into the rain, out of sight. Outside, the police found the burglar gone but his shoes stuck fast in the mud. They gave chase through glass-littered alleys, but the burglar eluded them in the darkness and heavy rain. They were left with his shoes, the car, and a driver's license he'd dropped inside that bore the name James Earl Ray. At dawn, Alton police found the suspect limping into town, soaking wet, his stockinged feet cut and bleeding. The take was $28.

Out on bond, Ray ran into a hometown friend, Walter Rife—a convicted forger, thief, and sometime pimp. Rife, according to Ray, had an idea involving U.S. Post Office money orders. On March 7, 1955, someone—presumably Rife, although he was never charged in the crime—had burgled the tiny post office at Kellerville, Illinois, for 66 blank money orders and the validating stamp that made them negotiable. Ray and Rife now embarked on a rambling spree through Kansas, Arkansas, Florida, and back to Missouri, cashing the money orders in clothing stores, art galleries, music stores—anywhere that would have them.

Postal authorities followed the resulting trail of serial numbers with ease. In 16 days the carefree duo cashed 32 of the stolen money orders before their arrest on the road back to Quincy. Recalling their short-lived joyride, Rife would later call Ray "just a country boy who didn't know how to act." When they took their ease in a bar, Ray "didn't know how to act around girls. He wouldn't dance. Couldn't dance. Didn't know what to say or do." And, perhaps Rife's biggest complaint, "He was a lousy forger. He'd walk into a store and just look guilty. He was heat personified."

Ray and Rife were both sentenced to the federal penitentiary in Leavenworth, Kansas, where, according to Rife, "they separate the men from the boys. It's a tough place, full of big-time people. A lot of people get murdered in Leavenworth." But James Earl Ray knew how to keep a low profile and do his time. "I saw him every day in the yard," recalled one fellow prisoner. "He never volunteered anything. He had to know you real well before he talked to you." On those terms, doing "his own time," with never a visitor from the outside, Ray served 33 months of his 45-month sentence at Leavenworth, again winning early release for good behavior.

Free again in April of 1958, he went to St. Louis, where his grandmother Maher now ran a shabby rooming house that served as a gathering place for the rest of the family, when they were at liberty. He worked part-time as a painter, but work, as it always seemed to do, fell off, and Ray looked to crime once more, earning his way as a Sunday bootlegger for the denizens of skid row.

Just before Christmas, according to his own account, Ray robbed a craps game in Madison, Illinois, then followed the big river south to New Orleans, hoping to get merchant seaman's papers and a berth that would take him out of the country. When that idea collapsed, he drove west around the curve of the Gulf coast into Mexico, and south to Veracruz, where he also found it impossible to get a berth without papers. Things were no better in the Pacific port of Acapulco. By February 1959 Ray was back in St. Louis and bootlegging again. When police began looking for him as a suspect in a grocery store robbery he claimed was not his, Ray fled to Montreal, laying low in that city's St. Catherine district.

Back in St. Louis by summer, Ray began frequenting Preacher Jim's skid-row mission, where he got to know an ex-con named Joseph Elmer Austin. Austin was a hard case, fresh from 33 years in prison, who, with an accomplice, had killed a man during an armed robbery. Austin and Ray teamed up in July to rob a Kroger's supermarket of about $1,200 and drove away in a stolen car with stolen license plates. A store camera made a clear portrait of Austin's scowling face. Mission workers identified Austin from the picture and recalled that his recent companion had been Ray, whom store personnel then recognized from police mug shots. The bandits eluded police efforts to find them but struck again in August, this time at an IGA grocery store in Alton, netting $2,200—another $15,000 lay untouched in the safe.

Their attempted getaway led police on a wild and peculiar car chase. As pursuing cruisers hurried toward a bridge leading over the Mississippi toward Missouri, they were astonished to see the getaway car hurtling back toward them and into Alton. Moments later the car went out of control and crashed into a garage and then a tree. Two men jumped out and ran into a dense thicket; when Austin sauntered out of the woods, he was arrested, and went back to prison for parole violation. Ray remained at large.

Two months later, with a new accomplice named James Owen, Ray robbed another Kroger's supermarket, this one in St. Louis. The operation netted $120, while an $18,000 payroll reposed in the safe. Ray, at the

Ray *(right)* and an accomplice are unwittingly photographed by a security camera as they rob a St. Louis Kroger's supermarket of $1,200 in 1959. The partner was caught a month after the heist, but Ray remained at large for three months before police arrested him.

wheel of the getaway car, craftily drove to a second car, where the men split up. But a witness had followed them and police soon had the tag numbers of both vehicles. Fifteen minutes later, they spotted one of the cars outside a cheap rooming house; there they arrested the accomplice and, after a tussle and some gunfire, Ray himself. In his room they found two loaded pistols. Ray had moved up in the world; the petty burglar had become an armed robber.

The morning of his trial, December 15, 1959, Ray made a clumsy effort to escape, assaulting an elderly deputy sheriff who came to his cell to escort him to the courtroom. The attempt failed, and Ray had a jury trial—his first—in which he conducted his own defense. He apparently had no firm grasp of the legal process. He had already signed a confession in which he admitted planning the St. Louis robbery; now, by taking the stand himself, he opened the way for the prosecutor to introduce his previous criminal record. In his testimony, as one lawyer present recalled it, "He didn't make a lot of sense. He rambled and got kind of wild."

Ray testified that he thought his "constitutional rights was violated," when the arresting officer had come rushing up the stairs to get him. "They didn't know who they was after—everybody shooting and grabbing me and they didn't know if I was paying for the room or anything." He even volunteered the damaging information that someone had allegedly tried to bribe the arresting officer, offering him $200 to forget about the two loaded guns he had found in Ray's room. "Now I deny the charge that anyone offered him any money," Ray inelegantly replied, "due to the fact I don't think any of my relatives has $200. I know none of my friends has, and I haven't." The jury reached a guilty verdict in only 20 minutes. Under Missouri's stiff habitual-criminal law, the judge sentenced him to 20 years in the state penitentiary. James Earl Ray arrived at the maximum-security prison at Jefferson City on March 17, 1960, a week after his 32nd birthday.

Jeff City wasn't much of a change for Ray. "In many ways prison life is like life on the outside," he wrote. "You have a place to live, a place to eat, a job to do, rules to follow and people you have to get along with." In Ray's view, the difference was in the high cost of breaking the rules. "If a prisoner cheats a guard or an administrator, the price could be a stint in the hole, as solitary confinement is called. If the prisoner cheats another prisoner, the price could be his life." He easily settled back into prison routine. He occupied himself in his spare time by lifting weights to keep in shape and reading voluminously. Although Ray enjoyed detective and spy novels, he also studied self-improvement books and medical texts; he soon began using terms like tachycardia for erratic heartbeat, intracranial tension for headache, and solar plexus for stomach in discussing himself with prison medics.

Beyond the gray walls, the 1960s unfolded without really touching the lives of those within. "It's hard for people to believe," Ray pointed out in 1993, "but when I was in Missouri we had very little communications with the outside. The only communications we had in there was a radio. They had one station on the Mutual Network. Occasionally there would be newspapers. I think sometime after I was there for awhile I started getting newspapers. Then about a year before I escaped they started selling small transistor radios. And that's the only communications I had. But I really wasn't too concerned. I was always into trying to escape, things like that. And I wasn't concerned about what was going on outside. The Vietnam War and all that stuff didn't interest me at all." The days and years went by indistinguishably for the prisoners.

The degree of Ray's participation in the underground prison government and economy remains unclear. Some believe Ray had evolved into a skilled prison merchant, deftly manipulating guards to supply cash—prisoners were only permitted scrip—and drugs that could be sold at an enormous profit inside. On the other hand, Ray's record had been one of lying low, going along, being, as one fellow inmate later described him, "concrete"—unshakably silent about himself and the activities of his comrades.

As a prisoner, Ray had always studiously avoided trouble and may very well have kept it at a distance in Jeff City, where officials regarded him—later, ominously—as a loner. Ray discounted this. "I think you're better off if you are a loner," he told one reporter. "I don't think there's anything sinister about someone being a loner. I'd much rather do something where I don't have

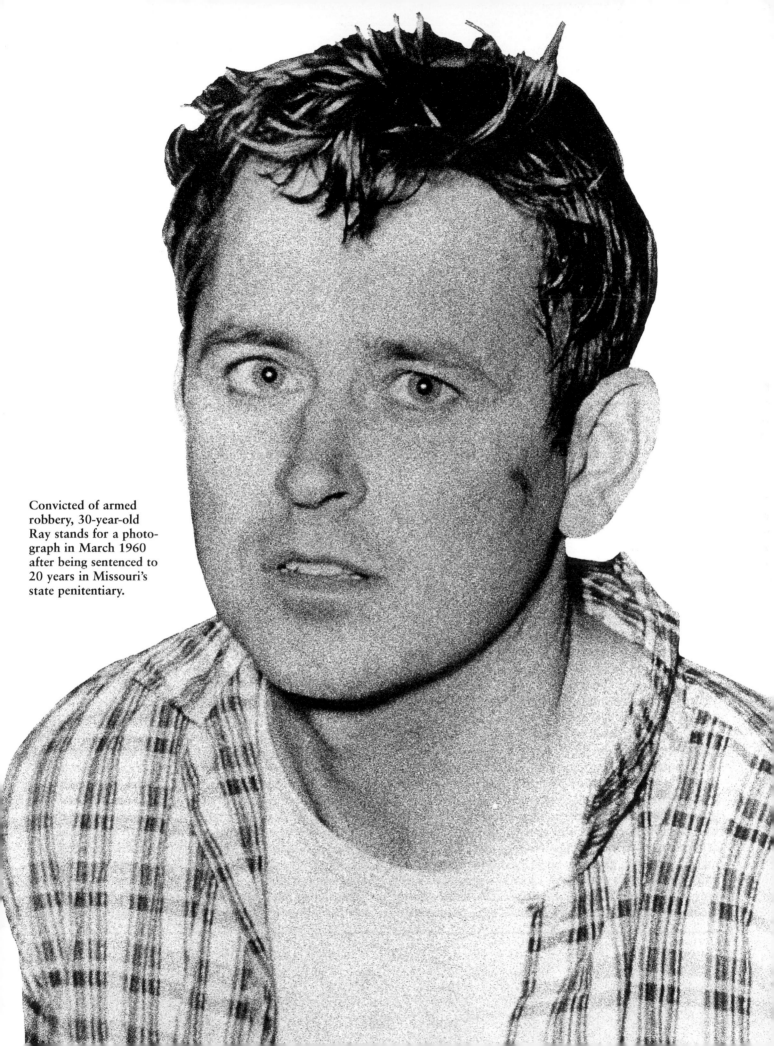

Convicted of armed robbery, 30-year-old Ray stands for a photograph in March 1960 after being sentenced to 20 years in Missouri's state penitentiary.

I was more concerned about escaping and food and things like that than I was about racism.

to worry about later on someone testifying against me in court." In fact, he pointed out, he'd had accomplices in the crimes that had landed him in Jeff City and accomplices inside who'd helped him get out.

Still, as Ray himself has attested, he itched to be always active, and his entrepreneurial instincts were strong. One former Jeff City inmate has said he worked for Ray in a book-lending enterprise. "He had about three hundred books in his cell," the man recalled. "One pack of cigarettes would get two books for one week. There was about five cartons a month in it for me." Cigarettes being one form of legal tender inside a prison, a man who at 16 could save more than $1,000 from 18 months' tannery wages would be able to trade his way to a considerable nest egg in seven years.

Ray's racial attitudes in those days have been the focus of considerable study and speculation, as historians have tried to improve the fit between a nonviolent petty thief and the assassin of a black civil-rights leader. Some anecdotes turned out to be apocryphal. For example, Ray, watching Martin Luther King Jr., on television, reportedly snarled that "somebody should kill that nigger"; but at the time Jeff City's inmates had no television beyond a sports screen set up in the exercise area. Further evidence of rabid racism has been found in his declining a transfer to the honor farm because he didn't want to live in an integrated dormitory.

"I agreed to go out," Ray said in a 1993 interview, "until I found out that there was marijuana out there. At that time blacks were using this marijuana and whites, they were hooked on what you call moonshine, homemade liquor. If you got caught with marijuana, at that time, you entered a guilty plea and you'd get two years. If you went to trial, you got 10 years." He noted that his prison job was in the night bakery, where the work force was racially diverse. "I was more concerned about escaping and food and things like that than I was about racism." In fact, growing up in primarily white towns and serving in an Army still racially segregated, Ray's only close contact with African Americans likely came at the integrated prison farm in Pontiac, a decade earlier.

As he has said many times, escape was Ray's real preoccupation in Jeff City. He trained constantly, preparing himself for life on the run. He scrutinized the prison routines around him, watching for opportunities, and he lay on his bunk and schemed. He made his first attempt to break out when he had been in for 20 months. He built a ramshackle ladder from lengths of wood that he'd hoarded secretly in the dry-cleaning plant. Held together with string, the shaky structure collapsed and fell on him, producing some jagged cuts; that effort apparently went undetected.

Hours later, Ray had another ladder, fashioned from wood and threaded pipes that could be screwed together. This time, he wrote later, he made it nearly to the top before the ladder gave way. For that attempt Ray drew six months of solitary confinement in a narrow room with nothing but a straw mattress and a blanket, and a square meal every third day.

Nearly five years passed before Ray tried again. One night in 1965, while the other prisoners watched the week's outdoor movie, he shinnied up a pole, climbed out a window 12 feet from the floor, and hid for 27 hours inside a ventilator hut on the roof of the building while guards searched for him. After that caper, Ray was charged with trying to escape, and when his attorney asked why he did these things, Ray asked for a mental examination—perhaps in hopes of building an insanity defense for the upcoming trial. But when he saw a fellow prisoner at the state mental hospital writhing in the throes of electroshock treatment, he thought better of it. In his 39-day stay at Missouri's State Hospital No. 1 at Fulton, authorities "just didn't find anything unusual," recalled hospital superintendent Donald B. Peterson. Examination uncovered "nothing in his mental makeup or background to indicate anything but a recidivistic criminal whose crimes were all associated with money." A report summed him up as "Sociopathic personality, antisocial type with anxiety and depressive features"— like most convicts.

Since Ray had never left the grounds, the charges against him at Jeff City were dropped. He remained inconspicuous; Warden Swenson even wrote him off as "innocuous." "If James Earl Ray had amounted to a hill of beans here," Swenson later said, "I would have a card on him in this pack of Big Shots and Bad Actors"—a bundle of three-by-five cards—"and Ray isn't in here." As of nine o'clock on the morning of April 23, 1967, Ray wasn't in Jeff City, either.

From the roadside near the Missouri State Honor Farm, where he'd leaped from the bakery truck, Ray cautiously made his way on foot and by train to Chicago, where his brother Jerry was then living. Once in the city, Ray lay low for a few days, then, on May 3, answered a newspaper advertisement for a dishwasher at the Indian Trail Restaurant in Winnetka, a northern suburb. His employers knew him as John Larry Rayns—an old alias of the brother who'd come to see him in Jeff City the day before his flight.

The fugitive worked at this pleasant, family-owned business for eight weeks, earning $813.66, before quitting abruptly, saying he had to "get back to the boats." Perhaps echoing an old desire to ship out, Ray had told them he was a merchant seaman. After he quit, his employers wrote him that they were sorry to see him go. Indeed, he was reluctant to leave, but he had the petty criminal's faith in the FBI and was worried that they would be able to track him down through his current Social Security number. Also, he later explained, he couldn't afford to stay in any one place too long, and he couldn't risk friendships.

Ray had taken the job—his last on the outside—apparently because he needed what he now called capital, and perhaps even more, he needed to stay out of trouble, living quietly under his brother's name among strangers. The only stir his employers recalled in connection with Ray was a man who came to visit and "three or four pressing calls" in the last week of his employment—possibly from his brothers.

Now he bought a seven-year-old Chrysler, paying $100 in cash to the owner. In addition to the car, the transaction gave him some valuable identification: the car title and a temporary driver's license, in the name of John L. Rayns. He drove as far as East St. Louis, Illinois, where the car broke down; he replaced it with a red Plymouth, bought from a dealer for $200. He spent two weeks visiting in East St. Louis and in his old town of Quincy, claiming to have "told my friends I was leaving the country and to tell my family. I didn't tell anybody which country I was going to. The last thing I did was get a new .38 pistol from a friend. But I didn't pay him for it then. I was just too short of capital."

Almost certainly Ray has withheld much about his activities in the St. Louis area during these days, to protect himself or his family and friends. He was an escaped convict, and anyone helping him—even by their silence—was guilty of aiding a fugitive. Ray may have made contact with local criminals he'd known before Jeff City, and a convenient place to meet these old pals would have been a downscale tavern in St. Louis called the Grapevine—named not just for the source of wine but for every prison's internal communication system. The Grapevine's liquor license was in the name of Ray's sister, Carol Ray Pepper, but the place really belonged to his brother John Larry, himself an ex-con. Some believe it was at the Grapevine that Ray learned of a $50,000 bounty reportedly placed on the head of Martin Luther King Jr. by St. Louis businessman John Kauffman and attorney John Sutherland.

Assassination conspiracists speculate that the St. Louis offer may have reached Ray's ears in the summer of 1967, after his escape, possibly through his brothers. Some believe he learned about it much earlier, while he was still an inmate at Jeff City—the bounty, in this theory, was part of his motive for escaping. In constructing such conspiracies, every common acquaintance that Ray shared with Kauffman and Sutherland becomes portentous—even the fact that they all knew someone whose wife tended bar at the Grapevine looms large. It may very well have been that the denizens of the seamy neighborhoods along this segment of the Mississippi River simply kept bumping into one another; one theorist's conspiracy is another's coincidence.

James Earl Ray has also been suspected of participating in a lucrative bank robbery in Alton, his hometown and the scene of some of his minor crimes. On July 13, 1967, two masked gunmen held up the Bank of Alton and got away with more than $22,000; the crime remains unsolved. Ray has steadfastly denied that he was one of those bandits, saying such a job was too risky, and he needed to keep his nose clean. But he was in the

Murder in Harlem

The man who called himself Malcolm X was a kind of mirror image of Martin Luther King Jr. Where King was a Christian, Malcolm was a Muslim. While King labored for full racial integration, Malcolm X urged separate equality. King espoused nonviolence as a path to racial integration; Malcolm urged blacks to take up arms against their oppressors. Curiously, both leaders shared the same fate: In a decade of inexorably rising violence, both were assassinated. Both were 39 when they died.

Malcolm X had come to his ministry from the ghettoes of Boston and New York, the son of the Reverend Earl Little, a preacher who followed the back-to-Africa teachings of black nationalist Marcus Garvey. Jailed at 21 for burglary, Malcolm underwent a religious conversion in prison, joining the Nation of Islam—the Black Muslims—which in the 1950s were becoming a powerful force for racial pride and discipline in African American communities. On his release in 1952, Malcolm went to Chicago and met the leader of the Nation of Islam, Elijah Muhammad, the former Elijah Poole of Georgia, who accepted him into the movement and named him Malcolm X. After training briefly in Chicago, Malcolm X established a mosque in Philadelphia; in 1954, the charismatic speaker, not yet 30, was sent to lead the movement in Harlem.

Not everyone welcomed Malcolm's rise to power— some saw him as a threat to Elijah Muhammad. As a beloved partner, he had learned the innermost secrets of his mentor, including some of dubious morality. The catalyst for division apparently came on December 1, 1963, soon after the assassination of President John Kennedy. When a questioner at a rally asked Malcolm's opinion of that killing, he replied, "Chickens coming home to roost never make me sad, they make me glad." Elijah Muhammad forbade Malcolm X to speak in public for 90 days. Within weeks, Malcolm had left the Black Muslim movement, and on March 8, 1964, he established two new organizations, The Muslim Mosque, Inc., and the Organization of Afro-American Unity, aimed at materially "solving the unending hurt that is being done daily to our people here in America." After a 1964 pilgrimage to Mecca, however, Malcolm seemed to have moderated his blanket condemnation of whites.

But his enemies hadn't forgotten his defection. On February 14, 1965, Malcolm X, his wife, and four daughters escaped unharmed after three gasoline bombs were thrown into the living room of their Queens apartment. The bombing could have been the work of Black Muslims, he acknowledged, or of the Ku Klux Klan, whom he'd just denounced in Selma, Alabama. "It doesn't frighten me," he said. "It doesn't quiet me down in any way or shut me up."

Only a week later, on February 21, Malcolm stood before some 400 people in Harlem's Audubon Ballroom. He had just arrived and had barely uttered the Arabic greeting, *As-salaam alaikum*—May peace be with you—when his assassins struck.

The five black men had come to New York that morning from Paterson, New Jersey, and had arrived early to take up their positions around the room. All were Muslims, but they belonged to the Newark mosque and were able to slip past Malcolm's security. Talmadge Hayer, a 22-year-old who'd grown up very much as Malcolm X had, poor and angrily oppressed in New Jersey, took a seat near the podium. He'd been recruited, he said later, by two fellow Muslims. As Malcolm's sins against Elijah Muhammad mounted, two other men were drawn into the conspiracy.

As Malcolm began to speak, one of the conspirators jumped up in the back of the room, yelling "Man, get your hands out of my pocket." With the crowd's interest momentarily diverted, another assassin stood up in the second row, opened his trench coat, leveled a shotgun at Malcolm, and fired; the swarm of shot struck him squarely—and fatally—in the chest. Then Talmadge Hayer pulled out his .45 automatic and a comrade brought out his 9-mm. Luger, and the pair blazed away at the fallen leader's body. Someone shot Hayer in the leg, and as he dragged himself toward the door, the crowd grabbed him; when they turned him over to police, his left leg was broken. His partners got away.

Within two weeks police had arrested Norman 3X Butler and Thomas 15X Johnson, both from the Bronx and both in the Black Muslim militia unit, the Fruit of Islam. Hayer, while denying membership in the group, confessed to the killing but claimed to have acted alone. He declared that Butler and Johnson were innocent—indeed, there was evidence that they were elsewhere at the time. But the jury thought otherwise. Found guilty of murder, all three men were sentenced to life in prison. In New York's penitentiaries, all adopted Muslim names: Talmadge Hayer became Mujahid Abdul Halim; Johnson, Khalil Islam; and Butler, Muhammad Abdul-Aziz.

When Elijah Muhammad died in early 1975, Hayer broke a 14-year silence. He recanted his 1965 confession and offered another: He and four Muslim brothers—Leon, Wilbur, Willie X, and Ben—had carried out the assassination because of their great love for their leader and their fear that Malcolm X might bring him down. As before, Hayer said that Johnson and Butler were innocent. And, as before, his confession carried little weight. The three men served almost 20 years of their life sentence before being released in the mid-1980s. No other arrests were made in the case.

TALMADGE HAYER   THOMAS 15X JOHNSON   NORMAN 3X BUTLER

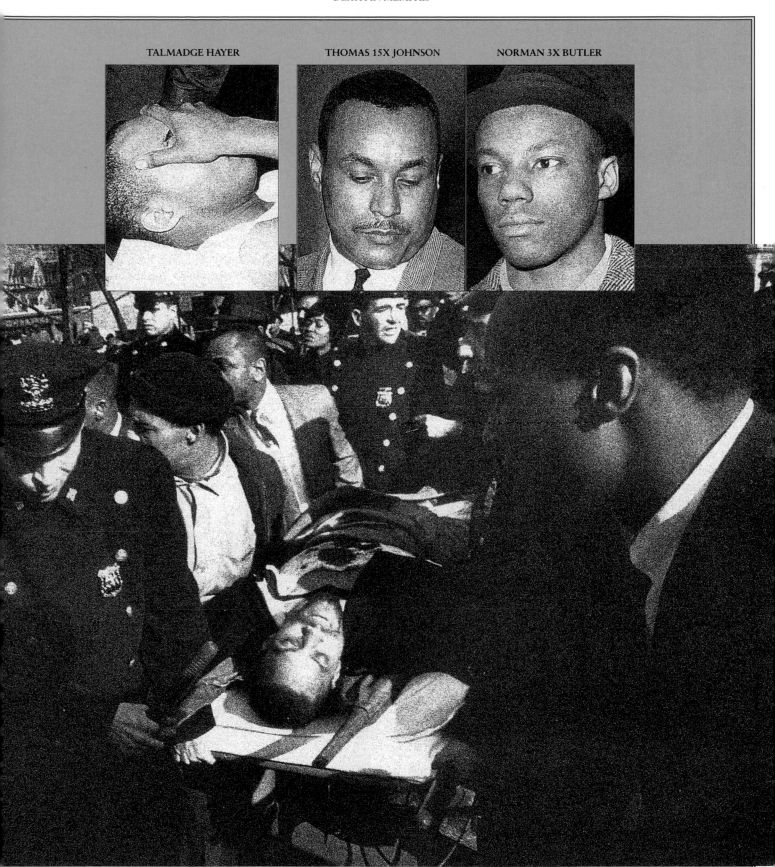

The bullet-riddled body of militant black leader Malcolm X is borne
from a Harlem hall on April 21, 1965. Tried and sentenced to
life imprisonment for the shooting were *(top, from left)* Talmadge
Hayer, Thomas 15X Johnson, and Norman 3X Butler.

area when the bank was robbed, and he had no alibi. Historians attempting to explain how Ray was able to move around the country for more than a year after his escape have pointed to this bank job as a possible answer: An $11,000 cut would have more than covered his expenses.

On July 15, two days after the bank was robbed, Ray left East St. Louis and spent that night in a motel in Indianapolis; the next day he drove to Detroit, crossed the border into Canada at Windsor, Ontario, and drove on to Montreal. Back in the St. Catherine district he had visited in 1959, he took a $75-a-month room at the Har-K apartments, signing a six-month lease in the name of Eric S. Galt. It was the first time he used this alias, which Ray said he had invented on the way to Montreal, after observing a highway exit sign for the town of Galt.

Again, conspiracists were drawn to his choice of aliases. Some said he'd borrowed it from the ultraconservative protagonist of an Ayn Rand book, *Atlas Shrugged.* Others pointed at yet another ominous coincidence: A Canadian citizen named Eric St. Vincent Galt, who resembled Ray, lived near Toronto. Some theorists have pointed to this as evidence that Ray was already receiving help from an organized conspiracy. They maintained that Ray couldn't have done the research to find this name in such a short time on the loose and that his randomly hitting on so useful an alias was unlikely without the help of others more adroit than he. Pressed on this point, Ray has always insisted he had no help in choosing the alias.

Ray's next goal was to replenish his dwindling capital, which he claimed to have accomplished by rob-

bing a prostitute and her pimp. Then he began serious work on getting the identification that would help him ship out of Montreal, Canada's busiest port, as a merchant seaman. He began frequenting the Neptune Tavern, a disreputable waterfront bar several blocks from his room, letting it be known that he'd gotten into some trouble back in the States and was looking for money and identification. According to his own account, he shadowed inebriated sailors who resembled him, hoping to roll one for his service papers and use the credentials to find a berth, but this scheme never worked out.

It was in the Neptune, Ray asserted, that he had his first contact with a shadowy, elusive man known to him only as Raoul, thirtyish and Latin or French Canadian. "He was about 5'8", weighed 140 pounds or so and had slightly wavy dark red hair that might have been the result of a dye job," Ray later wrote. He thought Raoul spoke with a Spanish accent. After some cautious exploratory talk over a beer, according to Ray, Raoul offered to get him money and a passport if Ray would help him with some "projects." Ray demurred, explaining that before he ventured into what sounded like contraband running, he wanted to try another ploy.

A travel agent had once told Ray that he could get a Canadian passport if a Canadian citizen who'd known him for two years would verify his citizenship. Thinking he could charm some woman into doing this for him, Ray bought a gentleman's wardrobe—including two suits—and no doubt for the first time in his life, he got himself a manicure. Then he headed for Greyrocks, a pleasant resort north of Montreal where he'd heard a lot of single women vacationed.

There, with a degree of charm he had never shown

Perhaps coincidentally, Ray adopted this Toronto man's name for an alias: Eric S. Galt.

Ray says he first met Raoul, his alleged handler, at this Montreal waterfront bar in 1967.

before, he struck up an intimate friendship with an attractive woman. He told her he was in business with his brother in Chicago. She agreed to meet him again when she got back home to Ottawa, the national capital. But when he looked her up in Ottawa, Ray learned that she worked for a government agency. He dropped the idea of asking her for help, figuring she would feel obliged to turn him over to the Mounties. Found and interviewed later, this woman told investigators she would not have helped.

Back in the Neptune Tavern, according to Ray, he and Raoul set up their first joint venture. On August 17, Ray said, they headed for the border in his battered red Plymouth, stopping in Windsor, Ontario, long enough for Raoul to hide three packages under the backseat. Raoul then took a taxi across the border. Ray, alone in his car, went through customs without incident, and in Detroit picked up Raoul, who retrieved and disposed of his packages. Then they went back to the Canadian side and repeated the whole operation.

This kind of relay was a favorite method for drug dealers using hired smugglers to carry heroin into the United States from Canada in those days. Ray claimed that Raoul paid him $1,500 for one day's services. According to Ray, Raoul then told him to head for Birmingham, Alabama; he was to stay out of trouble, get some new identification, and stand by for instructions on where they would next get together.

Few students of the Martin Luther King assassination believe that Raoul actually existed, and indeed, the mystery man often rings clangingly false in Ray's own descriptions of him. Some authorities concluded that Raoul was Ray's code word for everyone who worked with him in this interval, including his brothers, or perhaps his way of referring to himself—a kind of inner Ray. Others have maintained for decades that Raoul was real and still holds the key to a larger conspiracy that either hired Ray to murder King or framed him for the act.

James Earl Ray made for Chicago, arriving there on August 22, 1967. He gave his old Plymouth to his brother Jerry in payment for $100 borrowed earlier, then took the train south. He reached Birmingham on August 25 and checked into the Granada Hotel under his Galt alias. The next day he moved to the Economy Grill and Rooms. On August 28, according to Ray's memoir, Raoul met him at the nearby Starlite Cafe, and gave him $2,000 to buy a car. The following afternoon he bought a 1966 Ford Mustang painted Springtime Yellow—a pale hue that was almost white—spending more than he'd ever spent on a car before: $1,995, cash.

Lying low in a Los Angeles apartment *(below)* on Serrano Avenue, Ray still found time in December 1967 to visit New Orleans, where he stayed in the Provincial Motel *(left)* and, he has claimed, met with the shadowy Raoul.

In fact, Ray's description of himself in this interval has been that of a puppet animated by Raoul's strings. On his mentor's instructions, Ray got an Alabama driver's license in his Galt alias, opened a safe-deposit box in that name, and ordered movie-making equipment from a Chicago mail-order house, for reasons that remain murky. He claimed that Raoul wanted the stuff; some observers believed that Ray planned to go into the pornography business with his brothers. He also bought a Polaroid still camera and joined a Canadian lonely-hearts club, perhaps in another effort to locate a female pushover who would vouch for him as a Canadian citizen—he apparently still had a strong interest in leaving the United States.

On October 6 Ray gave up his Birmingham room and safe-deposit box and headed for New Orleans, where, he later explained, he had a telephone number for Raoul. Customs records show an Eric S. Galt crossing the border at Laredo, Texas, on October 7. Ray said that he was again teamed up with Raoul to transport a spare tire—a common smuggling container—into Mexico. According to Ray, Raoul paid him another $2,000 for taking the contraband across.

Ray spent five weeks in Mexico, much of it in the pretty Pacific village of Puerto Vallarta, which was just becoming well known as a resort. The inept, penny-pinching Ray of old appears to have vanished in Mexico, where he managed to have both girlfriends and fun, and where he might have remained, had he been able to present a legitimate set of credentials to the local authorities. But in November he turned the Mustang north toward Los Angeles, arriving there, he later claimed, on the 19th.

Under his Galt alias, Ray settled into apartment number 6 at 1535 North Serrano Avenue and became a regular at the Sultan Club, a bar in the run-down St. Francis Hotel three blocks away. And there, in the illusion capital of the world, he embarked on an intensive—and, for him, expensive—self-improvement program. He made five visits to a psychologist named Mark Freeman, in hopes of learning self-hypnosis, improving his memory, and gaining confidence. He attended two months of dance classes and ran a personal ad in a local newspaper: "SINGLE MALE. Cauc. 36 yrs. 5'11". 170 lbs. Digs Fr. cult. Desires discreet meeting with passionate married female for mutual enjoyment and/or female for swing sessions."

In the midst of this burst of activity, Ray made a quick trip back east. He'd become friendly with Marie Martin, one of the Sultan Club's cocktail waitresses, and had made the acquaintance of her cousin Charles Stein, a middle-aged hippie. Martin wanted Ray and Stein to bring Stein's two young nieces home from visiting in New Orleans. The two left on December 15 and drove Ray's Mustang day and night for two days; they stayed in separate motels when they reached New Orleans. December 17 and 18, Ray registered as Galt at a place far nicer than his usual flophouses—the Provincial Motel, on Chartres Street in the French Quarter.

On that trip, Stein commented later, Ray impressed him as a "cat on a mission." Ray has claimed that he met with Raoul in New Orleans but denied that he'd been "summoned" there; investigators concluded he must have been trying to sell some property that had been stolen in California. The pair, with Stein's nieces, were back in Los Angeles by December 21. Ray spent a Christmas he later described as "just another day and another night to go to a bar or sit in your room and look at the paper and drink a beer or two and maybe switch on the TV." Christmas, he said, "don't mean anything to a loner like me."

But Ray appears to have been looking for somewhere else to go. He wrote to the American Southern Africa Council, in Washington, D.C., to inquire how he might legally immigrate to what was then Rhodesia (now known as Zimbabwe). Some theorists have speculated that Rhodesia, which was cracking apart in a racial civil war, would have been attractive to Ray the arch-racist, and that, at least to his mind, the country might in fact have welcomed the assassin of a charismatic black American leader.

Ray discounted that in a 1993 interview. "When I got out of prison I was thinking about several countries," he said. "In fact, when I went to Chicago, the first country I wrote to, I wrote to the Canadian consulate, and they sent me some things about immigrating to Canada. But Canada is a little bit too close to the United States. I checked about going to Colombia, South America, and found out you didn't need no passport to get in there. But Colombia is a poor country and you need money.

And, of course, I'd already checked on Brazil. I checked on numerous countries. Primarily, I was interested in getting in an English-speaking country because I didn't have much money and if I wound up in some country where I couldn't speak the language it would be difficult to make a living. So I wanted to go to Australia or Rhodesia or somewhere like that." As for wanting to fight in race wars, he said, "I thought if I got in one of those countries like that, under the guise that I wanted to be a mercenary, once I got there I could hide in the bush or something and get out of there and try to get somewhere else."

After the new year, Ray moved into the St. Francis Hotel, the establishment that housed his hangout, the Sultan Club—the hotel manager later remembered him as shy, neat, and quite presentable in his dark suits. Continuing his self-improvement program, Ray visited another hypnotist and read three recommended books on mind-control. Still planning, he said, for expatriate life, he hit on bartending as the ideal occupation, since it would provide mobility and a good income. On January 19, 1968, he enrolled in a bartending school for a six-week course. The head of the school described him as "a nice fellow with a slight Southern accent, very intelligent, with ability to develop in this type of service." On March 2, graduation day, Ray was forced to put on a bow tie and pose for a photograph. In an apparent effort to mask his identity, he closed his eyes just as the shutter snapped.

Almost two weeks earlier, Ray had consulted a plastic surgeon, Dr. Russell Hadley, about getting rhinoplasty—a nose job. He wanted his face to be completely forgettable and different from all of his earlier mug shots, which showed a thin, sharply pointed nose, and his left ear protruding. He'd read that the nose and ears are a face's most distinctive features, and the easiest to alter. Taming that ear was to be his second operation, with a second surgeon. On March 5 he kept his appointment for "Reduction of Prominent Nasal Tip," a $200 office procedure. Back in his room at the St. Francis, Ray removed the bandage and manipulated his still-numb nose into a different shape than what the doctor had intended. He kept his appointments for post-op checkups on March 7 and 11, but did not keep the appointment that would have included a photograph recording his after-surgery appearance. A week later he left Los Angeles, designating General Delivery, Atlanta, Georgia, as his forwarding address.

Because James Earl Ray had no known ties to Atlanta, it seemed a curious choice, and assassination theorists were quick to point out that the Georgia metropolis was the home of Martin Luther King Jr.; the site of his Ebenezer Baptist Church; and the headquarters of his civil-rights organization, the Southern Christian Leadership Conference, or SCLC. By an odd coincidence, King was not in Atlanta as Ray prepared to set out on the road east—he was in Los Angeles. Speaking at the Second Baptist Church on Sunday, March 17, King said he had seen hatred become the "national malady," and he ended his talk by declaring, "Hate is too great a burden to bear. I can't hate." But others could.

Now the paths of James Earl Ray and Martin Luther King Jr. began to braid together. Ray has said it was all just coincidence or, perhaps, a by-product of his being framed. But most other observers viewed the coming together of these men as Ray's first steps in stalking the leader he intended to kill. Thus, as King flew east toward Memphis on March 18, Ray's not-quite-white Mustang pushed across the southwestern desert toward New Orleans, his first stop on the way to the Georgia capital. On March 20 King crossed into Mississippi, and then into Alabama, where his civil-rights movement had begun a dozen years before.

The next day Ray delivered a package in New Orleans for his friend Marie Martin, the waitress from the Sultan Club; he may also have transacted some business of his own. King spoke in Linden and Ca, Alabama, before flying on to Atlanta. The following night, March 22, Ray spent the night as Eric S. Galt in Selma, just 30 miles from Ca. It had been in Selma two years earlier that King had led one of his most famous civil-rights marches. Ray spent the night of March 23 in Birmingham, where he claimed to have picked up Raoul for the 160-mile drive to Atlanta. When they arrived on March 24, King was speaking in New York.

Ray checked into a shabby apartment house off Peachtree Boulevard, still using the Galt alias, and stayed there until March 28. He bought a map and marked four areas—simply to orient himself in a strange city, he would assert; one mark was on his apartment building. Two other marks were near King's home and his SCLC headquarters; a fourth indicated a parking lot in a public-housing development called Capitol Homes, a spot that would figure in Ray's flight from Memphis a week later.

In fact, as Ray reconnoitered in Atlanta on March 28, King was in that fateful Tennessee city, leading the striking, and mostly black, garbage workers of Memphis in a demonstration for the right to unionize. In a sense, that day sealed King's fate. The march spawned a flurry of peripheral vandalism and arson, and a brutal crackdown by police; for the first time, one of King's nonviolent demonstrations had spun out of control.

On March 29 Ray drove from Atlanta back to Birmingham and visited the Aero-Marine Supply Company.

There he bought a high-powered .243-caliber Remington Gamemaster rifle, plus a 7-power Redfield variable telescopic sight, which the salesman mounted on the rifle, and a box of 20 Norma hollow-point cartridges. Ray decided to make this purchase in Alabama, he later said, because he had a valid Alabama driver's license and other identification for his Galt alias. But he didn't use that alias for the rifle purchase. Showing no identification at all, he gave a phony Birmingham address and signed himself, for the first and only time, as Harvey Lowmeyer. This was apparently his misspelling of the name of Harvey Lohmeyer, a former prison mate of his brother John's.

Later that day, Ray called the store and said he wanted to exchange the rifle for something bigger; he said he was taking his brother's advice, and they would be hunt-

Blinking in an attempt to disguise his appearance, Ray *(far right)* displays his 1968 diploma from this Los Angeles bartending school.

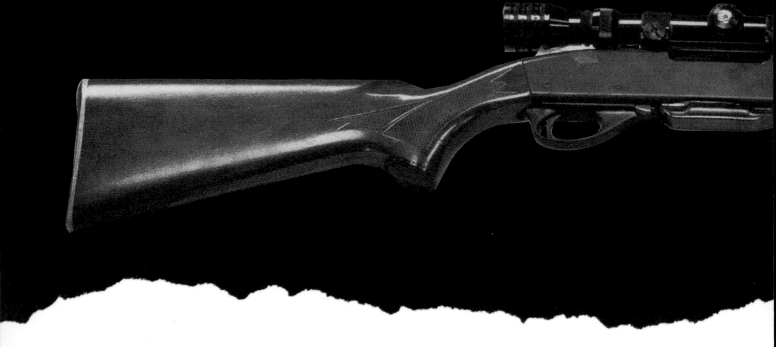

ing really big deer. Ray spent that night in Birmingham, and the next day exchanged his rifle for the same model in the larger 30.06 caliber and new bullets, twice as heavy as those he had bought the day before. The salesman remounted the telescopic sight on the new rifle and then, since the altered rifle no longer fit into its original carton, packed it into a Browning shotgun box.

Ray would tell authorities that Raoul had sent him back to make the exchange and that Raoul had said he needed the rifle to show to some prospective customers who wanted to order weapons in bulk. But no one has ever explained why, in a country where firearms are so readily available, Raoul's alleged clients would have bothered with an off-the-shelf deer rifle. The .243-caliber weapon, with a muzzle velocity half again that of the rifle used to kill John Kennedy, would have been more than adequate for an assassin.

According to Ray, on Raoul's instructions he drove north, but aimlessly, like someone killing time, taking an opportunity to try out the rifle in the countryside. By dusk on Saturday, March 30, he said, he'd advanced only about 150 miles, to Decatur, Alabama. The next day, Ray said, he drove another 50 miles or so to Florence, Alabama, and the next, April 1, he stopped at a motel in Corinth, Mississippi. On Tuesday, April 2, Ray claimed, he stopped at a motel just outside of Memphis, on the Mississippi side of the line. Raoul allegedly met him there, examined the rifle, and took it with him; Ray told investigators he never saw the weapon again. Later he indicated that Raoul didn't appear until the next day, in Memphis.

If his Atlanta landlord's memory was correct, however, Ray must have driven back from Birmingham to Atlanta after exchanging the rifles, because he paid another week's rent on Sunday, March 31. King, meanwhile, had returned to Atlanta on March 29, and then, on March 31, he'd spoken at the National Cathedral in Washington, D.C.—if Ray were stalking the minister, he lagged him by a day. The records of Atlanta's Piedmont Laundry indicated that Ray dropped off some dirty clothes on the morning of Monday, April 1. Later that day, King announced—no doubt with some misgivings—that he would be returning to Memphis on April 3 in order to march once more beside the striking garbagemen of that city.

Ray surfaced again on April 3, in Memphis, where he checked into the New Rebel Motel at 7:00 p.m., under the Galt alias. Martin Luther King Jr. and his entourage had arrived before noon and had moved into rooms at the Lorraine Motel, a black hostelry on Mulberry Street. King's room, on the second floor, was reached by iron outside stairs and a walkway that ran along the front of the building and served as a common balcony for all the second-floor rooms.

Incidents and threats of violence had been building steadily around King. The March 28 demonstration in Memphis had dissolved in disorder and looting; 60 people had been injured and one killed as police dispersed the crowd with night sticks, mace, and guns. King had been rushed to refuge in the local Holiday Inn. Now he felt impelled to return to Memphis, to lead another march, to prove that his cherished nonviolent ideals

could solve the problem, that those who disagreed with his methods could not destroy his movement for change.

King understood that he would have to depend on careful planning by his own organization to avoid a repetition of the earlier disturbances and that he could not count on help from any law-enforcement agency. To local police and the FBI, the apostle of nonviolence was a charismatic outside agitator importing trouble to Memphis. To them, he was the harbinger of a kind of racial anarchy and chaos, a dangerous man. On the morning of April 3 King's plane flight from Atlanta to Memphis had been delayed for more than an hour by a bomb threat against him.

"It was very difficult for him," recalled the Reverend Samuel Kyles, King's host in Memphis. "A lot of his support had backed off because of his stance against the war, and you have the young Turks who were saying now that nonviolence hasn't worked, it's not going to work. The media portrayed him as a buffoon, had him, after the march, sitting on top of a pile of garbage holding his nose." Worse, Kyles pointed out, the earlier disturbance in Memphis had infected King's plan for a mammoth poor-peoples' march on Washington that spring. The government, and FBI director J. Edgar Hoover in particular, Kyles said, wanted the second Memphis march to fail.

That evening at a rally, King gave his last public address, a rousing and prophetic speech in which he discussed the recent threats that had been made against his life. "Like anybody," he told the crowd, "I'd like to live a long life. Longevity has its place, but I'm not con-

cerned about that now. I just want to do God's will and He's allowed me to go up to the mountaintop. And I've looked over. And I've seen the Promised Land. So I'm happy tonight. I'm not worried about anything. I'm not fearing any man. 'Mine eyes have seen the glory of the coming of the Lord.' "

That same evening, April 3, Memphis television stations broadcast a news story on King's visit to Memphis, including footage of the minister standing on the balcony outside his room at the Lorraine Motel. Clearly visible behind him in the picture were his door and his room number, 306.

At 1 pm on April 4, James Earl Ray checked out of the New Rebel. At around three o'clock, giving his name as John Willard, he checked into a rooming house owned by Bessie Brewer, at 422½ South Main Street. The rooms Brewer offered him were on the second floor, above a jukebox-repair shop called Canipe Amusement Company, Cohen & Company Dry Goods, and a tavern, Jim's Grill. The newcomer took room 5B, on the second floor, toward the back of the building. Its narrow window overlooked a shrub-covered lot strewn with urban debris and, across Mulberry Street, the Lorraine Motel, which was just over 200 feet away; the door of King's room, 306, was visible from 5B, but it was partly obscured unless one leaned out of the window. An unobstructed view of the Lorraine's balcony could be had from the bathroom at the end of the hall. Through a 7-power Redfield telescopic sight, room 306 appeared to be only about 30 feet away.

At 4 p.m., half a mile from Bessie Brewer's rooming

house, Ray bought a pair of binoculars from the York Arms Company, paying $41.55. After 4:30, the other tenants on the second floor of the rooming house complained that someone was in the bathroom for a long time; the man next door to it told them it was the new guy in 5B.

At 6 p.m. King stepped onto the balcony outside his room. With him were fellow civil-rights activists Ralph Abernathy, Jesse Jackson, Andrew Young, and Samuel Kyles. "Martin was leaning over the railing, talking to Jesse," Kyles, a Memphis minister, recalled. "The last person in the world that he spoke to was Jesse Jackson. In the middle of their conversation I said, 'Hey, guys, come on, let's go.' And he was still talking to Jesse, leaning over. I got about five steps and heard this noise. I thought it was a car backfiring."

King suddenly stiffened as a single bullet tore into the right side of his jaw, fragmented on its way through his neck, and severed his spinal cord. The enormous energy of the projectile threw King against the wall of his room.

"By the time I looked back," said Kyles, "Martin had already fallen. His leg was laying through the railing. I was the first one to get to him. There was a crushed cigarette in his hand, because the tension had gotten so much—he wouldn't smoke publicly. I took the cigarette out of his hand." When, moments later, police ran into the courtyard, the men on the balcony raised their arms to point at what they took to be the source of the shot—the back of Bessie Brewer's boardinghouse.

Inside the house, several tenants heard a shot they thought came from the bathroom and said they saw a man walk out of the bathroom and down the hallway. Moments later, in front of the rooming house, a customer at Canipe Amusement Company reported seeing a white man drop a bundle in the shop's doorway and a white Mustang drive away. Memphis police officers picked up the bundle, which proved to be a green bedspread wrapped around most of Ray's worldly possessions: the Remington 30.06 rifle in its improvised cardboard carton; a partial box of ammunition; binoculars; and a blue travel bag containing two cans of Schlitz beer, a hammer and pliers, a shaving kit, underwear, a hairbrush, Georgia and U.S. road maps, a copy of that day's local newspaper, the *Commercial Appeal,* and the transistor radio Ray had brought out of Jeff City.

The rifle and binoculars bore Ray's fingerprints and no one else's; the radio bore his prison number, partly filed down. If assassins had indeed framed Ray, they had done a masterful job of it; if James Earl Ray had killed King, he had left a wide, deep trail that just about anyone could follow.

Twenty-five years after the event, James Earl Ray still claimed that he was not the man who shot Martin Luther King Jr. He was just a patsy, he explained, framed by someone using a rifle similar to the one he'd bought for Raoul, someone who conveniently left the rifle in the doorway of Canipe Amusement Company. Although that weapon had been fired and still had an expended round in its breech, it was neatly packed in the same Browning box in which it had come from the store. Why, Ray has asked, would an assassin risk taking the time to put the murder weapon away, and why was it that the FBI had never conducted a ballistics test on that weapon?

Close studies of how an assassin would have had to operate in Bessie Brewer's rooming house suggest that, while the location provided an easy shot, it must have been a logistical nightmare. The assassin had to trot back and forth between room 5B, from which King could have been seen only with difficulty, and the communal bathroom, where, to make the shot, the assassin needed to steady himself in a steep-sided bathtub. Some observers say that such clumsiness echoes the planning flaws in all Ray's crimes—that the King murder *looked* like an assassination by James Earl Ray.

The first time Ray told the story of that afternoon, he said that he'd been waiting in the Mustang when Raoul came pounding out of the rooming house, leaped into the backseat, and pulled a sheet over his head as Ray sped away. Ray has since called that account a joke on one of his early biographers, William Bradford Huie, who'd written extensively about the Ku Klux Klan. "Bedsheet, Klan—the joke seemed obvious to me," said Ray, "but I guess not everyone got it."

In subsequent accounts, Ray said that he met Raoul at Jim's Grill before renting the room upstairs. Once they had the room, Raoul sent Ray out to get infrared binoculars to show to their gun-running customers. Shortly after Ray got back from the York Arms Company with

Flanked by Jesse Jackson *(left)* and Ralph Abernathy, King stands on the Lorraine Motel balcony in Memphis, one day before a bullet struck him down.

ordinary binoculars, Raoul told him the gun dealers were coming to the flophouse, and he wanted to meet with them alone. He told Ray to pick him up at the rooming house around six but to disappear in the meantime, maybe take in a movie. Ray said he left the rooming house around five o'clock, then remembered that the Mustang's spare tire needed to be repaired. He'd just retrieved the repaired tire from the shop and was approaching the rooming house a few minutes after six when he saw police in the street and decided he had better steer clear of them.

Fearing the worst, he said, Ray drove out of town without stopping and learned from a radio news bulletin that King had been shot and then, an hour later, that he was dead. Behind Ray, Memphis had erupted in angry grief, and in the ensuing confusion police never issued an all-points bulletin for Ray's car. They were evidently lured by a still-mysterious hoaxer's tip that the man they wanted had headed northwest—opposite the direction taken by Ray. Thus, as he sped east from Memphis, no one was looking for him.

Ray drove all night to get back to Atlanta, where at eight o'clock the next morning he abandoned the white Mustang at the Capitol Homes apartment complex—one of the four places he'd marked on his Atlanta map. The car would not be reported to police for a week. He walked to the Piedmont Laundry and picked up his clean clothes, then left a note at his rooming house saying he wouldn't be back, and caught an early afternoon bus to Detroit, by way of Cincinnati. Reaching Detroit at eight o'clock in the morning of April 6, Ray took a taxi across the border to Windsor, Ontario, then went by train to Toronto. He rented a room at 102 Ossington Avenue,

Mortally wounded by an assassin, Martin Luther King Jr. is secured to a stretcher by medics at the Lorraine Motel.

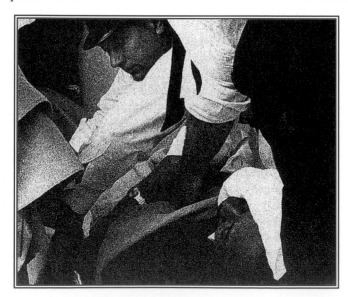

and lay low. South of the border, the largest manhunt in American history had been undertaken to search for King's assassin—a nondescript Caucasian male of medium build, identity unknown.

In urgent need of new credentials, Ray went to the public library and looked up birth notices from around the year of his birth, then selected 10 as possible aliases, Paul Bridgman among them. With the name of a real Canadian citizen his age, he hoped to get a passport issued. The next day, as Paul Bridgman, Ray applied for a duplicate birth certificate, to use as identification to get a passport. On April 11 he had a passport picture taken, using the name of Paul Bridgman, and as a belated but clever precaution, he called Bridgman's home pretending to be a government official. Learning that the real Paul Bridgman already had a passport, Ray reluctantly decided to scrap that alias.

Taking up another prospect from the birth notices, he called the home of Ramon George Sneyd and found that Sneyd had no passport. Conspiracy theorists have placed great emphasis on the apparent ease with which Ray, who had formerly rolled winos for their IDs, changed his method to one favored by real and fictional secret agents. A man with his limited background, they've argued, could not have been so slick.

That same day, Atlanta police found Ray's abandoned Mustang, registered to Eric S. Galt, and announced that Galt was the object of their search. Ashes in the ashtray—Ray didn't smoke—and clothes too small for Ray in the trunk led police to believe he'd at one point had company in his car.

On April 16 Ray went to a travel agency to purchase an airline ticket for London in the name of Ramon George Sneyd, asking for a round-trip booking, so as

Asked where the bullet came from, four King associates point across the street to the back of a boardinghouse where Ray had taken a room.

to avoid raising suspicion. When he asked about obtaining a passport, he learned that no birth certificate would be necessary; he gave the travel agency his application that day.

Two days later Toronto papers carried a photograph of Eric S. Galt, the chief suspect in the King murder; it was the picture of Ray with his eyes closed at his bartending graduation. A police artist had filled in eyes, producing a portrait that did not much resemble Ray. Still, the fugitive opted to change rooming houses the next day and moved to one seven blocks away, signing in as Ramon George Sneyd. On April 20 Toronto papers carried worse news, with fresh photographs: The man sought in the King assassination case was a petty thief and prison escapee named James Earl Ray; his string of aliases had confused the FBI for only two weeks.

On May 2 Ray's plane ticket and passport were ready, and he picked them up at the travel agency, paying $345 in Canadian money. At noon that day, Ray had a mysterious visitor. A man arrived at Ray's rooming house and gave him an envelope. Ray explained the visit matter-of-factly: He'd left his Sneyd birth certificate in a phone booth and the man was returning it. Conspiracists believe that the mysterious envelope contained payment for killing Martin Luther King Jr.

Ray flew from Toronto to London's Heathrow Airport, arriving on May 7. He exchanged his London-to-Toronto return ticket for a ticket to Portugal, whose former colony of Angola had embarked on civil war. He spent 11 days in Lisbon, making inquiries about ships bound for English-speaking African countries and trying to get himself hired as a mercenary. Meeting with no success, on May 17 Ray hopped a plane back to London. There he came across newspaper accounts of the international manhunt that had been mounted for him; the reward for his capture was $100,000.

Meanwhile, Canadian authorities had been drawn into the search for Reverend King's killer. Combing through 50,000 recently issued passports for a photograph that looked like James Earl Ray, Royal Canadian Mounted Police found the Sneyd passport. Checking with the real Sneyd—as it happened, a Toronto police officer—the Mounties found that he hadn't requested a passport; then they traced Ray's May 6 departure from Toronto for London on the phony document. Flashed to the FBI, Scotland Yard, and Europe's Interpol, the information was the basis for an "all-port" warning, which alerted immigration officials to detain the bogus Sneyd when he next presented the illicit passport.

Ray was running out of cash—an odd

Minutes after King's murder, an unidentified man left this bundle and Ray's rifle in the doorway of a nearby store.

Appropriating another Canadian's identity, Ray obtained this passport in the name of Ramon George Sneyd and fled to Lisbon.

circumstance if he had received a bounty for King's murder, as some conspiracists suggest—but he still had a pistol. On June 4 he walked into a branch of the Trustee Savings Bank in the blue-collar London neighborhood of Fulham and presented the cashier with a note: "Hand over the cash." Ray took off with £100—then about $240—in easy-to-spend £5 notes. Scotland Yard detectives discovered his fingerprints on the holdup note that he had left behind. This pathetic stickup was the act of a man in need; if there were people who'd hired or used James Earl Ray, they had surely abandoned him.

The next day Ray moved to yet another out-of-the-way hotel, where he kept to himself but "he was so obviously a troubled man," the proprietress recalled, "that he gave me the creeps." In London, between June 3 and June 7, a man calling himself Ramon George Sneyd made several telephone calls to a reporter on the *Daily Telegraph* who'd covered white-mercenary units fighting in Africa. The caller said he wanted to know about joining mercenary forces and needed assistance in tracing his brother, missing in the conflict in Portuguese Angola; the reporter referred him to an address in Brussels, Belgium—the Belgian Congo had also erupted in nationalist war.

On June 8, when Ray arrived at Heathrow Airport with his ticket for Brussels, the special-branch officer checking passports recognized his name and asked him politely, "Would you step into our office, Mr. Sneyd?" Police on the scene arrested Mr. Sneyd for carrying an unregistered pistol and then, after they had confirmed his identity through his fingerprints, asked him whether he was indeed James Earl Ray. The fugitive's long run from the law had come to an end; for once, he gave up without a chase.

After extradition hearings, Ray, charged with murdering Martin Luther King, was flown from London to Memphis on July 19, 1968, aboard a U.S. Air Force jet. He had retained the father-and-son legal team of Arthur J. Hanes and Arthur J. Hanes Jr. The elder Hanes was a former mayor of Birmingham and had defended the three Ku Klux Klansmen who killed Viola Liuzzo, one of the marchers in King's 1965 voting-rights demonstration in Selma. The Haneses had tried to prevent Ray's extradition from England on the grounds that he had acted as part of a conspiracy and therefore Ray's involvement in the killing, if any, had been a "political action," for which he could not be extradited. This argument failed, and they were left with the prospect of a trial by jury in Shelby County, Tennessee.

In an extraordinary setup that seemed aimed as much at psychological torture as at preventing the escape of this proven breakout artist, Ray was imprisoned in a cell that had its windows covered by sheet metal, so that no daylight came in. Bright electric lights burned day and night, and video cameras kept Ray under constant surveillance. "I soon lost track of time, and all sense of night and day," he complained.

While the Haneses interviewed witnesses and learned the nature of the state's case against him, Ray spent much of his time writing down his recollections for well-known southern writer William Bradford Huie, who'd negotiated a book deal with the Haneses. But when Huie published what the Haneses turned up in articles for *Look* magazine, Ray felt the lawyers had compromised his case and fired them. He next engaged a flamboyant Texan named Percy Foreman. After a cur-

A Scotland Yard van shuttles Ray back to a London jail several weeks after the fugitive's June 8 arrest at Heathrow Airport.

sory examination of the state's case, Foreman informed Ray in a letter that in view of "the overwhelming evidence that has been assembled against you," he foresaw "more than a 99% chance of your receiving a death penalty verdict" in a jury trial. The attorney advised Ray to plead guilty in order to escape Tennessee's electric chair.

"Foreman pretended he wanted to go to trial when he first come in on the case," Ray recalled in a 1993 interview. Then, according to Ray, the attorney applied unusual pressure to bring him to a guilty plea, including futile attempts to recruit Ray's tightly knit family to persuade the suspect to plead guilty. "He said something

about they might put my father in jail for this thing," Ray alleged. "So, really, what more or less convinced me to enter a guilty plea was he indicated he might not put forth his best efforts and things like that. He just didn't act like he was interested. So I finally agreed to enter a guilty plea."

On March 10, 1969, more than 11 months after the crime, James Earl Ray pleaded guilty to the assassination of Martin Luther King Jr., at the same time waiving the right to any appeal or review of his case or to a trial. He voiced one disagreement with the brief courtroom proceeding: He could not agree, he said, with the theories of Attorney General Ramsey Clark and FBI director

J. Edgar Hoover, who claimed that there had been no conspiracy. After a session lasting less than two and a half hours, Judge W. Preston Battle handed down a 99-year sentence.

Within three days, Ray repudiated his admission of guilt, saying that he'd been misled and coerced by his lawyer and by the federal government. He wrote to Judge Battle, informing him that "that famous Houston attorney Percy Fourflusher is no longer representing me in any capacity." In the letter, Ray also asked that he be given a new trial. On March 31, with the request still on his desk, Judge Battle died in his chambers, of natural causes. Ray carried his appeal for a new trial all the way to the Supreme Court, which in 1974 and again in 1976 refused to hear it. Since July of 1968, James Earl Ray has been confined in prisons in the state of Tennessee; he is now held in Riverbend Maximum Security Institution in Nashville.

Ray's stay has not been uneventful. He attempted to escape in 1971, and briefly succeeded in 1977 before being tracked down and returned to prison. In 1978 he married Anna Sandhu, a court artist sent to his escape trial by a Tennessee television station. The Reverend James Lawson, a black minister from Memphis and a former close colleague of King's, performed the ceremony. In 1981, searching for legal avenues out of jail in the prison law library, Ray was stabbed 22 times with shanks; he claimed that his assailants were

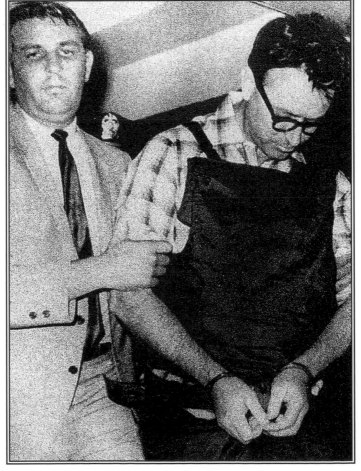

black inmates, moved to vengeance by recent publicity naming him the sole killer of King.

The Raoul-centered conspiracy that Ray alleged at his 144-minute hearing finally came under official investigation eight years later, when the U.S. House of Representatives convened a Select Committee in 1976 to spend 30 months and more than $5 million investigating the assassinations of John F. Kennedy and Martin Luther King Jr. This committee published its findings in January of 1979—and put few questions to rest. Based on its scrutiny of available evidence, the committee decided that Ray had killed King but that he had probably not acted alone; they suggested that there had been a conspiracy and outlined several plausible scenarios (*page 167*). The committee stopped short, however, of choosing one of these possible chains of events; and it refrained from naming any coconspirators. Ray remains the only person implicated in the crime.

"In these conspiracy books," Ray told a reporter in a 1993 prison interview, "there's thousands of people involved. I really don't think that it would take that many people, because there's too many blabbermouths. Something like that would get out. It just takes three or four people. Let's say in this King case, me and Raoul and some guy as a middleman and maybe five people, and one or two of them are Intelligence. That would be enough." Only he knows if that is the voice of experience.◆

Wearing a bulletproof vest as protection against possible assassins, Ray is escorted to a Memphis jail in July 1968.

Solitary as ever in this May 1977 photo, James Earl Ray ambles to his cell at Tennessee's Brushy Mountain State Prison, where he spent almost five years of a 99-year sentence.

A Host of Conspiracy Theories

James Earl Ray was never tried for the murder of Martin Luther King, and his plea of guilty, since recanted, tied up the case perhaps too neatly. As with all assassinations where motive is unclear, where coincidence suggests conspiracy, and where files are sealed—in this instance, until the year 2029—alternative theories abound. Ray himself has maintained that there was a conspiracy, but many observers doubt that even he knows who was ultimately behind the slaying. Some of the leading scenarios:

Loyd Jowers Did It.

In 1993 Memphis businessman Loyd Jowers claimed that he had arranged to have King shot from the tall shrubs facing the Lorraine Motel. Jowers, who is white, was supported in this claim by three others, all African Americans: two women, both former employees and one his former lover, and a man supposedly hired to enforce silence after the shooting. According to Jowers, two men had given him $100,000 to have King killed, assuring him that he ran no risk, as they would arrange a decoy to take the fall. Jowers said he'd paid a black marksman $10,000 for the shooting. After the murder, Jowers claimed, he disposed of the rifle.

Although skeptical law enforcement authorities were reluctant to grant the immunity Jowers wanted before telling all he knows, the district attorney agreed to investigate. Ray's London-based lawyer, Dr. William Pepper, claimed that Jowers and the other witnesses had come forward because they thought Pepper's 16-year-long investigation would expose them. The attorney told British reporters that he believed Jowers would reveal a trail leading back through the New Orleans Mafia to J. Edgar Hoover—and would eventually exonerate his client.

The FBI Did It.

Even before the Jowers confession, the FBI was a prime suspect among conspiracists. J. Edgar Hoover, omnipotent FBI director for 48 years, until his death in 1972, claimed to see, in the drive for black civil rights, a Communist-backed effort to cripple the United States government. Not content with his public expressions of contempt for Martin Luther King, Hoover directed a covert bureau vendetta against the dynamic leader and his organization, the Southern Christian Leadership Conference. Beginning as early as 1962, bureau tactics included illegal wiretaps and informants, forged letters, electronic eavesdropping in the minister's hotel rooms, and even an ultimate design to replace him with someone that the FBI—namely, Hoover—found more congenial.

An eight-man intelligence squad in the bureau's Atlanta office, according to former FBI agent Arthur Murtagh, "did almost nothing for a period of seven or eight years, except investigate King and try to destroy him." The investigators had given King the code name of Zorro, and said Murtagh, on hearing the news that King had been shot, at least one FBI man "jumped for joy, literally leaped in the air, yelling, 'They got Zorro. They got the son of a bitch.' " Hoover put the same Atlanta squad that had tried to discredit King in charge of investigating the murder.

In 1979 the House Select Committee on Assassinations did not discover any direct links between the FBI and the killing but declared that the bureau's "morally reprehensible, illegal, felonious, and unconstitutional" conduct had contributed "to the hostile climate that surrounded Dr. King."

Racists Did It.

The Ku Klux Klan, the Minutemen, and any number of segregationist organizations calling themselves White Citizens' Councils unabashedly wanted King silenced, and one white supremacist organization offered to help with Ray's defense. But no organization or individual has been implicated, and Ray, with no personal violence in his record, would have been an unlikely choice for the hired gun.

The Army Did It.

Afraid of the effect of King's antiwar oratory, the Army sent killers to Memphis and involved Ray as a patsy. Reported first by a Tennessee journalist, this scenario is fueled by the fact that Army intelligence units were watching King in Memphis and by the unexplained presence of a Green Beret unit in the city when he was killed.

The CIA Did It.

No conspiracy would be complete without the involvement of the Central Intelligence Agency. Some observers detect the hand of master spies in Ray's facility in obtaining false identities and credentials. They also cite an agency interest in King's movements and contacts; one anonymous account by a former CIA official claims that King was under the influence of Chinese communists and that he received communist money from secret contacts in Toronto. A former CIA agent reportedly told British researchers that an agency identity specialist named Raoul worked in Montreal in the 1960s.

Such reports, and the accounts of witnesses who said they saw suspicious movement in the bushes across the street from King's motel at the time of the shooting, fuel the suspicion that Ray was merely a pawn manipulated by some clever player—in this case, the CIA. One version holds that the CIA flew a specialist into Memphis to do the dirty work, while Ray was left to take the fall. Ray might be the first to agree.

Acknowledgments

The editors wish to thank these individuals and institutions for their valuable assistance:

Robert Andrews, Arlington, Va.; Assassination Archives and Research Center, Washington, D.C.; Ben Bagert, New Orleans; Jessica Bayne, HarperCollins Publishers, New York, N.Y.; Carolyn Bennett, The Foundation for Historical Louisiana, Baton Rouge, La.; Biblioteca Storica di Storia Moderna, Rome; G. Robert Blakey, Notre Dame Law School, Notre Dame, Ind.; Judy Bolton, Lower Mississippi Valley Collections, Louisiana State University, Baton Rouge, La.; Ida Pavy Boudreaux, Opelousas, La.; Leila Boyd, National Civil Rights Museum, Memphis, Tenn.; Ek Hart Bozeman, Winfield, La.; Jeff Britt, St. Joseph's, La.; Roger L. Busbice, Louisiana Old State Capitol, Center of Political and Governmental History, Baton Rouge, La.; Judy Calhoun, Baton Rouge, La.; Prof. Mark Carleton, Louisiana State University, Baton Rouge, La.; Thompson L. Clarke, St. Joseph's, La.; Jinx Coleman, New Orleans; David Culbert, Louisiana State University, Department of History, Baton Rouge, La.; Joan Dobson, Tex./Dallas History, Dallas Public Library, Dallas, Tex.; Charles East, Baton Rouge, La.; Hickman Ewing Jr., Memphis, Tenn.; Walter Fauntroy, Washington, D.C.; Mark Flanagan, McLean, Va.; William Joseph Gillespie, Lanark Village, Fla.; Francis Grevemberg, New Orleans; Judith Harris, Rome; Larry Howard, JFK Assassination Information Center, Dallas, Tex.;

Kenneth Hughes, Memphis, Tenn.; Bob Hunnicutt, Associate Technical Editor, *American Rifleman*, Bluemont, Va.; Glen Jeansonne, Ph.D., University of Wisconsin, Milwaukee, Wisc.; Rev. Samuel Kyles, Memphis, Tenn.; James Lesar, Assassination Archives and Research Center, Washington, D.C.; Hershal Long, Winfield, La.; Robert Mears, Downsville, La.; Dr. Philip H. Melanson, University of Massachusetts/Dartmouth, North Dartmouth, Mass.; Jonathan Meyers, Assassination Archives and Research Center, Washington, D.C.; Capt. Don Moreau, Baton Rouge, La.; Faye Phillips, Lower Mississippi Valley Collections, Louisiana State University, Baton Rouge, La.; Lt. Robert Priolo, Corcoran, Calif.; Andrew Purdey, Bethesda, Md.; Ed Reed, Baton Rouge, La.; Guy Riché, Baton Rouge, La.; Jerry Roden, New Orleans; Joseph Sabatier Jr., M.D., New Orleans; Isabelle Sauvé-Astruc, Conservateur, Musée des Collections historiques de la Préfecture de Police, Paris; George Sells, WAFB-TV, Baton Rouge, La.; Ann E. Smith, University Archives, Howard-Tilton Memorial Library, Tulane University, New Orleans; Virginia Smith, State Library of Louisiana, Baton Rouge, La.; Henry Stubbs, Baton Rouge, La.; Steve Tilly, National Archives and Records, Washington, D.C.; Stephen G. Tompkins, Nashville, Tenn.; Simonetta Toraldo, Rome; E. L. Trevillian, St. Joseph's, La.; Carl Weiss Jr., M.D., Garden City, N.Y.; Norbert Weiss Jr., Metairie, La.; Thomas Weiss, M.D., Metairie, La.; Nancy Zimmelman, Roseville, Calif.; David Zinman, Point Lookout, N.Y.

Bibliography

Books:

Blair, Clay, Jr., *The Strange Case of James Earl Ray*. New York: Bantam Books, 1969.

Blakey, G. Robert, and Richard N. Billings, *Fatal Hour: The Assassination of President Kennedy by Organized Crime*. New York: Berkley Books, 1981.

Breitman, George, Herman Porter, and Baxter Smith, *The Assassination of Malcolm X*. New York: Pathfinder, 1991.

Bremer, Arthur H., *An Assassin's Diary*. New York: Harper & Row, 1973.

Briggs, L. Vernon, *The Manner of Man That Kills*. Boston: Richard G. Badger, 1921.

Caplan, Lincoln, *The Insanity Defense and the Trial of John W. Hinckley, Jr.* Boston: David R. Godine, 1984.

Cassels, Lavender, *The Archduke and the Assassin*. New York: Stein and Day, 1984.

Clark, Champ, and the Editors of Time-Life Books, *The Assassination: Death of the President* (The Civil War series). Alexandria, Va.: Time-Life Books, 1987.

Clarke, James W.:
American Assassins: The Darker Side of Politics. Princeton, N.J.: Princeton University Press, 1982.
On Being Mad or Merely Angry: John W. Hinckley, Jr., and Other Dangerous People. Princeton, N.J.: Princeton University Press, 1990.

Collins, Larry, and Dominique Lapierre, *Freedom at Midnight*. New York: Simon and Schuster, 1975.

Curry, Jesse, *Retired Dallas Police Chief Jesse Curry Reveals His Personal JFK Assassination File*. Limited Collector's Edition.

Deutsch, Hermann B., *The Huey Long Murder Case*. Garden City, N.Y.: Doubleday, 1963.

Deutscher, Isaac, *The Prophet Outcast: Trotsky, 1929-1940*. London: Oxford University Press, 1963.

Donovan, Robert J., *The Assassins*. New York: Harper & Brothers, 1955.

Dupuy, R. Ernest, and Trevor N. Dupuy, *The Encyclopedia of Military History: From 3500 B.C. to the Present*. New York: Harper & Row, 1986.

Epstein, Edward Jay, *The Assassination Chronicles*. New York: Carroll & Graf, 1992.

Friedly, Michael. *Malcolm X*. New York: Carroll & Graf, 1992.

Gilfond, Henry, *The Black Hand at Sarajevo*. Indianapolis: Bobbs-Merrill, 1975.

Goode, Stephen, *Assassination! Kennedy, King, Kennedy*. New York: Franklin Watts, 1979.

Groden, Robert J., and Harrison Edward Livingstone, *High Treason: The Assassination of President Kennedy and the New Evidence of Conspiracy*. New York: Berkley Books, 1990.

Hair, William Ivy, *The Kingfish and His Realm*. Baton Rouge, La.: Louisiana State University Press, 1991.

Houghton, Robert A., with Theodore Taylor, *Special Unit Senator*. New York: Random House, 1970.

Huie, William Bradford, *He Slew the Dreamer: My Search for the Truth about James Earl Ray and the Murder of Martin Luther King*. New York: Delacorte Press, 1968.

Jansen, Godfrey, *Why Robert Kennedy Was Killed*. New York: Joseph Okpaku, 1970.

Jeansonne, Glen, *Messiah of the Masses: Huey P. Long and the Great Depression*. Ed. by Oscar Handlin. New York: 1993.

Kaiser, Robert Blair, *"R.F.K. Must Die!"* New York: E. P. Dutton, 1970.

King, David, and James Ryan, *Trotsky*. Oxford: Basil Blackwell, 1986.

Kohn, Hans, *The Habsburg Empire*

1904-1918. Princeton, N.J.: Van Nostrand, 1961.

Kovalyov, Eduard, *The Crime in St. Peter's Square*. Moscow: Novosti Press Agency, 1985.

Lane, Mark, *Rush to Judgment*. New York: Thunder's Mouth Press, 1966.

Lane, Mark, and Dick Gregory, *Code Name "Zorro."* New York: Pocket Books, 1977.

Lattimer, John K., *Kennedy and Lincoln: Medical and Ballistic Comparisons of Their Assassinations*. New York: Harcourt Brace Jovanovich, 1980.

Lesberg, Sandy, *Assassination in Our Time*. London: Peebles Press International, 1976.

McKinley, James, *Assassination in America*. New York: Harper & Row, 1977.

McMillan, George, *The Making of an Assassin: The Life of James Earl Ray*. Boston: Little, Brown, 1976.

McMillan, Priscilla Johnson, *Marina and Lee*. New York: Harper & Row, 1977.

Marrs, Jim, *Crossfire: The Plot That Killed Kennedy*. New York: Carroll & Graf, 1989.

Mason, John W., *The Dissolution of the Austro-Hungarian Empire, 1867-1918*. London: Longman, 1985.

Melanson, Philip H.:
The Martin Luther King Assassination: New Revelations on the Conspiracy and Cover-Up, 1968-1991. New York: Shapolsky, 1991.
The Robert F. Kennedy Assassination. New York: Shapolsky, 1991.

Merchant, Minhaz, *Rajiv Gandhi*. New Delhi: Viking, 1991.

Moore, Jim, *Conspiracy of One: The Definitive Book on the Kennedy Assassination*. Fort Worth, Tex.: Summit Group, 1991.

Morrow, Robert D., *The Senator Must Die*. Santa Monica, Calif.: Roundtable, 1988.

Morton, Frederic, *Thunder at Twilight*. New York.: Charles Scribner's Sons, 1989.

Payne, Robert:
The Life and Death of Mahatma Gandhi. New York: E. P. Dutton, 1969.
The Life and Death of Trotsky. New York: McGraw-Hill, 1977.

Posner, Gerald, *Case Closed*. New York: Random House, 1993.

Ray, James Earl, *Who Killed Martin Luther King? The True Story by the Alleged Assassin*. Washing-

ton, D.C.: National Press Books, 1992.

Reed, Ed, *Requiem for a Kingfish*. Baton Rouge, La.: Award Publications, 1986.

Remey, Oliver, Henry F. Cochems, and Wheeler P. Bloodgood, *The Attempted Assassination of Ex-President Theodore Roosevelt*. Milwaukee: Progressive, 1912.

Rosenberg, Charles E., *The Trial of the Assassin Guiteau*. Chicago: University of Chicago Press, 1968.

Salazar, Leandro A. Sanchez, *Murder in Mexico*. London: Secker & Warburg, 1950.

Sarin, Ritu, *The Assassination of Indira Gandhi*. New Delhi: Penguin Books, 1990.

Segal, Ronald:
Leon Trotsky: A Biography. New York: Pantheon, 1979.
The Tragedy of Leon Trotsky. London: Hutchinson, 1979.

Seigenthaler, John, *A Search for Justice*. Nashville: Aurora, 1971.

Shihab, Aziz, *Sirhan*. San Antonio: Naylor, 1969.

Sterling, Claire, *The Time of the Assassins*. New York: Holt, Rinehart and Winston, 1983.

Summers, Anthony, *Conspiracy*. New York: Paragon House, 1989.

Turner, William W., and John G. Christian, *The Assassination of Robert F. Kennedy*. New York: Random House, 1978.

U.S. House of Representatives, *The Final Assassinations Report: Report of the Select Committee of Assassinations*. New York: Bantam Books, 1979.

The Warren Commission Report: Report of the President's Commission on the Assassination of President John F. Kennedy. New York: St. Martin's Press, 1964.

Weisberg, Harold, *Frame-up*. New York: Outerbridge & Dienstfrey, 1969.

Williams, T. Harry, *Huey Long*. New York: Alfred A. Knopf, 1969.

Zinman, David H. *The Day Huey Long Was Shot*. Jackson, Miss.: University Press of Mississippi, 1993.

Periodicals:

Aaron, Leroy F., "The Emergence of Sara Jane Moore." *Washington Post*, Sept. 28, 1975.

"The Accused: A Loner Who Hated Israel." *Washington Post*, June 7, 1968.

"Admits Taking Part in Malcolm X Slaying." *Chicago Tribune*, Mar. 1, 1966.

"Agca Asserts K.G.B. Aided in Pope Plot." *New York Times*, July 9, 1983.

Apple, R. W., Jr.:
"Police Trace the Path of the Suspect from Turkey to St. Peter's Square." *New York Times*, May 15, 1981.
"Pope Is Shot in Car in Vatican Square, Surgeons Term Condition 'Guarded'; Turk, an Escaped Murderer, Is Seized." *New York Times*, May 14, 1981.
"Trail of Mehmet Ali Agca: 6 Years of Neo-Fascist Ties." *New York Times*, May 25, 1981.

"Archduke's Slayers Sentenced by Court." *New York Times*, Oct. 29, 1914.

"Assassinations: Eye of the Hurricane." *Newsweek*, Mar. 3, 1969.

Bigart, Homer:
"Black Muslim Guard Held in Murder of Malcolm X." *New York Times*, Feb. 27, 1965.
"Bremer Diary Details Effort to Kill Nixon." *New York Times*, Aug. 4, 1972.
"Bremer Guilty in Shooting of Wallace, Gets 63 Years." *New York Times*, Aug. 5, 1972.

Bilitz, Walter, "Black Nationalist Is Shot at Rally in NY." *Chicago Tribune*, Feb. 22, 1965.

Billen, Andrew, "I Hired Martin Luther King's Killer, Says Memphis Businessman." *The London Observer*, Dec. 12, 1993.

Bosworth, Warren, "Walker Target of Sniper Blast." *Dallas Times Herald*, Apr. 11, 1963.

Brecher, John, "Anyone Here Know Mr. Agca?" *Newsweek*, Dec. 27, 1982.

Buckley, Thomas, "Malcolm X Jury Finds 3 Guilty." *New York Times*, Mar. 11, 1966.

Chapman, William, "Suspect Is Native of Jordan." *Washington Post*, June 6, 1968.

Charlton, Linda, "Indira Gandhi, Skilled in Uses of Power, Dominated India for Two Decades." *New York Times*, Oct. 31, 1984.

"Chronicle of Ray's Whereabouts, from the Time He Fled." *New York Times*, Nov. 18, 1968.

Clark, Evert, "F.B.I. Accuses Galt of a Conspiracy in Dr. King Slaying." *New York Times*, Apr. 18, 1968.

Cooper, Richard T., "Ray's Getaway Via Toronto Hints at Uncommon Finesse." *Los Angeles Times*, June 11, 1968.

Corney, Cynthia, "Sirhan." *Washington Post*, Aug. 21, 1979.

Cortesi, Arnaldo, "Trotsky Dies of His Wounds; Asks Revolution Go Forward." *New York Times*, Aug. 22, 1940.

Crossette, Barbara, "Rajiv Gandhi Is Assassinated in Bombing at Campaign Stop; India Puts Off Rest of Voting." *New York Times*, May 22, 1991.

Daniell, F. Raymond:
"Long Forces Press Conspiracy Case." *New York Times*, Sept. 28, 1935.
"Throngs Pass Long's Bier as Friends Discuss 'Plot.'" *New York Times*, Sept. 12, 1935.

"Death of Trotsky." *The Times* (London), Aug. 22, 1940.

Dionne, E. J., Jr., "Evidence Cited for Theory that a Second Gunman Fired at the Pope." *New York Times*, Nov. 2, 1984.

"Doctors Voice Concern at Lack of Improvement." *Washington Post*, June 6, 1968.

Einstoss, Ron, "Verdict Was People's Will, Prosecution Says." *Los Angeles Times*, Apr. 18, 1969.

Elson, John, "And Now, Who Shot R.F.K.?" *Time*, June 7, 1993.

Farr, Bill, "After 17 Years, 'Ifs' Still Haunt Sirhan." *Los Angeles Times*, June 24, 1985.

"Father of Sirhan Asks, 'What Do You Think I Feel?'" *Washington Post*, June 7, 1968.

"A Fool for a Client?" *Time*, Nov. 10, 1975.

"For Perspective & Determination." *Time*, June 14, 1968.

"Freed in Trotsky Attack." *New York Times*, Apr. 18, 1941.

Friedrich, Otto, "Sad, Lonely, but Never Afraid." *Time*, Nov. 12, 1984.

"Gandhi Case Accused to Testify for State." *New York Times*, June 23, 1948.

"Gandhi's Killer Doomed." *New York Times*, June 22, 1949.

"Gandhi's Killers to Die Nov. 15." *New York Times*, Oct. 28, 1949.

"Gandhi's Slayer Doomed by Delhi Court to Hang." *New York Times*, Feb. 10, 1949.

"Gandhi's Slayer Hanged; Reported Unrepentant." *New York Times*, Nov. 15, 1949.

"Gandhi, Slain, Is Succeeded by Son; Killing Laid to 2 Sikh Bodyguards;

Army Alerted to Bar Sect Violence." *New York Times*, Nov. 1, 1984.

Graham, Fred P., "F.B.I. Says 'Galt' Is an Escaped Convict." *New York Times*, Apr. 20, 1968.

"'Gunman Shot Point-Blank, Then It Was Too Late . . .'" *Los Angeles Times*, June 5, 1968.

Hazarika, Sanjoy:
"India Investigates Plot Possibilities." *New York Times*, Nov. 3, 1984.
"Indian Police Arrest 3d Sikh in Gandhi Slaying." *New York Times*, Dec. 3, 1984.
"New Delhi Trial Starts for 3 in Gandhi Assassination Case." *New York Times*, May 18, 1985.
"Sikh Suspect Taken for Questioning." *New York Times*, Nov. 16, 1984.
"Suicide of Suspects in Gandhi Case Reported." *New York Times*, Aug. 21, 1991.

"Heir to Austria's Throne Is Slain with His Wife by a Bosnian Youth to Avenge Seizure of His Country." *New York Times*, June 29, 1914.

Howe, Marvine:
"Turk's Hometown Puzzled by His Climb to Notoriety." *New York Times*, May 23, 1981.
"Turks in Disagreement on Motive of Alleged Assailant." *New York Times*, May 16, 1981.
"Turks Say Suspect in Papal Attack Is Tied to Rightest Web of Intrigue." *New York Times*, May 18, 1981.

"India Holds Security Aide to Indira Gandhi in Conspiracy Inquiry." *New York Times*, Nov. 15, 1984.

"India Said to Widen Inquiry on Slaying." *New York Times*, Nov. 18, 1984.

"In the Night Kitchen." *People*, June 7, 1993.

Iyer, Pico:
"All in the Family." *Time*, Nov. 12, 1984.
"The Lions of Punjab." *Time*, Nov. 12, 1984.
"The Tamil Tigers' Threat." *Time*, Apr. 22, 1985.

Jackson, Donald, "The Evolution of an Assassin." *Life*, Feb. 21, 1964.

Kamm, Henry, "Bonn Is Fearful of Bulgaria Tie with Terrorists." *New York Times*, Dec. 11, 1982.

Kaufman, Michael T., "Rootless but Ruling for Unity, the Dynasty That Was Modern India Is Gone." *New York Times*, May 22, 1991.

Kihss, Peter:
"Hunt for Killers in Malcolm Case

'On Right Track.'" *New York Times*, Feb. 25, 1965.
"Third Man Seized in Malcolm Case." *New York Times*, Mar. 4, 1965.

Kisacik, Resit, "The Life Story of Agca." *Cumhuriyet* (Turkey), May 1981.

Kneeland, Douglas, "Now, Arthur Bremer Is Known." *New York Times*, May 22, 1972.

Landers, Jim, "Hijacker Arrested as Picket." *Washington Post*, Feb. 23, 1974.

Landers, Jim, and Timothy Robinson, "Posthumous Fame Sought by Hijacker." *Washington Post*, Feb. 23, 1974.

Lane, Mark, "Killer at Large." *Skeptic*, Mar./Apr. 1977.

Langman, Betsy, and Alexander Cockburn, "Sirhan's Gun." *Harper's*, Jan. 1975.

Larsen, David, "Five Jurors in Favor of Death Penalty from Start, One Says." *Los Angeles Times*, Apr. 24, 1969.

"Leon Trotsky." *The Times* (London), Aug. 23, 1940.

"Long Shot, Assailant Slain." *New Orleans Times-Picayune*, Sept. 9, 1935.

McWhirter, William A., "The Story of the Accused Killer of Dr. King." *Life*, May 3, 1968.

"The Making of a Lonely Misfit." *Time*, May 29, 1972.

"The Man Who Loved Kennedy." *Time*, Feb. 21, 1969.

Mathews, Tom, "The Lessons of Bobby." *Newsweek*, May 31, 1993.

"Mayor Cermak Is Dead." *Newark Evening News*, Mar. 6, 1933.

Mitra, Anirudhya, "The Inside Story." *India Today*, July 15, 1991.

Moldea, Dan E.:
"RFK's Murder: A Second Gun?" *Washington Post*, May 13, 1990.
"Who Really Killed Bobby Kennedy?" *Regardies*, June 1987.

Montgomery, Paul L., "Harlem Is Quiet as News Spreads." *New York Times*, Feb. 22, 1965.

Murphy, Jamie, "On the Trail of an Elusive Turk." *Time*, Mar. 25, 1985.

Nagorski, Andrew, "The Pope Plot: A Second Gun." *Newsweek*, Nov. 5, 1984.

O'Neil, Paul, "Ray, Sirhan—What Possessed Them?" *Life*, June 21, 1968.

Pace, Eric, "Sikh Separatism Dates Back to '47." *New York Times*, Nov. 1, 1984.

Posner, Gerald, "The Man with a Deadly Smirk." *U.S. News & World Report*, Aug. 30-Sept. 6, 1993.

"The Presidency: Fanatics' Errand." *Time*, Nov. 13, 1950.

"Prinzip Found Guilty." *New York Times*, Oct. 27, 1914.

"Protecting the President." *Time*, Oct. 6, 1975.

"Puerto Rico Revolt Endangers Truman." *Life*, Nov. 13, 1950.

"Putting Agca's Word on Trial." *Newsweek*, June 10, 1985.

"Ray, Starting 99-Year Term, Is Assigned to Maximum Security Section." *New York Times*, Mar. 11, 1969.

"Reagan's Close Call." *Newsweek*, Apr. 13, 1981.

Rensberger, Boyce:
"Bremer's Way of Life Likened to 3 Assassins." *New York Times*, May 21, 1972.
"Clues from the Grave Add Mystery to the Death of Huey Long." *Washington Post*, June 29, 1992.

Richards, Bill, and Donald P. Baker, "Pilot Critically Hurt during Shoot-Out at Baltimore Airport." *Washington Post*, Feb. 23, 1974.

Rogers, Warren, "'Not Again!': Eyewitness to the Killing of RFK." *Washington Post*, May 23, 1993.

Salpukas, Agis, "Suspect, to Neighbors, Was Withdrawn Loner." *New York Times*, May 17, 1972.

"Says Dr. Weiss Wept over Long Reign in State." *Morning Advocate*, Sept. 10, 1935.

"Senator Long Dies at 4:10 A.M." *Morning Advocate*, Sept. 10, 1935.

Shuster, Alvin, "Ray Is Being Held in Close Security." *New York Times*, June 9, 1968.

"Sirhan Asked Two about Kennedy." *San Francisco Chronicle*, Feb. 18, 1969.

"Sirhan Family Shares Grief with Kennedys." *Washington Post*, June 7, 1968.

"Sirhan Sirhan Denied Parole for 10th Time." *Washington Post*, May 24, 1989.

"Sirhan's Picture of Kennedy—'A Saint.'" *San Francisco Chronicle*, Mar. 6, 1969.

"Sirhan's Practice on Target Range." *San Francisco Chronicle*, Feb. 19, 1969.

Smith, Dave:
"Sirhan Takes Witness Stand, Admits He Killed Kennedy." *Los Angeles Times*, Mar. 4, 1969.
"Sirhan Wants to Plead Guilty, Lawyer Says." *Los Angeles Times*, Feb. 26, 1969.

Smith, Terence, "Suspect Is a Strong Nationalist Who Hoped to Return to Jordan: Early Life Termed Bitter." *New York Times*, June 7, 1968.

Smolowe, Jill:
"Agca's Surprise." *Time*, July 1, 1985.
"The Third Man." *Time*, July 15, 1985.

Soble, Ronald L., "Sirhan Denied Parole; His Next Hearing to Be Delayed." *Los Angeles Times*, May 29, 1987.

Starrs, James E., "Scientific Insights into a Louisiana Tragedy." *Scientific Sleuthing Review*, summer 1991.

"Statement Just before the Shooting." *Washington Post*, June 6, 1968.

Stevens, William K., "Indira Gandhi Assassinated by Gunmen; Police Seal Off 2 Areas as Crowds Gather." *New York Times*, Oct. 31, 1984.

"Suspect Said to Have Lived in Germany." *New York Times*, May 15, 1981.

"Sylvia Ageloff Indicted." *New York Times*, Sept. 1, 1940.

Tanner, Henry:
"Attack on Pope a Conspiracy, Court Says." *New York Times*, Sept. 25, 1981.
"Pope's Assailant Sentenced to Life." *New York Times*, July 23, 1981.
"Turk Says He Tried to Kill the Pope." *New York Times*, July 21, 1981.

"Three Sikhs Charged in India in the Killing of Indira Gandhi." *New York Times*, Feb. 13, 1985.

"*Times* Newsmen on Scene: 'Gunman Shot Point-Black, Then It Was Too Late.'" *Los Angeles Times*, June 5, 1968.

"To Be an Assassin Ideal of Prinzip." *New York Times*, July 2, 1914.

Tompkins, Stephen G., "25 Years Later, Continuing Series: Domestic Spying." *Commercial Appeal*, Mar. 21, 1993.

Toth, Robert C., "Ray Flying to U.S. for Trial; Expected to Land in Memphis." *Los Angeles Times*, July 19, 1968.

"Tracking Agca." *Time*, Sept. 27, 1982.

"Tragedy May Alter Politics of Europe." *New York Times*, June 29, 1914.

"Trial of Gandhi's Killer Ends." *New York Times*, Dec. 31, 1948.

Trials: "A Deadly Iteration." *Time*, Mar. 7, 1969.

Trials: "Death without Dread." *Time*, Mar. 14, 1969.

Trials: "Sirhan through the Looking Glass." *Time*, Apr. 4, 1969.

Trials: "The Sirhan Verdict." *Time*, Apr. 25, 1969.

Trials: "Toward the Gas Chamber." *Time*, May 2, 1969.

Trials: "The Wanderer." *Newsweek*, Jan. 13, 1969.

"Trotsky." *The Times* (London), Aug. 23, 1940.

"Trotsky's Assailant Indicted." *The Times* (London), Aug. 28, 1940.

"Trotsky, Wounded by 'Friend' in Home, Is Believed Dying." *New York Times*, Aug. 21, 1940.

Trumbull, Robert, "Gandhi Is Killed by a Hindu; India Shaken, World Mourns; 15 Die in Rioting in Bombay," *New York Times*, Jan. 31, 1948.

Vahey, William H., Jr., "Idealism Is Held Motive of Weiss in Slaying Long." *Washington Post*, Sept. 29, 1935.

Waldron, Martin:
"Bremer, in Red, White and Blue, Was Conspicuous." *New York Times*, May 29, 1972.
"Ray's Arrest Ends Hunt That Began with His Escape from Jail." *New York Times*, June 9, 1968.

"The Wallace Shooting: The Savage Secret behind a Smile." *Life*, May 26, 1972.

Walz, Jay, "3 Whose Names Ray Used Resemble Him." *New York Times*, June 12, 1968.

Watson, Russell, "A New Chapter in the Pope Plot." *Newsweek*, Dec. 6, 1983.

Weinraub, Bernard:
"India Holds Dozen in Gandhi Killing." *New York Times*, July 14, 1991.
"Theory of a Tamil Plot to Kill Gandhi." *New York Times*, May 28, 1991.
"Woman May Have Set Off Bomb Fatal to Gandhi." *New York Times*, May 26, 1991.

Weisman, Steven R.:
"Death Sentences in Gandhi Killing." *New York Times*, Dec. 3, 1986.
"Rajiv Gandhi." *New York Times*, May 22, 1991.

West, Richard, "President Escapes Assassin's Bullet." *Los Angeles Times*, Sept. 23, 1975.

Windeler, Robert, "Suspect Is a Strong Nationalist Who Hoped to Return to Jordan." *New York Times*, June 7, 1968.

Wittner, Dale, "A Boy Who Shut Everyone out." *Life*, May 26, 1972.

"Woman Is Accused in Trotsky Murder."

New York Times, Aug. 27, 1940.
"Woman Who Introduced Killer to Trotsky Holds Home Relief Civil Service Job Here." *New York Times*, Aug. 23, 1940.

Other Sources:
"The Death of Former Senator Huey Long." *Congresssional Record*, (pp. 23210-23221), Sept. 10, 1985.
Final Investigative Report: Senator Huey P. Long. State of Louisiana, Dept. of Public Safety and Corrections, Case Number R1D013191. Louisiana State Police, June 5, 1992.
"The Los Angeles Police Dept. Records of the Robert F. Kennedy Assassination Investigation." California State Archives. Released Apr. 1988.
"Rehabilitation after Ethnic Violence" (brochure). Sri Lanka's Office of the Commissioner General of Essential Services, Feb. 1984.
"World Federation of Sri Lanka Associations Second Convention" (brochure). Aug. 1985.

Index

Picture Credits

The sources for the illustrations that appear in this volume are listed below. Credits for the illustrations from left to right are separated by semicolons; from top to bottom they are separated by dashes.

Cover, 4: AP/Wide World Photos, New York. 6: UPI/Bettmann, New York. 7: National Archives, Commission Exhibit, #2. 10: AP/Wide World Photos, New York, inset, National Archives. 11: AP/Wide World Photos, New York; National Archives—AP/Wide World Photos, New York; courtesy Time Inc. Picture Collection and WDSU-TV. 12: National Archives CE#4. 15: AP/Wide World Photos, New York. 16, 17: National Archives. 19: National Archives CE#2625. 21: Courtesy Time Inc. Picture Collection. 23: National Archives CE#2625. 24: National Archives CE#790. 28: National Archives CE#788. 30: National Archives CE#796—797. 34: National Archives CE#2966B; CE#1413. 38: AP/Wide World Photos, New York. 40: The Bettmann Archive, New York. 42, 43: Abraham Zapruder/Time Inc. (3)—Earl McDonald/National Archives. 44: National Archives; UPI/Bettmann, New York. 45: National Archives. 46: UPI/Bettmann, New York. 47: AP/Wide World Photos, New York. 48, 49: © 1963 Bob Jackson. 50: Archive Photos, New York. 52: The Bettmann Archive, New York—Library of Congress (LC#622342). 53: The Bettmann Archive, New York; Culver Pictures, New York; UPI/Bettmann, New York. 54: AP/Wide World Photos, New York. 55: UPI/Bettmann, New York (2); UPI/Bettmann Newsphotos, New York. 56: UPI/Bettmann, New York. 59: Bill Eppridge for *LIFE.* 60: Courtesy Time Inc. Picture Collection. 62, 63: Courtesy Time Inc. Picture Collection (2)—courtesy California State Archives, Roseville, Calif. 64: Courtesy California State Archives, Roseville, Calif. 65: Courtesy Time Inc. Picture Collection—courtesy California State Archives, Roseville, Calif. 66: Mel Price for Hollywood Park, Englewood, Calif. 67: Courtesy California State Archives, Roseville, Calif. 69-76: Courtesy California State Archives, Roseville, Calif. 78: Bill Eppridge for LIFE—UPI/Bettmann, New York. 79: UPI/Bettmann, New York. 80: Courtesy California State Archives, Roseville, Calif.—UPI/Bettmann, New York. 81: Courtesy California State Archives, Roseville, Calif. 82, 83: AP/Wide World Photos, New York. 84, 85: Michael D. O'Toole. 86: David Culbert. 88: Louisiana State Library, Baton Rouge, La. 89: Tulane University Library, New Orleans, La. 90: UPI/Bettmann, New York. 91: AP/Wide World Photos, New York. 92, 93: The Historic New Orleans Collection, New Orleans, La. 96, 97: Background, from The University Archives, Howard-Tilton Memorial Library, Tulane University, New Orleans, La.; private collection (3). 98: Private collection. 101: Henry L. Stubbs. 102: The Louisiana Collection, State Library of Louisiana, Baton Rouge, La. 103: The Louisiana State Library, Baton Rouge, La. 105: David Culbert. 106: AP/Wide World Photos, New York. 108, 109: Louisiana's Center for Political and Government History, Baton Rouge, La. 110: AP/Wide World Photos, New York—Louisiana's Center for Political and Government History, Baton Rouge, La.—courtesy Professor James E. Starrs. 113: UPI/Bettmann, New York. 114: The Louisiana Collection, State Library of Louisiana, Baton Rouge, La. 116: The Bettmann Archive, New York. 119: Private collection. 121: AP/Wide World Photos, New York. 122, 123: Osterreichische National Bibliothek, inset, *The Road to Sarajevo* by Vladimir Dedijer/Simon and Schuster, 1966, courtesy, Time Inc. Picture Collection. 125: UPI/Bettmann, New York, inset, Jefature De Vlicia Del D. 127: AP/Wide World Photos, New York—Sygma, New York. 129: AP/Wide World Photos, New York; Sygma, New York. 131: Credit unavailable; UPI/Bettmann, New York. 133: Reuters/Bettmann, New York—AP/Wide World Photos, New York. 134: AP/Wide World Photos, New York. 137: Art Shay for *Time* Magazine—Lee Balterman for *Time* Magazine. 139: Courtesy Time Inc. Picture Collection. 140: Rodney Dungen/Chicago Tribune, Chicago, Ill. 143: Courtesy Time Inc. Picture Collection. 145: AP/Wide World Photos, New York. 149: AP/Wide World Photos, New York; UPI/Bettmann, New York; AP/Wide World Photos, New York—UPI/Bettmann, New York. 150: Arthur Schatz for *LIFE.* 151: James Hansen/*Look* Magazine, courtesy Assassination Archives, Washington, D.C. 152: Courtesy Assassination Archives, Washington D.C. 155: Courtesy Assassination Archives, Washington, D.C.—from The James Earl Ray Extradition File/Justice Department, Washington D.C. 156, 157: Curtis Kopf. 158: AP/Wide World Photos, New York. 160: Joseph Louw for *LIFE.* 161: AP/Wide World Photos, New York. 162: AP/Wide World Photos, New York. 163: © 1993 Thames Television, London. 164: UPI/Bettmann, New York. 165: AP/Wide World Photos, New York. 166: Gerald Holly/*The Tennessean,* Nashville, Tenn.

This edition published in 2004
by the Caxton Publishing Group
20 Bloomsbury Street, London WC1B 3JH
Under license from Time-Life Books BV.

TRUE CRIME

SERIES EDITOR: Janet Cave
Administrative Editor: Jane A. Martin
Art Director: Christopher Register
Picture Editors: Jane Jordan (principal), Jane A. Martin
Cover Design: Open Door Limited, Rutland, UK

Editorial Staff for Assassination
Text Editor: Carl Posey
Associate Editors/Research: Megan Barnett, Jennifer Pearce,
Katya Sharpe
Assistant Art Director: Sue Pratt
Senior Copyeditors: Mary Beth Oelkers-Keegan (principal),
Elizabeth Graham, Colette Stockum
Picture Coordinator: Jennifer Iker
Editorial Assistant: Donna Fountain

Special Contributors: R. Curtis Kopf, Catherine Harper Parrott,
Roseanne C. Scott, Robert Speziale, Robin Tunnicliff (research);
Richard N. Billings, George G. Daniels, Margery A. duMond,
Laura Foreman, George Russell, Daniel Stashower (text);
John Drummond (design); Mel Ingber (index).

Correspondents: Elisabeth Kraemer-Singh (Bonn); Christine Hinze
(London); Christina Lieberman (New York); Maria Vincenza Aloisi
(Paris); Ann Natanson (Rome). Valuable assistance was also
provided by Mehmet Ali Kislali (Ankara); Danie Donnelly,
Katheryn White (New York); Ann Wise (Rome).

Consultants: James W. Clarke is a professor of political science at
the University of Arizona in Tucson, specialising in studies of
criminal violence and race relations. In 1991 he received the
university's Social and Behavioural Sciences Award for
Outstanding Teaching. A prolific writer in his own speciality,
Clarke is the author of *American Assassins: The Darker Side of
Politics, Last Rampage: The Escape of Gary Tison* and *On Being
Mad or Merely Angry: John W. Hinckley, Jr. and Other
Dangerous People.*

James E. Starrs is professor of law and forensic sciences at the
George Washington University in Washington, D.C., and an
internationally known consultant in his field. In recent years, he
has applied his legal and forensic knowledge to solving such
lingering mysteries as the cannibalism of Colorado prospector
Alfred Packer, the alleged suicide of pioneer explorer
Merriwether Lewis, the Lindbergh kidnapping, the case of
accused murderers Sacco and Vanzetti, and the death of Senator
Huey P. Long

Title: **True Crimes, Assassination**
ISBN: 1 84447 107 1